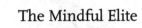

The Mindful Elite

The Mindful Elite

Mobilizing from the Inside Out

JAIME KUCINSKAS

Oxford University Press is a department of the University of Oxford. It furthers
the University's objective of excellence in research, scholarship, and education
by publishing worldwide. Oxford is a registered trade mark of Oxford University
Press in the UK and certain other countries.

Published in the United States of America by Oxford University Press
198 Madison Avenue, New York, NY 10016, United States of America.

Library of Congress Cataloging-in-Publication Data
Names: Kucinskas, Jaime, author.
Title: The mindful elite : mobilizing from the inside out / Jaime Kucinskas.
Description: New York : Oxford University Press, [2019] | Includes
bibliographical references.
Identifiers: LCCN 2018012940 | ISBN 9780190881818 (hard cover) |
ISBN 9780190881825 (updf) | ISBN 9780190881832 (epub)
Subjects: LCSH: Mindfulness (Psychology)
Classification: LCC BF637.M56 K83 2018 | DDC 158.1/3—dc23
LC record available at https://lccn.loc.gov/2018012940

This book is dedicated to my parents, my husband, and my daughter, who have filled my days with inspiration, curiosity, and joy.

Americans believe strongly in positive thinking. Positive thinking is great. It works best when based on a realistic assessment and acceptance of the actual situation.

URSULA K. LE GUIN, No Time to Spare, 2017, p.12

CONTENTS

ACKNOWLEDGMENTS

This book would not have been possible without the support of many people, to whom I am tremendously grateful. I owe thanks to the contemplatives for their support and trust along the way. I am particularly grateful to Adam Engle and Cliff Saron for going above and beyond in helping me get this project off the ground. I hope that the book lends insight to your experiences, and helps you make our world a better place.

I am also in debt to my dream team of academic advisors at Indiana University and Vanderbilt, who believed in my work from the beginning. Rob Robinson exemplified how one can be not only an exemplary sociologist, but a good person and mentor. I am grateful to Rob for encouraging me to study what I wanted, even when it was in its early stages. Brian Steensland provided an invaluable sounding board, helping me to see different angles when I was immersed in data collection. Fabio Rojas taught me to be a courageous qualitative researcher. Tim Hallett and Larry Isaac helped me keep swimming and refining the project into the book it has become.

I am fortunate to be part of an incredible team at Hamilton College. Our department colloquia have greatly improved the book. I am especially grateful to Yvonne Zylan for her analytic guidance, to Steve Ellingson for his tips on structuring the book and making it more coherent, to Dan Chambliss for his insights on writing an interesting book and his inspiration for Chapter 8, and to Ben DiCicco-Bloom for commiserating in the trials of being a new professor and first-time book author. I am also grateful to Emily Sigalow, Richard Seager, Rhys Williams, Robin Vanderwall, Kelly Besecke, Jeanne Penn, Elizabeth Beck, Meredith Grossman, Chris Willemsen, James Cook, and two anonymous reviewers for reading chapters of the book and providing valuable feedback.

I am lucky to have such a caring, generous extended family who has provided endless love, emotional support, housing, meals, and babysitting over the years. I would not be here, and this book would not be in print, without you: Liz and Paul Beck, Kim Kucinskas, Joy-Lee Pasqualoni Merlini, Mary, Jimmy, Kristin, J. W., and Kim Fischer, Rosemary Ng, Ashley Wei, Nicki Chavoya, Meredith Grossman, Greg Piesco-Putnam, and Kristin Pelkey. I am also thankful for the love and support of my new family members, Rhonda Sanderson, Richard Schuman, Adam Schuman, Dina Schuman, Garrett Schuman, and Rebecca Moses.

This book would not be nearly as readable without my husband Zack's many sacrifices, support, and invaluable feedback. Thank you, Zack and Adela, for making my world such an inspired, loving, and beautiful place every single day.

The Mindful Elite

Timeline of the Contemplative Movement, 1979-1999

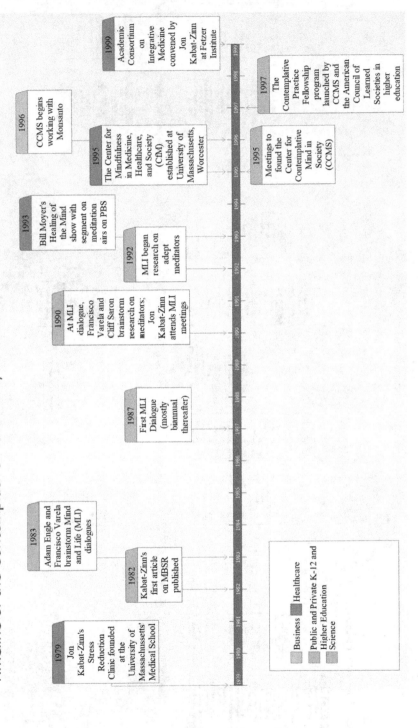

1979 — Jon Kabat-Zinn's Stress Reduction Clinic founded at the University of Massachussetts' Medical School

1982 — Kabat-Zinn's first article on MBSR published

1983 — Adam Engle and Francisco Varela brainstorm Mind and Life (MLI) dialogues

1987 — First MLI Dialogue (mostly biannual thereafter)

1990 — At MLI dialogue, Francisco Varela and Cliff Saron brainstorm research on meditators; Jon Kabat-Zinn attends MLI meetings

1992 — MLI began research on adept meditators

1993 — Bill Moyer's Healing of the Mind show with segment on meditation airs on PBS

1995 — The Center for Mindfulness in Medicine, Healthcare, and Society (CIM) established at University of Massachusetts, Worcester

1995 — Meetings to found the Center for Contemplative Mind in Society (CCMS)

1996 — CCMS begins working with Monsanto

1997 — The Contemplative Practice Fellowship program launched by CCMS and the American Council of Learned Societies in higher education

1999 — Academic Consortium on Integrative Medicine convened by Jon Kabat-Zinn at Fetzer Institute

Legend:
- Business
- Healthcare
- Public and Private K-12 and Higher Education
- Science

The Contemplative Movement, 2000–2012

2000
Susan Kaiser Greenland founds Inner Kids

2001
Oasis Institute founded at CIM to train MBSR teachers

2001
Wellness Works in Schools founded by Kinders; Inner Resilience founded by Linda Lantieri; Trish Broderick adapts MBSR program for kids; PassageWorks founded by Rachel Kessler; Holistic Life Foundation established by Ali and Atman Smith

2002
Goldie Hawn starts her mindfulness education program, MindUP

2002
Steven Hickman founds the University of California San Diego Center for Mindfulness

2003
MLI Summer Research Institute and Varela Awards begin

2003
Garrison Institute, hub of mindful education, founded

2003
MTT Dialogue; MLI goes public

2004
Sue Smalley founds Mindful Awareness Research Center (MARC) at UCLA

2004
The Garrison Institute launches the Initiative on Contemplation and Education (ICE)

2004
Program in Creativity and Consciousness Studies established at University of Michigan by Ed Sarath

2005
Hal Roth awarded grant to develop contemplative center at Brown University; Contemplative Studies Initiative and Concentration established

2005
Dalai Lama visits Stanford, which catalyzed founding of the Center for Compassion and Altruism Research and Education (CCARE)

2006
Buddhist Geeks podcast begins

2006
Emory Collaborative for Contemplative Studies founded

2007
Shamatha Project, a longitudinal study of meditation's effects on love and forgiveness, begins

2007
Liz Stanley and Amishi Jha brainstorm Mindfulness-Based Mind Fitness Training (MMFT) program at MLI Summer Research Institute

2007
Mindful Schools starts teaching children

2007
Garrison holds first mindful education conference

2007
CCMS begins work with Army chaplains

2007
Google Search Inside Yourself program starts

2008
Center for Investigating Healthy Minds (CIHM) founded at the University of Wisconsin by Richard Davidson

2008
David Black starts Mindfulness Research Guide website

2010
Institute for Mindful Leadership founded by Janice Marturano

2010
Headspace meditation app founded

2010
First Wisdom 2.0 conference held

2010
Official opening of CIHM at University of Wisconsin

2011
Buddhist teacher Kenneth Folk moves to San Francisco to train tech leaders in meditation

2011
Mind and Life offers Contemplative Studies grants to broaden the field

2011
First Buddhist Geeks conference

2011
Interaxon builds neuroscientific feedback headband for meditation

2012
Contemplative Sciences Center launched at the University of Virginia

2012
MLI hosts first annual International Symposium for Contemplative Studies

Legend: Healthcare ☐ Science ☐ Public and Private K-12 and Higher Education ☐ Business ☐ Military ☐

PART I | An Introduction to the
Mindful Elite

| The Contemplative Elite and Capitalism
A Case of Contradictions, Successes, and Shortcomings

A Meeting at the American Enterprise Institute

On February 20, 2014, the most eminent Buddhist leader in the world—the 14th Dalai Lama—walked on stage wearing his bright red robe. He sat among a row of distinguished-looking white men in dark suits and ties. Sitting off to the left, the Dalai Lama polished and repolished his glasses. The suit in the middle, Arthur Brooks, the president of the neoconservative American Enterprise Institute (AEI), an economist and frequent author of op-eds and blogs for the *New York Times* and the *Wall Street Journal*, began introductions. The AEI event featured the Dalai Lama and the Mind and Life Institute (MLI), the most prominent organization bringing Buddhism into science.[1] The title of the first session, "Moral Free Enterprise," conveyed AEI's agenda for the meeting.

It was a meeting of seemingly strange bedfellows. MLI was established in the late 1980s by progressive, politically liberal meditators who had come of age during the American counterculture of the 1960s and 1970s. MLI's founders sought to bring together Buddhist and scientific worldviews to see what each could learn from the other. As an organizational leader of a broader contemplative movement, MLI has worked to legitimize and spread secularized forms of Buddhist meditation in professional institutions. This movement, which is the focus of this book, promotes contemplative culture, which is a secularized cultural amalgam of the values, ideology, and meditation practices from multiple Buddhist lineages, including Theravada, Tibetan, and Zen traditions, as well as humanistic American intellectual and spiritual traditions, to leaders and professionals in powerful institutions. I refer to the meditation movement as the *contemplative movement* because "contemplative" is used by many of the dominant organizations in this field. Buddhism directly and indirectly influenced all of the programs in my sample, including "mindfulness" and "mind training" programs. "Mindfulness," or "paying attention in a particular way: on purpose, in the present moment and nonjudgmentally" as defined by contemplative leader Jon Kabat-Zinn (1994a: 4), is a central part of this movement. Other traditions, such as yoga, humanist psychology, and neuroscience are also woven into contemplative culture.

Both contemplative organizations and AEI seek to reform society—but the leaders of each have considerably different starting points, ideologies, and approaches of doing so. On one hand, contemplative organizations seek to reform society by promoting contemplative practices, such as meditation, in "intervention" programs in healthcare, education, business, the military, sports, and other institutions to transform individuals. Drawing from Buddhist ideology, they hope that through contemplative practice, individuals' self-awareness, sense of interconnectedness with others, and compassion for others will increase. With greater self-awareness and social concern, they believe people will be able to better address collective social problems such as materialism, inequality, and injustice. On the other hand, AEI represents the interests of the capitalist establishment, which is often associated with supporting increased materialism and consumption. AEI is one of the most vocal proponents of government policies that support free market capitalism, financial deregulation, and limited government.

As Brooks continued to speak about the meeting of these different minds, the Dalai Lama carefully folded the cloth used to wipe his glasses and tucked it into the folds of his robe near the center of his chest. Next he adjusted his robe and put on the trademark red visor that he often wears during public talks. Now he was ready for discussion.

"So here's the question," Brooks asked quickly, raising his right hand to accentuate the question's importance. "Is the free enterprise system still the best system to pursue our happiness, to lead a good life? Have we become too materialistic? Do we need to reorder our priorities toward higher ends?"

———

The 2014 AEI event provoked a lot of questions not only from journalists of nationally renowned publications such as the *Washington Post*, the *New York Times*, and *Vanity Fair*, but among the founders of the contemplative movement. How did the Dalai Lama and MLI—and their shared cause of bringing

Buddhist ethics and meditation practice into the American mainstream—arrive on center stage in capitalistic American culture? How did Buddhism and countercultural variants of meditation, which had often been associated with anti-materialist hippies and flighty New Age believers in the United States in the aftermath of the 1960s and 1970s counterculture, become so nonthreatening—and even appealing—to neoconservative business leaders that they could publicly welcome it?

And what were the contemplative leaders, as advocates of Buddhist ethics, which include nonattachment to material goods, doing at an event sponsored by a prominent neoliberal think tank devoted to free market capitalism, the production of profit, and the deregulation of capitalism? Did the AEI event support the contemplatives' mission to popularize meditation and Buddhist culture as a way of reforming American society? Or were the contemplatives and their ideas co-opted? Had they abandoned their commitment to Buddhist values as the price of gaining popularity?

There is much to learn from the mindful elite movement. By examining how the contemplative movement popularized meditation and other related mindful practices among professionals over the past forty years, I begin to answer the above questions in this book. By knowing more about where the movement has come from, it is possible to better understand both its successes and shortcomings, and those of other elite-driven change initiatives.

"Somehow Mind and Life Got Taken"

If men define situations as real, they are real in their consequences.

—W. I. THOMAS

This theorem by W. I. Thomas is perhaps the closest sociologists get to agreeing on an overarching social "rule." It explains that people often act upon what they perceive as real. People's interpretations produce actions that have consequences. Thus if people act as if something is real, even if it is not, the effects of the action are likely to be the same as if the event really happened. Therefore, in the case of the AEI event, what was most important was not what actually happened, but how what happened was interpreted and publicized post hoc.

After the event Arthur Brooks wrote on the AEI's blog that the organization was "honored to hear the Dalai Lama report he had learned something from us as well." Their conversation, he wrote, "helped remind him [the

Dalai Lama] why he has moved away from the negative view that capitalism 'only takes money, then exploitation.' Provided that societies stay mindful of the challenges that capitalism creates and never forget the paramount importance of inclusion and equal opportunity, we can and should celebrate the miracle of free enterprise—and the billions of souls it has helped free from desperate poverty" (Brooks 2014: 1). From Brooks' statement, it sounded as if the Dalai Lama was embracing free market capitalism, and the economic ideology that underlay it.

David Rose, a reporter for *Vanity Fair* who was invited to the event, wrote that "To be sure, nabbing the Dalai Lama for his first-ever appearance at a think tank was a huge and symbolic coup . . . it's hard to think of a more dramatic way of trying to get across the notion that conservatism, at least as envisioned by AEI, has changed" (2014). Danielle Pleta, vice president of AEI, told Rose that the event was "a really big deal for us. It underscores the fact that the Right needs a new vibe." Brooks also bluntly communicated to Rose (2014) that "We are trying to remake the debate, and we're going to win. It's not a question of if, but when." How did he want to remake the debate? Brooks sought a "complete ideological remodeling of the American Right." Brooks wanted to refashion the Right as a " 'free market movement' that steals the clothes of the Left, by demonstrating that free markets offer a much more effective and empowering way to tackle social problems than the state . . . We're moral warriors for people who can't fight for themselves. What I really want is for the free enterprise movement to become like the civil rights movement: something that transcends politics" (Rose 2014). Brooks used the Dalai Lama as a tool in his campaign to create a new moral image for neoconservatives; the Dalai Lama seemed to unintentionally provide a stamp of moral approval for AEI's economic beliefs.

It was evident to many that the Dalai Lama had considerably different economic opinions than AEI, which were not discussed in AEI's public reports of the event. In a private interview, the Dalai Lama told Rose (2014) that "Strictly speaking, I am socialist, so I am Leftist." The Dalai Lama also mentioned in response to a question at one of the AEI discussion panels that "so far as social economic theory is concerned, I am a Marxist" (2014). These comments were not reported in the transcripts of the event or in AEI's reporting of it. In a private conversation, Paul Wolfowitz, former Deputy Secretary of Defense under George W. Bush and an AEI Visiting Scholar, conceded to Rose (2014) that the Dalai Lama's "political means for expressing compassion was somewhat different than Brooks' . . . But symbols are important." Merely by his presence and by his subtle support for the organization's economic tenets, the Dalai Lama provided a powerful symbol of moral legitimacy for the AEI.

How did the progressive, liberal members of MLI respond to the AEI event? The simple answer is: not well. In response to the MLI collaboration with AEI, many early MLI leaders were furious. One MLI scientist stated it simply, "Somehow, Mind and Life got taken." To the progressive, left-leaning leaders of meditation in science whom I spoke with, the AEI event was like watching in slow motion their evil twin coopt their tactics as well as their moral spiritual leader and the most prominent celebrity sponsoring their cause. The Dalai Lama was both an important public face of MLI and a funder of the organization's work. Not only did it seem that the spiritual leader had been manipulated into providing moral legitimacy for free market capitalism, but MLI had been dragged into the event. This was politically antithetical to the anti-materialist, implicitly politically liberal view that the contemplative meditators adhered to. Furthermore, the event provoked the question of whether MLI and AEI were in fact similar. Were both organizations proponents of the free market that were stealing "the clothes of the Left" to advance the interests of moneyed elites?

As an organization, MLI did not do a good job clarifying to members or the public why it collaborated with AEI and what the event symbolically meant for the organization. Although MLI posted a blog before the AEI event explaining that they were participating in the dialogue because they wanted to engage in conversation with all others, no matter how different their beliefs were, they did not report on the event further after it occurred. A MLI administrator I spoke with suggested the organization was going through a transitional period at the time. It was struggling to deal with its rapid growth over the past few years, had internal conflicts between older and newer members, and had disagreements over how much to cater to the Dalai Lama. Overall, it was clear that MLI lacked the organizational capacity and manpower to effectively deal with the backlash from the event.[2]

Other strategic choices MLI leaders have made over the years, which I discuss in more depth throughout this book, set them on the path to arrive on AEI's stage. Contemplative leaders work with affluent patrons and sympathizers who are members of esteemed organizations in powerful institutions like science, healthcare, education, business, and the military. Many members and their professional allies are part of organizations with divergent missions from the contemplative cause. To gain access to mainstream professional audiences, resources, and legitimacy, contemplatives have adapted Buddhist modernist meditation to appeal to a variety of audiences in numerous ways. Furthermore, the contemplative movement has a thin collective identity; they share some meditation practices, but lack an explicit shared spiritual or religious identity, sacred texts, common teachers, and a uniform ethical code.[3] The movement does not have a single regulatory body to distinguish and enforce the boundaries of who should teach contemplative practice, what their training should entail, best practices in teaching, and what kinds of individuals and organizations are appropriate collaborators in spreading Buddhist-inspired meditation as a means of social progress. Although these various factors have contributed to the contemplatives' success in rapidly spreading among new professional audiences, they also led to MLI's presence at the AEI event.

The AEI meeting left contemplative leaders reeling and confused. They were made aware that the choices they had made in promoting Buddhism in secular society had tragically and counterintuitively led them to this event. As MLI member and UC Davis neuroscientist Cliff Saron told me the following summer over coffee, something that "had been wrong was made manifest." The event made MLI and leaders of other contemplative organizations realize that they had to do some soul searching; they needed to collectively decide on what their values, standards, and mission truly were.

The Purpose of the Book

How did Buddhist forms of meditation come to be associated with a capitalistic, professional elite? What has gone right and what has gone wrong in the promotion of meditation from the perspectives of Buddhist meditation's early secularizers, devout practitioners, and critics? How do organizations in this meditation movement respond to the threat of cooptation? In light of the AEI event and the rapid increase in elite interest in meditation in the past decade, these questions are important to consider. They are important not only in understanding how a previously countercultural Buddhist-inspired practice of mindful meditation has become popular among mainstream Western audiences, but in understanding more broadly how elite-driven cultural change occurs, and what its strengths and its shortcomings are.

When I first began to study the spread of mindful meditation in the United States in 2009, it seemed inconceivable to me that tough Wall Street and Silicon Valley executives, military leaders, and top athletes would, of their own accord, go to a Buddhist temple, bow to a teacher, chant, and practice sitting meditation. Buddhist meditation was widely seen as a practice of select Asian immigrants, leftist hippies, and New Age spiritual seekers, rather than leaders of the most powerful institutions in American society. Yet today elites of all stripes—professionals, intellectuals, the wealthy, and celebrities—not only practice different Buddhist-inspired forms of meditation, but declare over national, international, and social media that meditation is secular, legitimate, and good for you. Mindful meditation is promoted as a panacea for all that ails us.

Mindfulness is understood by popular audiences as an individual contemplative attention practice, in which a meditator focuses on the rising and falling of the breath while sitting in a grounded, meditative posture. Lay proponents as well as some researchers say it increases physical and psychological health, hones attention skills, enhances productivity, increases emotional awareness, and cultivates ethical social values and skills, such as compassion.[4] These benefits of sustained meditation practice are largely supported by a rapidly growing body of scientific research. Since 1980, scientists have published thousands of academic articles on meditation and mindfulness.[5] News sources as varied as the *New York Times*, *Time* magazine, CNN, ABC News, CBS News Sunday Morning, and Fox News have reported on the positive effects and burgeoning popularity of mindfulness meditation.

With this increased legitimacy and widespread media coverage, Western converts are meditating more than ever. While it is nearly impossible to know exactly how many people are influenced by Buddhism in the United States, sociologists Robert Wuthnow and Wendy Cadge (2004) estimated that about 30% of Americans are very or somewhat familiar with Buddhist teachings. Most of the people they surveyed viewed Buddhism favorably, believing it to be a "tolerant" and "peace loving" religion. A 2007 PEW Religious Landscape survey estimated that about four in ten American adults (39%) meditated at least once per week (Duerr 2011)—a number that has likely grown since then. In part because of its health benefits, meditation has emerged as the next big thing in business: in 2009 alone, Americans spent $4.2 billion on mindful practices for their health (Wilson 2014: 2).

To investigate how Buddhist-inspired forms of meditation came to be embraced by esteemed American professionals, I went directly to the sources of the ideas. From 2010 to 2012, I spoke with leaders of the contemplative movement as they were becoming more unified across various institutions including science, healthcare, education, business, and the military. From 2014 to 2016, I conducted follow-up visits and interviews to assess how they were coping with their work's successes and failures.[6]

In meeting with contemplative leaders, I was struck by how many of them had completed graduate-level education and held socially esteemed jobs. Most were part of financially comfortable households that did not struggle to pay their monthly bills. Compared to the average American family, most respondents were well above average in terms of their financial resources; some were downright wealthy. A handful of contemplative leaders were among the ultra-rich who did not have to work to subsist and could donate considerable resources to the movement to support fledgling contemplative programs and organizations. In short, the contemplative leaders were among America's educational, professional, and economic elite. In speaking of *elites* throughout the book, I refer to people who occupy privileged, high-level social positions in at least one of the following socioeconomic factors: education, occupation, and economic status.

I began investigating the contemplative movement both as an outsider and as a novice meditator.[7] Over time, the complexity of the mindfulness movement has come into full focus for me. It defies overly simplistic binary explanations thrown around by the media and by practitioners alike that characterize the movement as overwhelmingly good or bad, Buddhist or secular, or authentic as opposed to selling out. Instead, it is important to examine which parts of the movement are beneficial and which may have blind spots or deleterious consequences. Which elements of contemplative culture are promoting the Buddhist dharma, and which have been wiped of religious sources? And in what ways have the contemplatives displayed authenticity to their mission and purposes of promoting Buddhist-inspired contemplative practice, and in which missions, values, and purposes have they fallen short?

Although contemplative leadership, and the broader movement in its wake, is composed of a wide range of elites with varying niches of expertise and commitments to Buddhism, members share a belief that meditation practice and science can be brought together to help relieve suffering for people facing a wide range of individual and social problems. Despite their good intentions for spreading Buddhist-inspired meditative practices, along the way contemplative leaders have made strategic decisions about how to popularize and legitimize meditation with positive and negative consequences. While they have exposed various new audiences to meditation, the mindful elites at the helm of the movement seemed unaware of their privileges and of the possible negative short- and long-term consequences of their programs.

Making visible the strengths and weaknesses of the contemplative movement is important not only in developing a better understanding of mindfulness meditation in America—and internationally—but is crucial to understanding more broadly how elites can organize across institutions to initiate social reform, while also unintentionally abetting a status quo that privileges some at the expense of others.

What Kind of Social Change Is This?

Cultural Diffusion

Scholars of religion may look to the supply-side growth of Buddhist temples and the demand-side seeking by the spiritually inclined, the chronically ill, and the stressed to explain the rise of the mindfulness movement. They may point to the growing segment of the U.S. population that religiously or spiritually self-identify in nuanced, unique ways, rather than based on a single explicit religious identity. A 2015 PEW study suggested that while the proportion of American Christians has shrunk (from 78.4% in 2007 to 70.6% in 2014), the percentage of religiously unaffiliated people—who are atheist, agnostic, or "nothing in particular"—has grown (from 16.1% to 22.8%). In addition, unaware of all the behind-the-scenes contemplative organizing, meditators might assume that meditation has become popular in America because "it works"—as some of the meditators I spoke with suggested based on their experiences. Although these factors likely all contributed to the current popularity of contemplative practice, they suggest that it became popular through a scattered process of cultural diffusion in which Buddhist dharma centers and practitioners across America gradually converted others around them to adopt Buddhist meditation.

Scholars define cultural **diffusion** as a general means of social change, through which "a practice," which may be "a behavior, strategy, belief, technology, or structure," spreads "from a source to an adapter, via communication and influence" (Strang and Soule 1998: 266). As diffused practices spread, they generally are innovated by those that transmit them, empowering their carriers (Strang and Soule 1998: 267). Through various processes of diffusion, Buddhist-inspired contemplative practices have certainly spread widely in the past four decades. However, my research uncovered a less visible, more specific process of diffusion that has driven the mainstreaming of meditation: contemplative practice was popularized and legitimized deliberately by a movement of elite meditators.

Elite Movements

Because elites are often hard to access, we know little about how they sponsor and execute movements.[8] Yet, they are an important source of mainstream culture, as scholars have suggested for over a century (Marx, in Tucker 1978: 172–173). Consequently, as a sociologist, I wondered how this case can help us better understand how previously marginalized, stigmatized cultures can be brought into mainstream, everyday life by elites to initiate broader cultural and political change. I wanted to know how elites can collectively pool their resources and mobilize cultural change across institutions, and what associated weaknesses of this approach to social reform might be. I found that, as an elite movement, contemplative mobilization was a chimera of sorts. It shared common features of cultural diffusion, social movements, organizational innovation, and field development, yet could not definitely be placed as one of these conceptual categories. It was, in the end, an admixture of the ideal types of all these forms of social change.

The contemplative movement is a collectivity that aligns with common definitions of social movements. **Social movements** are defined by how they act *"with some degree of organization and continuity outside of institutional or organizational channels for the purpose of challenging or defending extant authority,* whether it is institutionally or cultural based, in the group, organization, society, culture, or world order of which they are a part" (italics added for emphasis; Snow, Soule, and Kriesi 2007: 11).[9] As an elite movement comprising insiders across professional social sectors, the contemplatives are collectively institutionalizing a previously stigmatized spiritual subculture in their secular workplaces. They seek to create a humanist society imbued with Buddhist values, ideology, and meditation practice. They see this societal vision as an alternative to the status quo, which they view as driven by bureaucratic habitual action based on instrumental rationality, greed, and materialism. They are organized through personal, religious, and professional networks, across and outside of their workplaces, as well as through central field-building organizations (such as the Center for Mindfulness in Medicine, Health Care, and Society [CfM], MLI, and the Center for Contemplative Mind in Society [CCMS]). For decades contemplative leaders[10] quietly mobilized; they constructed an elaborate apparatus of professional movement organizations that extolled meditation practices, developed scientific and cultural legitimacy for them, and translated them to appeal to new audiences.[11] They used unobtrusive consensus-driven strategies to develop their programs and organizations that did not provoke organized opposition by people of other faiths or ideological systems (like science).[12]

The contemplative movement is similar in many ways to what movement scholars call **New Social Movements (NSMs)**. In contrast to "older" movement studies, which focused on how chronic social problems could incite movements, how movements accumulated resources, and activists' rational decision-making processes, NSM theory highlighted the cultural side of movements. Based on movements of the 1960s and 1970s such as the environmental, women's, and gay rights movements, NSMs emphasized the importance of ideology and identity to mobilization.[13] In contrast to the labor and poor people's movements studied during the first half of the twentieth century by movement scholars, NSMs' members emphasize "new or formerly weak" identities, often focusing on parts of their personal lives, and reacting to a "credibility crisis" doubting the efficacy of conventional democratic politics (Larana et al. 1994: 6–8).

Members of NSMs tend to act out movement tactics individually rather than in large groups. Consequently, the boundaries between individual and collective action are more blurry. Although NSM activists may use "radical mobilization tactics of disruption and resistance," (Larana et al. 1994: 8) such as nonviolent civil disobedience inspired and supported by a larger movement, the movements themselves are likely to have a decentralized, segmented structure, rather than a formal hierarchical organizational structure. Furthermore, NSMs may appear to be less of a collective group because members typically come from different socioeconomic backgrounds and have varying political values and ideologies, even though they share some pragmatic goals (Larana et al. 1994: 6–8).

Like NSMs, the contemplative movement seeks to transform individuals' beliefs, values, and behavior in hopes of initiating wider processes of social change. The movement seeks to transform people's personal everyday lives by teaching them to meditate and do other contemplative practices. Over time, contemplatives gain a *practice-based identity*, based on a commitment to a regular personal meditation practice. Contemplatives share the belief that doing habitual contemplative practice will be beneficial to their health and well-being, and they aspire to practice regularly.[14] While some practitioners engage deeply in Buddhist religious practices such as Tibetan Buddhist visualizations of deities, others favor secularized contemplative practices such as yoga or mind–body scans, in which they pay attention to sensations arising in different parts of their bodies.

The contemplative movement aligns with NSMs from the 1960s and 1970s in several other ways as well. Rather than seek structural or legal reform through conventional politics, they instead focus on individual change. Believing that the "personal is political," they first seek to improve their own lives and the lives of those around them. Because of their emphasis on personally altering one's worldview and behavior, rather than collective action, there is a blurry line with regards to when movement outcomes are individual or collective. Furthermore, like NSMs, the contemplative movement has a decentralized structure; contemplative organizations are located across the United States and increasingly around the world.

Building a Multi-Institutional Field Through Institutional Entrepreneurship

Unlike conventional social movements and NSMs, the elite-driven contemplative movement does not use radical, contentious tactics to disrupt the status quo (Gamson 1975; Giugni 1998; McAdam 1999; McAdam et al. 2001). Instead, contemplatives hope to initiate social reform by establishing a new field of secular contemplative meditation practice, which overlaps with and is anchored in esteemed organizations in science, education, business, healthcare, the government, and other institutional sectors. As such, in addition to exemplifying elite-led diffusion and, in various respects, a movement, the contemplatives show how collectivities can build multi-institutional fields by embedding training programs in a variety of new fields. In accordance with Fligstein and McAdam (2012), I define **fields** as meso-level structures that overlap and are embedded in a variety of other social fields. In contrast with formal organizations, which are "objective," legally designated entities with clear boundaries, fields are constructed social orders within which actors consensually recognize and define the field (Fligstein and McAdam 2012: 64).

Rather than comprising a base of economically, politically, or organizationally marginalized people challenging the status quo (as in classic social movements or field theory: Fligstein and McAdam 2012; Gamson 1975), or a mix of people from different classes (like NSMs), the contemplative movement is composed mainly of affluent, educated professionals. At the core of the contemplative movement is a group of institutional entrepreneurs who work across various professional fields, such as science, healthcare, education, and the military. **Institutional entrepreneurs** are socially skilled actors who usually occupy high-level positions and have access to resources that aid them in implementing change from the top down within the organizations and institutional fields they are a part of.[15] After changes are implemented within respected, successful organizations, they tend to be copied by other similar kinds of organizations, which in competitive markets or uncertain environments seek to appear cutting-edge, competent, and legitimate (DiMaggio and Powell 1983; Meyer and Rowan 1977).[16]

Yet, the contemplative leaders differ from depictions of institutional entrepreneurs in several respects: they come from a variety of professional backgrounds and institutional sectors and are united by a larger movement. From the movement, they gain support and funding from a network of contemplative organizations, which are outside of and have different missions than contemplatives' professional institutions. This network supports them in implementing **consensus-based tactics**, which emphasize cooperation, compromise, and adaptation to dominant institutional cultures instead of contestation and opposition to dominant institutional norms and practices. Such consensus-building tactics have been acknowledged (for existing scholarship, see Klandermans 1988; Kucinskas 2014; McCarthy and Wolfson 1992; Michaelson 1994), but have received little attention in recent research and remain insufficiently understood in scholarship on movements (Pellow 1999) or on how fields develop (e.g., Fligstein and McAdam 2012).

Contemplative leaders use a number of consensus-based strategies to win over new audiences. The movement draws upon its leaders' privileged positions in society generally and their access to affluent networks and esteemed organizations specifically to bring a previously stigmatized or unknown practice into multiple powerful institutional fields gradually and covertly. Although some contemplative institutional entrepreneurs have the power to implement contemplative programs from the top (as occurred with the seed company Monsanto, as discussed in Chapter 4), many do not. Instead, many contemplative leaders had to carefully, and sometimes covertly, develop their contemplative programs before sharing them more broadly in their institutions. Program developers deliberately adapted contemplative practice to resonate in their professional contexts to avoid coming across as esoteric, too New Age, or dogmatic.

By identifying the specific mechanisms and strategies leaders of the movement used, I contribute to social scientific understanding of how movements can gradually build coalitions of support to establish broad new fields that are anchored in multiple existing powerful organizations and institutions, rather than directly confronting dominant systems of power.[17] This study also informs knowledge of institutional entrepreneurship, which has focused on studying single or small groups of actors and has not sufficiently examined the broader multilevel and multi-institutional contexts in which entrepreneurship is embedded (Batillana et al. 2009; Lounsbury and Crumley 2007). The contemplative case shows the importance of taking into account external cultural influences and organizational support from movements and other sources outside of discrete organizations and institutional fields.

Outline of the Book

In each chapter I show different facets of the contemplative movement as it unfolded over time. Although this book is intended to appeal to scholars, students, and meditators, I suspect certain chapters will resonate more with some audiences than others. However, all chapters contribute important pieces to the puzzle of how the mindful elite movement has popularized meditation across multiple institutions using consensus-based tactics, where they have been successful, and where their work has fallen short.[18]

I provide background information on the contemplative movement in Part 1. Chapter 2 has a brief historical overview of the contemplative movement's Buddhist modernist historical antecedents in America from the 1830s to the 1970s. In Chapter 3, I describe the purpose of the burgeoning contemplative work bringing meditation to secular audiences in the last decades of the twentieth century, as described to me by their founding members. I share why they believe meditation is important, how they think meditation will benefit society, and how they seek to implement social reform.

In Part 2 (Chapters 4 through 7), I delve into the repertoire of unobtrusive consensus-based tactics the contemplatives used to popularize Buddhist-inspired contemplative practices among secular professional audiences in science, education, healthcare, business, and the military from 1979 through 2016, when I stopped collecting data. In Chapter 4, I describe how contemplative leaders built an impressive contemplative field across powerful institutions by developing elite networks. They then used professional organizational legitimacy and credibility from elite universities, Fortune 500 businesses, and public figures to popularize meditation among secular elites.

To avoid a backlash from other professionals, the contemplatives took care not to challenge the explicit institutional rules or structures in place. Instead, as discussed in Chapter 5, they crafted mindfulness and meditation to fit within the institutions they brought it into. Once they gained access to powerful players and organizations in academia, healthcare, business, and education, they brought intervention programs in. In quiet spaces constructed for mindful practice, contemplative educators then began teaching people how to do contemplative practice, and how to bring the practices into their everyday lives "off the cushion" (as shown in Chapter 6).

There are strengths and limitations to the contemplatives' elite-driven approach to social change, as I discuss in Chapter 7 and in the last part of the book. With the growing popularity of mindfulness meditation, the movement has increasingly received both positive and negative attention from the media, Buddhist meditators, and others. While some publications applaud the contemplatives' commitment to improving the well-being of employees, children, teachers, doctors, nurses, and so on, critics question contemplatives' adaptability to capitalist institutions, their authenticity, and their commitment to Buddhism. In making such dramatic changes to Buddhist practice, critics wonder, is mindfulness attached to everything? Have mindful practitioners deserted their Buddhist roots to become a new elite engaged in a relentless push for increased productivity and profit? In Part 3 of the book, I address these questions. In Chapter 8, I examine critiques of the movement and the contemplatives' response. I conclude the book in Chapter 9 with an assessment of what we can learn from the contemplative movement about consensus-based, elite-driven approaches to cultural change.

Elites' Unobtrusive Consensus-Based Tactics: The Bigger Picture

Since the heyday of the social movements in the 1960s and 1970s, when the civil rights movement, the antiwar movement, the women's movement, and the environmental movement filled the streets and other public spaces, many changes have occurred in the world. Like some other scholars of social movements and activism (Lounsbury 2001; Sampson et al. 2005), I suspect the locus of social and culture change has shifted in the United States. Collective civic work is not just occurring via protest on the street or through the conventional political process in local, state, and federal government.[19] In addition, many political and cultural change-makers mobilize by leveraging power through society's major institutions, such as science, education, business, and the media. Through these institutions, movements can challenge localized cultural understandings within organizations as well as broader mainstream cultural currents in the public sphere (Armstrong and Bernstein 2008; Raeburn 2004). However, scholarship on mobilization and cultural change is only just beginning to understand the diverse ways activists initiate broader social change by mobilizing through powerful organizations and across institutional sectors (e.g., Raeburn 2004; Soule 2009).

The contemplative movement shows how social reform can be initiated by teaching elites a new praxis (a combination of philosophy and practice), which is justified by a compelling, optimistic, science-based ideology and practices that promise simultaneously to cultivate self-development, professional success, and social progress. Who wouldn't want that, right? Yet a primary focus on individual change, rather than deeper institutional change, can unintentionally limit a movement's ability to achieve lofty goals. As a result, I hope that for the reader, one of the main takeaway points of this book is to think more deeply about the strengths and weaknesses of this middle-way approach to social reform.

| A Brief History of Buddhist-Inspired
American Spirituality, 1830s–1970s

ALTHOUGH RECENTLY MINDFULNESS HAS been heralded as a new scientifically supported health craze or as a trendy productivity tool, many of the
arguments in support of meditation practice have been around a long time.
The contemporary mindfulness movement did not appear in a vacuum.
There have been important antecedents in American culture, philosophy,
and religion for over a century, which suggest that Buddhism helps foster
personal growth, aligns with science, and is more inclusive of people from
different religious traditions than Christianity. Hence, to better understand
Buddhist-inspired contemplative practices in America, it is necessary to
trace the historical seeds of contemporary Buddhist-inspired spirituality in
the United States.

In contrast to more traditional ethnic Asian Buddhists, American Buddhist
modernizers and converts who do not have ethnic ties to Buddhism have dramatically adapted Buddhism over the past 175 years, in a complex interplay
with converging forces of modernization, scientization, and Westernization
(McMahan 2008). During different historical periods, particular elements
of Buddhism were popularized through varying media. These prior seeds
of Buddhist-inspired American spiritual culture, which reached mainly select groups of religiously liberal white Americans with quite watered-down,
transformed versions of Buddhism, have been romanticized and passed down
over the generations. The current contemplative movement builds upon
such spiritual lore. However, contemporary mindful contemplative culture
by far surpasses its Buddhist-inspired spiritual antecedents: it has been the
most successful in breaking into mainstream American culture, propelled by
esteemed professionals and a network of contemplative organizations.

Buddhism's Early American Sympathizers

Small, select groups of white American religious liberals first became fascinated by Buddhism in the nineteenth century, based on European reports of Asian Buddhism and discussions about Buddhism at the 1893 World's Parliament of Religions. Early sympathizers like the Transcendentalist Henry David Thoreau romanticized Buddhist philosophy and adapted parts of it to fit into their own belief systems. Influenced by Unitarian denominations, Transcendentalism, and other new spiritual groups, like Theosophy, from the mid-nineteenth century until the early twentieth century, Americans' interest in the historical figure of the Buddha and Buddhist beliefs and ethics surged. However, these early Buddhist sympathizers had far less interest in Buddhist practices, such as meditation, than people do today (Wilson 2014).

Such groups had a cosmopolitan fascination with religious diversity and believed many paths could lead to a universal underlying spiritual experience. They brought together eclectic religious and spiritual influences from different Christian denominations and Asian religions like Buddhism and Hinduism. Although they romanticized Asian religions, Americans also believed American culture was more rational and sophisticated. American religious liberals rather liberally took, interpreted, and adapted resonant elements of Buddhist culture that appealed to Protestant Americans.

Buddhism's sympathizers thought Buddhism shared American Protestants' commitments to cultivating individual spiritual growth and progressive social progress toward world equality and spiritual enlightenment (Tweed 2000; 2013). Like Buddhists, some nineteenth-century religious liberals believed that people could cultivate an immanent sacred quality and experience transcendence through spiritual quests, as well as through silence, solitude, and serenity (Prebish and Keown 2010; Schmidt 2012). In the face of heightened immigration in the late nineteenth century, and subsequent marginalization and persecution of outsiders, Buddhism's champions also saw it as a more tolerant, scientific, and nonsectarian alternative to orthodox Christianity (Tweed 2000: 98).

The Transcendental spiritual and literary movement, which first became popular in the 1830s and 1840s, was the first major American cultural movement to take a serious interest in Buddhism. Building upon concurrent European Romanticism's emphasis on emotion and individualism, as well as Unitarianism's beliefs in individual reason and multiple possible paths to salvation, Transcendentalists sought truth, self-transcendence, and social development through the cultivation of inner spiritual experience. Through personal spiritual seeking, they thought that they could discover an underlying universal religious experience. Some of the most famous Transcendentalists, such as Ralph Waldo Emerson and Henry David Thoreau, were particularly fascinated by Hinduism and Buddhism (Versluis 1993). For example, Thoreau wrote in *Walden* (1982 [1854]):

> Sometimes, in a summer morning . . . I sat in my sunny doorway from sunrise til noon, rapt in revery, amidst the pines and hickories and sumachs, in undisturbed solitude and stillness, while the birds sang around or flitted noiseless through the house, until by the sun falling in my west window, or the noise of some traveller's wagon on the distant highway, I was reminded of the lapse of time. I grew in those seasons like corn in the night, and they were far better than the work of the hands would have been. They were not time subtracted from my life, but so much over and above my usual allowance. I realized what the Orientals mean by contemplation and the forsaking of works. (c.f. Fields 1992: 62)

Thoreau's passage reveals his fascination for contemplative practice in solitude in nature, which he associated with "Oriental" practices. Emerson and Thoreau's literary work inspired broader popular interest in Hinduism and Buddhism among religious liberals in the United States both during their time and in subsequent generations.

Interest in Buddhism continued to grow over the following several decades, becoming particularly fashionable among religiously liberal Americans from 1879 to 1912. During the late nineteenth century, Theosophy brought tales of Buddhism to a wider circle of American elites. Theosophy was based on an elaborate mythology about a group of spiritual adepts called Mahatmas, Brothers, or Masters created by founder Helena Blavatsky. The Great White Brotherhood of Mahatmas included famous religious and historical figures such as the Buddha, Jesus, Lao Tzu, Moses, and Plato. These spiritual adepts had reportedly undergone intensive esoteric training that gave them supernatural powers such as clairvoyance and the ability to inhabit bodies (Washington 1995).

Theosophists were particularly interested in Buddhism. Buddhist elements such as the law of karma, reincarnation, and meditation practice were part of their belief system (Washington 1995: 33–36). They made Buddhism appeal to their spiritual followers by depicting it as more of an occult "science" than a religion (Schmidt 2012). They also emphasized the utilitarian benefits of meditation. Theosophist leader Annie Besant described meditation as helping to foster an "increased energy in work, . . . steadiness, self-control, serenity; the man of meditation is the man who wastes no time, scatters no energy, misses no opportunity" (Schmidt 2012: 175–176). Thus, at the turn of the twentieth century, meditation was already being described by select spiritual seekers as a moral, scientific, and therapeutic practice with practical benefits. In addition to fostering self-integration, mental equilibrium, self-awareness, and efficacy in one's job, it was prescribed as an aid to treat addiction or self-centeredness (Schmidt 2012).

In 1893, during the World's Parliament of Religions in Chicago, Buddhism received further acclaim as a rational tradition aligned with science. At the meetings, Sri Lankan Buddhist Anagarika Dharmapala and Japanese Zen master Soyen Shaku discussed Buddhism's compatibility with science. Their talks and subsequent speaking engagements in the United States and Europe raised awareness of Buddhism among the general public in the West. Their talks provoked strong responses from the press and religious leaders, who compared Buddhism with Western religions and debated its merits and deficiencies.

Following the World's Parliament of Religions, German theologian and philosopher Paul Carus became an advocate of Buddhism in the West. His sympathetic arguments in support of Buddhism would resurface among mindful meditators a century later. Like Dharmapala and Shaku, Carus thought that Buddhism aligned with science. Because Buddhism did not require belief in God or a substantial soul, Carus argued that it was more scientific than Western religions were. Buddhism, he thought, was uniquely capable of harmonizing "the findings of science, the conclusions of reason, the demands of morality, and the requirements of interreligious cooperation" (Tweed 2000: 66).

Carus espoused other beliefs about Buddhism that have carried through to the present day. He wrote that Buddhists discern empirical truth based on their personal experience and that proven by science (Tweed 2000). Buddhism, according to Carus and other Buddhist sympathizers of his time, did not require faith. Carus additionally suggested that Buddhist cosmology's doctrines of karmic law aligned with evolutionary theory and the Buddhist "dynamic nonsubstantial self" dovetailed with the emerging discipline of psychology (Tweed 2000: 104–105). A century later, in his 2005 book, *The Universe in a Single Atom*, the 14th Dalai Lama made remarkably similar arguments in defense of Buddhism's compatibility with reason and science.

Carus distinguished between "pure Buddhism," which could apparently be identified by Westerners, and the "superstitious" beliefs and ritualistic practices of Asian Buddhists. He advocated for a "purification" of Buddhism and other religions by science (Tweed 2000: 105). This critical interpretation of ethnic Asian Buddhism revealed an implicit sense of cognitive superiority to Asian practitioners. Like his arguments, this prejudice has lingered among some convert practitioners in the present day.[1]

The Marginality and Decline of Early American Interest in Buddhism

Ultimately the dominant Christian majority's critique of Buddhism was more influential than the voices of its select sympathizers. Even during the height of Buddhist popularity in America at the turn of the twentieth century, few Americans practiced Buddhist meditation. Although tens of thousands of people were interested in Buddhism, during the period from 1893 to 1907, only about two to three thousand white Americans actually considered themselves Buddhists (Tweed 2000: 46).

In his 2000 book *The American Encounter with Buddhism, 1844–1912*, Thomas Tweed attributes Buddhism's marginal early influence on American culture, and its decline by 1912, to a number of cultural and institutional reasons. Buddhism, he argues, was too different from mainstream American culture. Sociologist of religion Rodney Stark (1987) theorized that new religious movements (NRMs) succeed in converting adherents by maintaining "a medium level of tension with their surrounding environment"; NRMs need to be "deviant, but not too deviant" and take care to "retain cultural continuity with conventional faiths of the societies in which they appear or originate" (c.f. Tweed 2000: 111–112).

When tales of Buddhism first trickled into nineteenth-century American society, Anglo-Saxon Protestant culture, with its emphasis on God, hard work, frugality, and sobriety, dominated American culture. American culture was also marked by a sense of individualism, optimism, and a penchant for activism. White Christians thought that through religious values and concerted effort, they could uplift members of their community to improve society as a whole. Many Americans proudly thought their Anglo-Saxon Protestant culture was superior to others, and that the United States played a pivotal role in the world's social development (Tweed 2000).

At the same time, the United States was undergoing a period of rapid social, industrial, and intellectual development. With industrialization and increased immigration, cities grew quickly. An intellectual revolution coincided with these changes. Science gradually displaced the Protestant establishment in the American education system (Reuben 1996). Developments in physical and social sciences such as biology, geology, and anthropology undermined biblical accounts of human origins (Reuben 1996; Tweed 2000: 93). In the end, religion was relegated from being a foundational part of American moral education to a marginal discipline that investigated the "scientific" study of comparative religions. In Religious Studies and more broadly, interest in other religions surged among Americans as European missionaries' and travelers' reports on the Middle East and the East became increasingly available.

In the face of such dramatic changes, people continued to privately gain comfort from religion in different ways. Among some groups, religious liberalism thrived. Among others, Christian orthodoxy became an appealing response to the many societal changes as a means to defend the preeminent role of Christianity in American culture. In this context of Christian religious revival, many mainline *and* orthodox Christians were hostile to Buddhism. They viewed it as a "strange," "heathen," "pagan" religion contradicting central tenets of American culture (Tweed 2000: xxx, 1–2, 6). Although some small pockets of religiously liberal Americans appreciated elements of Buddhism, such support only antagonized Christian opposition. Christian opponents denounced Buddhism as a cold, passive, pessimistic religion. Reverend J. T. Gracey, for example, of Rochester, New York, wrote to Christians that Buddhism was a "helpless, hopeless bondage, driving men to despondency or paralyzing all moral purpose." (c.f. Tweed 2000: 132). Even some of Buddhism's primary proponents, such as Paul Carus, viewed it as too pessimistic and passive. Such interpretations of Buddhism struck optimistic, activist-oriented Americans as discordant and a poor fit with their culture.

Interest in Buddhism declined for other reasons as well. Early American Buddhist converts failed to create stable institutions to sustain their spiritual beliefs and practices because they were generally skeptical of institutions. Although a few Buddhist organizations were established during this time, such as the American Madha Bodhi Society and the Dharma Sangha of Buddha, they were small, disorganized and lacked resources. In addition, because most Asian Buddhist teachers of Western convert groups did not permanently reside in the United States, there was a shortage of teachers. American convert Buddhists also had a few Buddhist texts to learn from; few texts had been translated to English (Tweed 2000).

The Counterculture

In the mid-twentieth century, earlier portrayals of Buddhism as scientific, not religious, and therapeutic revived. Once again, select groups of progressive spiritual Americans believed that, in contrast to mainline Christian churches—as well as Jewish synagogues—Buddhism was a more cosmopolitan, inclusive tradition that could promote social progress.

Popular interest in Zen grew from 1957 to 1963 based on the influence of D. T. Suzuki (a Columbia University professor of Buddhist philosophy and Zen teacher), Alan Watts (a British Episcopalian priest and writer on Buddhism), and the Beat poets (Seager 1999). Beat writers, such as Jack Kerouac, Gary Snyder, and Alan Ginsberg, described Buddhism as a "spiritual revolt with political overtones" (Seager 1999: 42). They reacted against white, upper-middle-class, suburban culture, which they characterized by social conformity and stale institutions. They were tired of their parents' churches and synagogues, which they saw as exemplars of routinized bureaucracy lacking in spiritual depth (Winter 1961). Instead, they drew upon Henry David Thoreau's reflections and meditation practice while living at Walden Pond (Schmidt 2012). Like Thoreau, the Beats glorified individual spiritual seeking through meditation and solitude. They delved more deeply into Buddhist dharma teachings than Thoreau, but in his spirit concluded contemplative practices were a means of opposing materialistic mainstream American culture and its social conformity. Kerouac offered up Buddhism to young people as a way to protest the resignation and obedience to dull middle-class life. Snyder advocated bringing together and building upon the tradition of social revolution in the West and the Buddhist awareness of the illusory nature of self (Seager 1999: 42).

In addition, due to changes in U.S. immigration law in 1965, Asian immigration to the United States increased. Buddhist teachers, such as Vietnamese monk Thich Nhat Hanh and the 14th Dalai Lama, could share their traditions with American audiences. Meditation instruction became increasingly accessible and appealing to American youth in the late 1960s and 1970s (Seager 1999; Wilson 2014).[2] However, the most important factor in the emergence of the contemplative movement was the popularization of *vipassana* (insight) meditation in the early 1970s.

The Formation of a Community of Scholar-Practitioners

Beat interest in Buddhism as a countercultural ideology gained traction in the 1970s when lay American practitioners returned from Asia and began teaching adapted versions of Buddhist *vipassana* meditation to young people. Alongside the rise of insight meditation, a critical community of scholar-practitioners, who practiced both science and meditation, coalesced in the 1970s. These scholar-practitioners, who came to establish the foundation of the contemporary contemplative movement, then created organizations to bring new adapted forms of meditation into hospitals, schools, businesses, and other powerful social institutions from 1979 (with the founding of Jon Kabat-Zinn's Center for Mindfulness in Medicine, Health Care, and Society) through today.

The American *vipassana* movement grew out of the Buddhist modernist teachings of Burmese monk Mahasi Sayadaw and lay Indian teacher S. N. Goenka. Both teachers were part of a reformation of Theravada Buddhism in Southeast Asia in the early to mid-twentieth century in response to British colonialism in Burma. Theravada *vipassana* meditation became a political tool of Burmese elites that was taught to laity in an effort to establish a post-colonial national-religious identity (Pagis [forthcoming]).

Sayadaw and Goenka went on to gain considerable followings of American lay meditators in the 1970s. Similar to prior Buddhist-inspired forms of American spirituality, the teachers attracted groups of white religious liberals who were skeptical of religious institutions. Sayadaw downplayed the impor-tance of the Buddhist monastic community, doctrine, cosmology, religious ritual, and sectarian divides. Mindfulness in this tradition was defined as a translation of *sati*, which in Pali means "memory" or "remembrance," and with respect to meditation refers to training in "awareness, attention, or alertness" (Wilson 2014: 15). Sayadaw and Goenka focused on teaching meditators to hone their attention. Sayadaw in particular taught practitioners to continuously label or "note" experiences that arose during practice.

Mindful meditation practice, as taught from Buddhist Theravada traditions from Burma, Thailand, and Sri Lanka as well as from other Buddhist traditions such as in lineages of Tibetan Buddhism, was used not only to hone people's attention, but to help participants gain awareness of often taken-for-granted cognitive and emotional patterns. By focusing on the breath and watching their thoughts arise, practitioners were taught to realize the impermanence of the mind, their emotions, and who they are. With greater awareness of ever-present flux and impermanence, meditators learned to deconstruct and decondition themselves from their cognitive and behavioral habits (Goleman 1976). They then reduced grasping to material objects, others, and who they thought they were (Goleman 1976; Varela, Thompson, and Rosch 1991). With mindful meditation practice, practitioners believed they would shift from less skillful, biased mental states of anger, hatred, greed, and attachment to more skilled mental states motivated by clarity, concentration, lovingkindness, compassion, and generosity (Weick and Putnam 2006).

Joseph Goldstein and Jack Kornfield, two former Peace Corps volunteers who studied Theravada *vipassana* meditation in Asia, were among the first Americans to teach it in the United States. Influenced by their Asian Buddhist modernist teachers, they continued to adapt Buddhist meditation practice in the United States. Like Mahasi Sayadaw, they taught meditation practices outside of religious contexts to lay audiences. They first taught mindful breathing exercises from Goenka's beginning meditation instruction. Only gradually, over time, did they work up to instructing practitioners on how to cultivate love and kindness toward others (Fronsdal 1998).

In the summer of 1974, Buddhist *vipassana* meditation attained new heights when teachers began building new institutions in America. Chogyam Trungpa convened a host of countercultural icons and meditators to teach summer courses at the newly formed Buddhist Naropa Institute in Boulder, Colorado. Meditators such as Kornfield, Goldstein, former LSD researcher and Harvard psychology professor Ram Dass (born Richard Alpert), Beat poet Alan Ginsberg, and others descended upon Boulder to teach (Fields 1992; Fronsdal 1998; Wilson 2014). After meeting at Naropa, Kornfield and Goldstein traveled around the United States and taught meditation mainly to young adults in their twenties and thirties for the following two years (Fields 1992). In 1976, with Sharon Salzberg and Jacqueline Schwartz, Kornfield and Goldstein established the Insight Meditation Society's Retreat Center in Barre, Massachusetts.

Throughout the 1970s, at meditation teachings such as Goenka's in India, at Naropa, and at the Insight Meditation Society, *vipassana* meditation took hold among a subset of countercultural youth and public intellectuals.[3] A network of American scholar-practitioners, who were both intellectuals and meditators, convened at places such as the dinner table of David McClelland (chair of the Harvard Department of Psychology) and retreats at the Lindisfarne Association, a progressive intellectual and spiritual hub in New York.[4] Meditators who would become central leaders of the contemporary contemplative movement, such as Kabat-Zinn, American Zen Roshi Joan Halifax, philosopher and neuroscientist Francisco Varela, activist Mirabai Bush, young philosopher-to-be Evan Thompson, and budding psychologists Richard Davidson, Daniel Goleman, and Cliff Saron, were among the mix. They crossed paths with and got to know Buddhist *vipassana* teachers, countercultural spiritual icons, and public intellectuals—such as Insight Meditation Society founders Salzberg and Goldstein, Ram Dass, and Ginsberg—who taught at Naropa and also frequented McClelland's dinner table.

Bush, the founder of the Center for Contemplative Mind in Society, recounted her experiences with this network of people in the 1970s while living at McClelland's house:

Every night we had dinner in that big dining room. And it was a big old Victorian house with this long mahogany table. And so every night there'd be like 12 or 15 people for dinner. And every [night], David would come back from

Harvard and he'd sit at the end of the table and he'd have a question or a theme for the evening (laughs). He would say, "I've been thinking about . . ." and then this conversation would start with everybody. It was SO much fun.

Political scientist Thomas Rochon (1998) theorized that cultural change occurs through a two-step process. First a critical community has to emerge.[5] "The creation of new ideas," Rochon writes, "comes from a relatively small community of critical thinkers who have developed sensitivity to a problem, an analysis of the sources of the problem, and a prescription for what should be done" (1998: 22). Critical communities often promote a new value system and work together on the conceptual clarification of new ideas. Then, social, political, and cultural movements bring critical communities' ideas to broader audiences. These movements use the critical communities' ideas as frames that are applied to influence the issues they care about.

The countercultural academics and meditators in the social circles at Harvard, Naropa, and Lindisfarne formed an initial critical community of scholar-practitioner meditators committed to both meditation and the scientific method. They wanted to bring together these two approaches to testing and refining knowledge. Some young scholar-practitioners, such as Harvard psychology graduate students Richard Davidson, Daniel Goleman, and Cliff Saron, began conducting research on meditation in the mid-1970s (e.g., Davidson et al. 1976; Davidson and Goleman 1977).

However, in the late 1970s, the countercultural era came to a close. Scholarship and interest in meditation became more suspect in mainstream science. Critics unleashed a backlash against the scholarship on Transcendental Meditation (TM) that had been conducted during the 1970s; they claimed that TM researchers had overgeneralized from their findings and were trying to scientifically prove that their own practices were beneficial.[6] Various contemplative leaders mentioned that as graduate students they were warned by their academic advisors that if they wanted serious careers in science, they should study more mainstream topics in their disciplines. Meditation was seen as too "fringe," "woo-woo," "mystical," or "religious" to bring into their work. Consequently, some of the young countercultural scholar-practitioners did not publicly disclose their interest in meditation for a decade or more. Instead, they entered the American mainstream and established their professional careers.

However, the future contemplative leaders remained influenced by the latent Buddhist currents in American spiritual culture, which included the alignment of science, personal development, and Buddhist-inspired spirituality from the nineteenth century; the Beats' countercultural vision of

American society; and more contemporary currents of Buddhist modernism such as Insight Meditation. Jack Kerouac's (1976 [1958]) *Dharma Bums* included a prophetic vision from Gary Snyder's character, Japhy Ryder, of how their "poetry-and-buddhist milieu" (Fields 1992: 223) would shape the 1960s counterculture and beyond:

> . . . see the whole thing is a world full of rucksack wanderers, Dharma Bums refusing to subscribe to the general demand that they consume production and therefore have to work for the privilege of consuming, all that crap they didn't really want anyway such as refrigerators, TV sets, cars . . . and general junk you finally always see a week later in the garbage anyway, all of them imprisoned in a system of work, produce, consume, work, produce, consume, I see a vision of a great rucksack revolution, thousands or even millions of young Americans wandering around with rucksacks, going up to mountains to pray . . . all of 'em Zen Lunatics who go about writing poems that happen to appear in their heads for no reason, and also by being kind, and also by strange unexpected acts keep giving visions of eternal freedom to everybody and to all living creatures . . .
>
> What we need is a floating zendo . . . a series of monasteries for people to go and monastate and meditate in, we can have groups of shacks up in the Sierras or High Cascades . . . Who's to say the cops of America and the Republicans and Democrats are gonna tell everybody what to do? (Kerouac 1976: 97–99)

The contemplative movement built upon the countercultural vision outlined by Snyder's character in *Dharma Bums*. Many of the older contemplative founders came of age during the 1960s and 1970s and were part of the counterculture. The contemplatives sought a change in consciousness to curb American materialism and foster greater kindness. They wanted to build meditation programs as a means of personal liberation. However, they chose to spread Buddhism differently than some prior American groups of converts whom were wary of institutions. Contemplatives instead embraced institutions, viewing them as places full of opportunities for improvement. Unlike Thoreau or the Beats, who chose to separate themselves from the materialism, social hierarchies, and normative pressures of mainstream society, the contemplatives decided to bring their practices into them. After contemplative leaders grew up and became successful professionals, they found ways to tactfully bring their practices into their workplaces, with support from contemplative organizations (established outside of their workplaces) and localized support, which they developed among sympathetic colleagues. With feedback from others in their workplaces, they learned to market Buddhist-inspired meditation practices as aids for productivity, employee health, and other instrumental purposes.

Embracing the Novelty, Familiarity, and Optimism of Mindful Meditation

Over the past two centuries, proponents of Buddhist modernism have advanced various explanations that articulate why Buddhism is beneficial and well suited for Western converts. Rather than being a completely new fad, the current mindfulness movement takes advantage of and builds upon prior spiritual, religious, and secular cultural streams that aligned with and supported Buddhism in American history.

Interestingly, when you search for meditation on the internet today, the search yields hundreds of images of attractive, fit, white meditators sitting alone, with their legs crossed, in nature. These seemingly serene, Lycra-wearing meditators represent what meditation now means to many people in the West, despite the fact that this is rarely what American meditators look like. American meditators often learn about meditation from and with others in a variety of secular, spiritual, and religious settings, rather than in solitude in the woods. They also represent a wide range of ages and body types. Furthermore, although the contemplatives, who are the focus of this book, are mostly white, there are a great many Asian ethnic meditators in the United States (Seager 1999).

Yet, from this imagery of meditation as a form of mental repose in solitude, we can trace ideas about Asian-inspired meditation that date back to the Transcendentalists, such as Thoreau's reflections at Walden Pond, and the Beats' stories of meditating on mountains. Current ideas about mindful meditation continue to build upon arguments from a long lineage of Buddhist sympathizers who have drawn attention to the similarities between scientific and Buddhist perspectives. Ideas from the Theosophists, from Anagarika Dharmapala and Soyen Shaku, from Paul Carus, and others have been periodically brought to the surface, in ever new adapted forms, to legitimize meditation.

Mindfulness meditation is more resonant to Americans today than it was during prior historical periods because it is tied to these other, familiar, romanticized American spiritual movements. As sociologist Rodney Starks (1987) argued, Buddhist-inspired meditation can be presented as simultaneously different and familiar enough. It can be edgy and fresh, but not so different as to be weird. The contemplative movement has been more successful at integrating into mainstream American culture during the current historical period because it has both built upon resonant cultural antecedents (like Buddhism's affinity with science and therapeutic personal development) and has distanced itself from stigmatized cultural baggage (such as Buddhism's association with the occult or New Age/ religious remnants of the counterculture). Furthermore, unlike prior American Buddhist antecedents, the contemplatives have been better at institutionalizing their culture through a field of contemplative organizations embedded throughout American society, as will be discussed in the chapters that follow.

CHAPTER 3 | The Contemplatives (1979–)

THE CONTEMPLATIVES SEEK TO incorporate Buddhist-inspired meditation into their rational, data- and science-driven workplaces in various powerful institutions.[1] Although the contemplative meditators draw from many different Buddhist and non-Buddhist contemplative traditions (including Tibetan Buddhism; Zen; Burmese and Thai Theravada Buddhism; insight meditation; Advaita Vedanta; mindfulness; and yoga), they are a distinct subset of meditators in America, who are connected by their commitments to doing and spreading secularized Buddhist-inspired practices, which align with science, for the benefit of practitioners and broader society. Contemplative practitioners tend to be lay converts, or non-monastics, who found Buddhist meditation and began doing it during their youth or adulthood. They are typically affluent, educated, and white and are more willing to adapt Buddhist meditation to appeal to a broader audience than most other Buddhists. They by no means represent religious Buddhist Americans, and have quite a different public approach to Buddhism than ethnic Asian Buddhists in America (Cadge 2008). Yet, by and large, they are undeniably interested in sharing lessons from the Buddhist dharma, or teachings, with others. Despite being a small, particular subset of converted American Buddhists, they have, over the last forty years, had a disproportionate influence on how Buddhism and mindfulness are perceived and adopted in America.

The contemplative movement is what social movement scholars call an *alterative* movement. Alterative movements inspire partial change in individuals' cognitive patterns and behavior. They believe that these partial changes will gradually lead individuals to fully transform (Kucinskas 2014; McAdam and Snow 1997). As more individuals undergo personal transformation, alterative movements expect that society will change (McAdam and Snow 1997).[2]

Like many youth of their generation raised during the American counterculture of the 1960s and 1970s, early contemplative leaders were disillusioned with the American government, the global political economic system, and elements of American culture that they viewed as too self-centered and materialistic. In the spirit of the activism of the countercultural generation and American progressivism, founding contemplative leaders sought to reform stodgy institutions such as science, healthcare, education, and business, inspiring change with a subversive new spiritual "consciousness." They hoped this consciousness, which was cultivated through meditation practices, would reverberate out and alter mainstream American culture. However, in doing so, contemplatives took care to tread a middle path between being "radical" protesters and bureaucrats reproducing the status quo. They also diverged from the paths of more fully devoted Buddhist meditators who retreated into contemplative solitude in the mountains or religious centers to leave consumer-driven culture behind (as many countercultural meditators did in the 1970s). Through this approach, the contemplatives created a path for professionals and other "mainstream" Americans to explore Buddhist-inspired variants of meditation that, from sociologist Rodney Stark's (1987) perspective, promised a new, appropriately fresh, and subtly subversive means of progress and development, without the trappings of being perceived as weird, countercultural, religious, or directly oppositional.

To reach broader secular audiences and people from other faith traditions, early contemplative leaders founded several organizations through which they could convene professionals sympathetic to meditation.[3] The first two pathbreaking organizations seeking to bring Buddhist-inspired practice to secular professional institutions, the Center for Mindfulness in Medicine, Health Care, and Society (CfM) at the University of Massachusetts in Worcester, and the Mind and Life Institute (MLI), which formed the base of this movement, were founded by scholars who were part of the countercultural critical community of scholar-meditators discussed in the last chapter.

Jon Kabat-Zinn, a Ph.D. in molecular biology and a Buddhist practitioner, established his Mindfulness-Based Stress Reduction (MBSR) program at the University of Massachusetts Medical School in 1979 to help patients, doctors, nurses, and others cope with chronic illness and to offer an alternative model of care. His eight-week program, now considered by many the "gold standard" mindfulness program, includes twenty to twenty-six hours of formal training during weekly group classes (typically 1.5 to 2.5 hours per class), an all-day six-hour retreat, and regular practice at home (about forty-five minutes per day, six days per week). In MBSR classes, participants focus on their breath, do body scans, and practice lovingkindness and compassion meditations and hatha yoga (Van Dam et al. 2017)

MLI began in 1987 with a series of dialogues between the Dalai Lama and scientists, and in the early 1990s researchers there started conducting research on adept meditators, as described in Chapter 1. In the late 1990s and the beginning of the twenty-first century, other programs, such as the Center for Contemplative Mind in Society in Northampton, Massachusetts, emerged to bring contemplative practice into higher education, business, law, and later the military.

Mindfulness in K-12 education arose in a more ad hoc grassroots manner, with various programs starting around the country around 2000. Buddhist meditators began creating ways to bring their practices to children and youth in classrooms and afterschool programs. However, over the next several years, leaders of many of these new programs began connecting with each other, as well as with leaders of the burgeoning contemplative movement, such as Kabat-Zinn and members of MLI.

Contemplative organizations that convened professionals from various fields have increasingly converged over the last decade with the rapid growth in popularity of mindfulness meditation and contemplative conferences. Dozens of new programs have been developed to bring mindfulness to ever-widening circles of people to improve their lives at work in business, the military, sports, in the public sphere, and at home.

Countering a Self-Centered Materialistic Society

On July 21, 2011, I joined MLI co-founder Adam Engle for lunch near his home in Boulder, Colorado. With the support of the Dalai Lama, MLI has worked over the past four decades to bring together Buddhism and science. Within the first five minutes of our conversation, it was clear that Engle wanted to change the world. He spoke with conviction about the "urgency" of the social problems we face globally, which now "can do a lot more damage" than in the past. He criticized capitalism, which "makes some people rich" at the expense of the majority of the population. This, Engle argued, was "not sensible on a human basis." Economic growth depended on "people buying into the noise of materialism," which led to various detrimental outcomes. Engle worried that we have collectively "crossed the threshold where that mentality adopted by seven to ten billion people leads to extinction, not survival. So that economic incentive paradigm has to shift to enough for everyone."

Engle thought that "bringing people back to their senses is a much greater challenge than it ever has been." But despite how the problems Engle identified were deep structural economic problems, he thought critical dialogue about extant social problems was impossible because of the "many special interests that are dominating the dialogue and too much demagoguery." There is "too much stupidity on the news" and "very sophisticated, powerful modalities that are actively working on a constant basis to keep us from sensibility." He concluded that the best way to initiate social change was to start with individual change.

Like other contemplatives, Engle said he founded MLI in order to cultivate individual change and self-development through meditation practice, so that people would be more sensitive to collective problems and more capable of dealing with them. Engle thought that "if we could get a large enough world population practicing [contemplative practices], we could get the kind of consciousness that we need to have a world that works." Engle's "whole purpose in being involved in Mind and Life," he said, "really, aside from serving the Dalai Lama was, since 1998, was basically because I'm a social activist. And I thought, 'Most of the problems that we have in life, right now, are man-made problems and we're not going to get the solutions unless we address the attitudes that created them and maintain them.'"

Various founders of the first major contemplative organizations described their frustration with living in a society that they characterized as full of selfishness, greed, and materialism as a motivation for their work promoting meditation. Kabat-Zinn also discussed how fostering individual mindfulness could help address deep-seated problems in our political economic system:

> The awareness we are speaking of when we are using the term "mindfulness" also encompasses the motivations for our actions, for example, the ways we are driven by self-aggrandizement or greed. In the financial crisis of 2008– 2009, we've seen the effects of greed played out on a massive scale in the banks and insurance companies. Healing that disease won't just be a matter of bailouts, stimulus packages, and magically creating greater confidence in the economy. We need to create a different kind of confidence and a new kind of economics, one that's not about mindless spending but is more about marshalling resources for the greater good, for one's own being, for society, and for the planet. Mindfulness can help open the door to that by helping us go beyond approaches that are based on conceptual thought alone and are driven by unbounded and legally sanctioned greed.[4]

Kabat-Zinn did not think American government interventions would solve social problems exacerbated by underlying greed and self-centeredness.

Instead, like other contemplatives, by teaching mindfulness, he hoped to shift the locus of individuals' actions from a predominantly cognitive, self-centered approach to one that draws upon embodied, intuitive knowledge and a greater awareness of others' experiences. This, he believed, would benefit the "greater good" of society and the planet by counteracting an over-emphasis in the West, and in particular in professional institutions, on individual attainment and instrumental objectives to the detriment of subjective, personal development.

The Buddhist Path to Transformation

The contemplatives believe that Buddhist forms of meditation practice will teach people to become more aware of their own and others' suffering, and of the illusory nature of reality and the self as people typically perceive it. Consequently, meditators will become aware of the interdependence between living beings, and will be driven to reform society. This ideology is rooted in Buddhism modernism, or forms of Buddhism that have been liberally adapted to align with modern society.

When Shakyamuni Buddha first taught the Buddhist teachings, or the dharma, about 2,500 years ago in India, he taught the "Four Noble Truths": the truth of suffering, the cause of suffering, the cessation of suffering, and the path to the cessation of suffering. The truth of suffering states that there is suffering. The cause of suffering suggests it originates in the mind from ignorance and mental delusions such as attachment, anger, jealousy, and other negative thoughts. These arise from grasping at existence, and illusory objects and outcomes in existence. Cessation of suffering comes from the cessation of negative mental states and relinquishing of grasping at existence, objects, and outcomes, which Buddhism suggests are illusory, cause suffering, and will not lead to happiness or Enlightenment. The core teachings of Buddhism are meant to foster wisdom or insight (the ability to see through the illusory nature of the world) and compassion. Buddhists believe meditation is a way to cultivate these traits.[5]

Increasing Awareness of an Interconnected World

Drawing from Buddhism, many contemplatives' ultimate aims were teaching attention, mindfulness, lovingkindness, and interconnectedness. They hoped to do so to reduce the suffering of those they instructed. For example, when I asked mindfulness educator Julia Martin what she seeks to accomplish with her program, she replied:[6]

> One is to reduce suffering. People suffer so much unnecessarily. So that suffering is stress-related. So to reduce their stress and therefore reduce their suffering and have more equanimity with their life—And then the other is to see that we're all in this together, that we have this interconnectedness that's beyond words. And if people can get that in whatever level they get it, there's more kindness and compassion towards self and toward others, which also reduces suffering.

Reducing suffering and promoting interconnectedness, kindness, and compassion are primary motivations in Buddhism. Mindful proponents hoped that beneficial consequences of meditation practices would ultimately accumulate to large-scale national and global cultural change, with increased collective well-being, democratic action, and less materialism.

It may seem naïve that contemplatives thought they could counteract a materialistic, selfish consumer culture and an ineffective political system by sitting on a cushion and focusing on themselves. But, like Buddhists, contemplative leaders thought that meditation practice would make people more compassionate and aware of their interdependence with others. Engle aspired to build a society in which people "realize that we're all in this together. Fundamentally," he said, "we're all like an aspen hill, where we appear to be independent, but we're connected in our root structure in one human family." Furthermore, he thought that because "virtually all of the contemplative-based practices are rooted in a compassionate understanding of the human condition," it was a foundational praxis from which to mobilize social reform.

Hal Roth, a religious studies professor at Brown University and founder of the Brown Contemplative Studies Initiative, expressed similar hopes. He optimistically thought that contemplative culture "has the potential to save humanity. I don't want to speak in such a grandiose fashion, but I really feel like it has the potential anyway to do that." He thought meditation practice could "turn people into more reflective, self-aware [people], aware of the larger context in which each of us as individuals live, and therefore be more other-regarding, more empathetic, and more compassionate human beings. I think it's all tied up together."

Thus, counterintuitively, Roth and other contemplatives believed that by focusing on themselves, people will become more aware of their broader social surroundings and more considerate to others. To understand why they thought this, it is very important to understand that this made sense to them through a lens of Buddhist-derived contemplative ideology. Through a combination of belief in a contemplative ideology (in which the self is viewed as an illusion, and a greedy one at that) and sustained meditation practice, meditators came to see the world in a very different way than non-meditators did.

Some meditators struggled with how to explain what they had learned from their long-term meditation practices.[7] In an attempt to communicate to non-meditators how they experienced the world, some people used metaphors and analogies. Greg Burdulis, a former Buddhist monk and a life coach for Fortune 100 business executives, tried to explain how meditation practice transforms practitioners to be more aware of their interdependence with others by using the metaphor of an individual realizing he is like a wave in the ocean: "When the person becomes transparent to the universe, I'm not saying the person doesn't exist . . . but it's not about HIM anymore. Rather, he is an aspect of the universe, not unlike a single wave in the ocean is part of the ocean." By developing their meditation practice, he thought practitioners over time shifted the focus of their attention and their actions away from themselves to become more inclusive and aware of others. This led them to let go of the ego, or the wave-identity, which sought to protect itself because it is "scared of rushing up onto the land and becoming annihilated." From a contemplative perspective, "the whole picture is so much bigger," Burdulis said. This explanation points non-practitioners to what Buddhist practitioners describe as an increased awareness of interdependence with others. Through meditation practice, he felt as if he had become decentered from his experiences in the world.

A Shambhala Buddhist and director of an education program thought meditation fostered compassionate action:

> . . . meditation, mindfulness and awareness practice allows you to see deep interconnectivity. Having seen and become aware of deep inner interconnectivity, you are connected, and therefore suffering there is not so different than suffering here. So therefore, because you are connected, you act. Compassion is the energy that flows between those connections . . . the traditional Buddhist expression of that is it's like wings of a bird. And so, the more awareness and mindfulness you apply, the more you see the deep interconnectivity. The more interconnectivity you find, the more you feel connected, and the more powerful your curiosity and connection is to look deeper into with more mindfulness and awareness, which generates more compassion, which generates more awareness and insight. So insight and compassion are constantly, working together in that way.

Like the educator above, contemplatives thought that introducing secular audiences to Buddhist-inspired meditation practices would foster a feedback loop in which their personal development will lead to greater insight, sensitivity, and compassion for others around them. Over time, as a result of contemplative practice and compassionate action, contemplatives believed the two behaviors reinforced each other, generating greater individual awareness and positive behavior that would gradually reverberate out.[8]

Social Change Through Mindful Interventions

Contemplatives assumed that by creating programs that taught meditation to develop subjective self-awareness, they would initiate broader waves of cultural change. As Engle alluded to, contemplative organizations sought to deeply transform participants in their programs:

> A way to look at this is that a lot of the problems that we face today, both individually and societally, come from the minds . . . And the truth of the matter is that it's going to be impossible to really develop the outer change that we're really interested in unless we also address the inner attitudes that had created that space in society. You can't change, you name it—sexism, racism—unless you start with the underlying attitudes that create that . . . So in a broad sociological view, what we're really about is to change the cultures of the world attitudinally and use contemplative-based training methods to do that . . . We're trying to change the world by providing *interventions* that people can use. (Emphasis added)

As they founded their meditation intervention programs, contemplative leaders such as Engle made several crucial decisions. Rather than just recruiting more people to meditation one at a time, contemplative organizations developed intervention programs they could embed in other powerful organizations and institutions. To pitch their programs, contemplative pioneers hearkened back to strains in American spirituality at the turn of the twentieth century that justified Buddhism by arguing it was aligned with science. However, contemplatives chose to speak first through the language of science rather than through poetry and literature as the Beats had done.[9] They studied meditation using the tools at hand, examining whether it had scientifically verifiable benefits. Foundational organizations in the contemplative movement (e.g., CfM and MLI) began studying meditation and scientifically documenting the benefits of their programs in their early years. This would prove crucial to their later success.

Based on their Buddhist-inspired, humanist ideology, contemplatives have been trying to bring the spirit, morality, and virtue back into secular organizations. Their perspective aligns with Max Weber's cautionary account in *The Protestant Ethic and the Spirit of Capitalism* (2012 [1934]), which warned of how, with increased bureaucratization, people would lose the religious spirit and values that contributed to the rise of capitalism. They would be left trapped in the structural encasings of organizations, driven by the pursuit of profit and other instrumental aims. In reaction to what they saw as the rise of unbridled instrumental rationality seeking materialistic ends, the contemplative leaders began promoting meditation in an attempt to bring values, subjectivity, and spirituality back into secular institutions through their organizations' support for intervention programs.[10] Yet, they used the persuasive rhetoric of science and rationality to make their case for the importance of preserving the softer spirit of personal moral development within organizations.

After creating programs that promoted Buddhist-inspired meditation, contemplative leaders were in for a pleasant surprise: more people showed up than they ever could have imagined. Why were so many people interested in trying meditation? What did they seek to gain from it?

Unlocking Human Potential: The Point of Mindful Meditation Practice

In his office in January 2015, CfM's executive director, Saki Santorelli, told me there are a lot of reasons why people want to learn to meditate.

"Every one of those 200 participants in that fall cycle that we just ended . . . they're coming to solve a Real. Life. Problem," he said. "Something is just not right. Even across a life that can feel generally right, something's not quite right. That's probably true for billions of people in the world."

"And what do they get?" he asked. "They don't need psychotherapy." He paused, and then continued, " If you could read it in a book and it could be transformational, we wouldn't need this kind of place . . . What people need is a place where they can actually be actively engaged. And what keeps people engaged is . . . the most interesting topic in the world."

He paused and turned toward me.

"What is this most interesting topic in the world?" He paused again, waiting. "I mean, when you come right down to it."

I hadn't the faintest idea. "Love?" I guessed, knowing this cheesy answer could not possibly be right, but that I had to say something.

"The most interesting topic in the world," he responded, "is *me*." He continued, "People come here because they are interested in *me*. Meaning *themselves*. And something's not quite right about *me* or I want to learn more about *me*, including 'How am I going to live with this condition for the next twenty or thirty or forty years?'"

But, he said, what is most important about learning mindfulness is that it is not just a cognitive, intellectual, or therapeutic education process. At the Center, Santorelli explained, mindfulness is not just about memorizing or learning "skills." Teaching mindfulness is a "kind of drawing out" not "a pouring in," he explained. "I'm committed as much as I can be, that MBSR [the Center's mindfulness program] is lighting a fire. It's igniting a fire with people to know more about 'who' or 'what' I actually am." He explained:

> They start with practice. Practice reveals not because *I* say so, but because *they* discover it. They discover that they have a breath, they discover that it feels a particular way, they discover something about the relative present moment, whatever *that* is. They discover something about what happens in their viscera when they have a particular thought or a particular emotion . . . They discover the ways that they're conditioned or limiting themselves or living today out of yesterday's memory, about whom or what I am or what I'm capable of. And they love it. . . . And whenever people discover a little bit more about who they are, they transcend. And ultimately, I think that's what's transformative—is that sense of transcending. Transcend some idea about who you think they are, even if it's a tiny little idea, and then you feel more room.

In Santorelli's view, once attendees began the process of learning mindfulness, they found it intrinsically rewarding and exhilarating. This feeling of transcendence kept people coming back.

Others found meditation useful for different reasons. Neuroscientist Ravi Chaudhary valued mindfulness because it helped him develop critical distance from challenges that arose in his life.[11] "I think if there's a one-lens summary of mindfulness it would [be to] not be super-reactive to unpleasant situations," he said. "There's difficult situations no matter what, but take a moment, sit back and accept that 'Okay, it is there and I am here. I am not part of it, but rather it is there and I am here.' And just trying to make a decision about it as if it's a presumed situation. [I] take it like [I] don't entangle myself with the situation." Chaudhary thought mindfulness practice provided him with a critical cognitive distance that enabled him to pause, reflect, and ultimately have greater self-control.

Some contemplatives did mindful check-ins as I spoke with them, showing how over time the practices had transformed how they inhabited the world. This was most evident in speaking with mindfulness coach Greg Burdulis. Unlike most people, as we sat talking, Burdulis was constantly checking in and noting his surroundings and his thoughts. Using Burmese Buddhist noting techniques, he identified sensory perceptions in the course of what would otherwise be a normal conversation. For example, while sitting on his front porch in the midst of the Rocky Mountains in Nederland, Colorado, he noted: "You feel this breeze?" he asked. "You hear the birds? You feel this gentle new connection that's like home? So nice? Do you notice how there is enough air here for your next inhalation? Somebody you just met offered you tea?" As he noted these aspects of our surroundings, he was touching and appreciating this wider panoramic view of experience, which is easy to miss when lost in deep conversation. To Burdulis, as to other meditators with honed attention skills, viewing the wide panoramic picture of their social environment, which they are interconnected with and a part of, is a richer, clearer, and more valid way of being in the world.

For non-meditators, Burdulis's stream-of-consciousness descriptions provide clues to how the cognitive habits he has honed over a decade of intensive meditation practice change the way he experiences the world. Through meditation, he has taught himself to continually self-reflect, question, and be skeptical of his personal perceptions and experiences. He has taught himself to view his personal experiences as inherently biased and socially conditioned. Instead, he shifts his cognitive focus to embodied physical sensations and detailed aspects of his surroundings.

From these practices, Burdulis gains great joy and a sense of equanimity. At times, his joy seemed to burst from him. From meditating, he said that he feels "this just like wows me . . . that goodness, that feeling of joy, that recognition of . . . better yet, the realization, the actualization of happiness." I saw him note and celebrate the good in each moment we shared. In addition, he described experiencing a sense of peace, as well as tenderness and sensitivity to others' pain.

The Contemplative Movement's Approach: Supporting Secularized, Buddhist-Inspired Interventions

Early contemplative leaders believe in the transformative power of contemplative practice, not just for the individuals practicing it but for society as a whole. As an alterative movement, they believed that if they could transform individuals (through intervention programs), they would initiate broader processes of social reform. Contemplatives thought that by learning about contemplative practice, and its associated worldview, practitioners would become more aware of their interdependence with others, sensitive to others' experiences of suffering, and empowered to more skillfully engage in democratic conversations about addressing large-scale social problems like inequality and materialism.

Yet, to popularize Buddhist-inspired practices among new secular, professional audiences, the contemplative movement took a different tack than prior instances of Buddhist-infused lay American spirituality. Contemplatives deliberately distanced contemplative practice from its religious roots and countercultural literary means of diffusion. Instead, they created organizations that (1) convened sympathetic elites, (2) built networks among professionals in targeted institutions, (3) built a substantial body of research on the benefits of meditation, and (4) developed intervention programs suitable and accessible to specific professional audiences that could be incorporated into powerful institutions.

Without a movement of affluent enthusiastic supporters, media attention, and philanthropic support, it is doubtful that meditation would have gained the popular attention that it has. As described in Chapter 2, Buddhism and meditation experienced periods of critique and disinterest, as well as periods of popularity, primarily in select liberal American subcultures. Buddhism largely fell out of favor, even among such groups, for over four decades in the early twentieth century. Contemplative leaders said that meditation became suspect in science as well in the mid-late 1970s and 1980s, when studies on Transcendental Meditation (TM) were dismissed as practitioners' biased pseudoscience and TM more generally was embroiled in a period of negative court cases and media attention (Tollefsen 2014; Wilson 2014). Furthermore, until the recent wave of popular support for mindfulness, meditation was never popular among large swaths of the American population, including most mainline and orthodox Christians, and professionals in science, healthcare, education, and business.

This has changed due to the contemplatives' work bringing Buddhist-inspired meditation to professionals through movement organizations and intervention programs embedded in powerful institutions. Interest in contemplative practice has grown among professionals, mainline Christians, Jews, and others, due to the strategic development of the contemplative mindfulness movement and the organizational support its central organizations provide. In the following chapters I discuss how the contemplative movement's organizations mobilize, and the strengths and shortcomings of their approaches.

PART II | Mobilizing Meditation Through
Consensus-Based Strategies

| Accessing Institutions

MIRABAI BUSH'S HOME AND office are tucked in the foothills of the Berkshires of western Massachusetts, nestled among the trees. During my two visits to her home, Bush greeted me with a warm smile, a cup of tea, and a plate of snacks. Rather than an interviewer, she treated me like a guest. She wore comfortable loosely fitting clothes and had glasses perched in her slightly disheveled blond hair. She told me her Hindu teacher, Neem Karoli Baba, had said to love everyone, and offering food was one way to show it.

As she made tea in her kitchen, I asked about a clay statue in her window. This statue, she explained, was a figure of Hanuman, a Hindu god that symbolized service. She said that she had also taken the bodhisattva vow in Buddhism, which meant that she had committed to living a disciplined contemplative life of compassion in order to alleviate the suffering of others. She had learned about Hinduism and Buddhism during her time in India in the early 1970s. She threw back her head and laughed: "I intended to go to India for two weeks and stayed two years," she said. Access to legendary religious gurus, like Neem Karoli Baba and Theravada Buddhist S. N. Goenka, had influenced her to stay. With Ram Dass (the former Harvard LSD researcher turned spiritual guru and countercultural icon), Daniel Goleman (future Emotional Intelligence expert), and Joseph Goldstein and Sharon Salzberg (future Insight Meditation Society founders), Bush learned about Buddhist meditation at Goenka's first *vipassana* retreat for Westerners in Bodh Gaya, India, in 1970.

Fascinated by meditation, after leaving India she helped her friends found the Insight Meditation Society, one of the foremost Buddhist *vipassana* centers in the United States. She went on to found and lead one of the first central contemplative organizations, the Center for Contemplative Mind in

Society (CCMS), which was at the vanguard of bringing Buddhist-inspired practices into business, higher education, law, and the military. In telling me how CCMS was founded, Bush identified the deliberate strategies used by the founders of the first major contemplative organizations, such as Center for Mindfulness in Medicine, Health Care, and Society (CfM), Mind and Life Institute (MLI), and others. Because these founders had friends in useful places, such as philanthropic foundations, top universities, and Fortune 500 companies, their tactics for spreading meditation were quite different than the tactics of marginalized populations. Instead, contemplative leaders could use unobtrusive, collaborative tactics. They developed collaborative relationships with institutional insiders via their social networks, using resources available through philanthropists they knew. The insiders they brought on board could then grant them access to reputable organizations in targeted institutions.[1] Over time, many of these insiders situated across institutions became leaders of the next generation of the contemplative movement.

Insider Aid in Institutionalizing Meditation

As discussed in the first part of the book, the mainstreaming of meditation is a relatively recent development. Many professionals I spoke with were still acutely aware of the stigmas that Buddhist meditation carried and the subsequent professional risks of proselytizing such practices. As a result, early contemplative leaders were cautious about how to share meditation with broader audiences. What did these meditators need to get over their risk aversion? To start, contemplative leaders needed to establish a foundation for their initiatives. They needed to create a supportive network of other reputable professionals who could help them brainstorm where to place their pilot programs. After embedding pilot programs in highly regarded fields such as science and business, and gaining the legitimacy associated with such institutions, then a second stage of mobilization occurred, in which more general processes of cultural diffusion could take place. During this second stage of cultural diffusion, other people interested in meditation could join the burgeoning movement, develop their own programs, build their programs' legitimacy upon the foundation created by movement leaders, and continue the process of bringing contemplative practices into new spaces.

The process through which contemplative organizations strategically brought meditation into new fields, such as science, higher education, law, and business, is depicted in Figure 4.1.[2] This model complements and builds upon the first three steps of Michael Lindsay's (2008) model showing

FIGURE 4.1. Assimilation into organizations' legitimacy

how elites can initiate social change through (1) articulating a vision for wider society, (2) drawing on resources available to them, and (3) building collaborations among leaders that leads to the formation of overlapping networks. However, likely because of their more adaptive religiously inspired culture (see Chapters 2 and 6), the contemplatives did not face the opposition Lindsay's evangelicals did. Like Lindsay, I do not argue these steps always occur in this sequence; they can occur iteratively or in different orders, as evident by comparing the creation of different subfields in this movement. While many organizations used these strategies, not all did. For example, some founders, particularly of mindful education programs, started bringing meditation into their work on their own before they convened with the larger movement.

First, early contemplative leaders privately convened professionals they knew were interested in meditation. They met in private spaces, such as members' homes or at foundations' retreat centers, when establishing their organizations' early working groups. As contemplative organizations grew, leaders continued convening and bringing new members into their networks and conferences. Second, based on these meetings and their extant social networks, contemplative leaders strategically identified where they could bring meditation. Third, using access granted through insiders within targeted institutions, contemplative organizations began developing meditation instruction programs for professionals. Early benchmark programs in a new professional area—such as a Contemplative Studies concentration at Brown University—then became beacons of legitimacy for other similar organizations in their institutional fields. These established programs legitimized previously stigmatized meditation practices in targeted fields by assimilating their contemplative programs into the established legitimacy and credibility of their host organizations.

Bush shared with me how this process unfolded with the CCMS's initiatives.

Convening and Cultivating Insider Networks Privately

"How," I asked Bush, "did you start moving contemplative practice into all these sectors?"

"At that time, in the early '90s, it was all kind of underground," she said. "Rob Lehman, who was then the president of Fetzer [a philanthropic foundation], and the president of philanthropic Nathan Cummings Foundation [lawyer Charlie Halpern], had funded Bill Moyers to do a program on alternative and complementary medicine called 'Healing and the Mind.'" The television program, which aired in 1993, featured Mindfulness-Based Stress Reduction (MBSR) founder Jon Kabat-Zinn, neuroscientists, and others. After the program, Lehman and Halpern, who had their own Christian and Buddhist contemplative practices, respectively, wondered if the practices could "be helpful in other sectors of American life than health and healing. Because," Bush said, "they were foundation heads and they were funding in lots of different areas. Charlie was a friend and he brought me in on it. The three of us brought together a series of working group meetings . . . We met, I think, once or twice a year for a few years."

Similar to leadership in other contemplative organizations, the CCMS working group began convening "miscellaneous," "interesting" professionals with an interest in Buddhist meditation, Bush said, whom they already knew or had heard about through mutual social connections. They met in private spaces, such as at foundations or retreat centers.[3] Included were meditators from different professional sectors such as Kabat-Zinn, Goleman, Robert Thurman (a professor of Buddhist studies at Columbia University), Francisco Varela (MLI founder and philosopher/neuroscientist), Zen Roshi Joan Halifax (who also helped found MLI), and philanthropist and Buddhist meditator Steven Rockefeller.

"We actually knew the answer before we asked the question," Bush said. Believing that Buddhist contemplative practice could benefit people in a lot of different organizations, they wanted to bring meditation into more institutional sectors of American society.

Strategically Staking a New Claim

Members of the CCMS working group, which included members of other contemplative organizations such as Kabat-Zinn and Varela, all believed that a tremendous amount of work needed to be done to get contemplative practice into more institutions. To spread contemplative practice as broadly as possible, the working group devised a strategy through which they could spread meditation through CCMS and the broader burgeoning field of secularized contemplative applications: they chose to develop mindful applications in new institutional areas where others were not already working. Representing what would become the third major contemplative organization after CfM and MLI, the CCMS working group deliberately decided "not to work in health and healing, or medicine," because Kabat-Zinn "was doing so much work there" or in science, where MLI was based. Instead, they chose to target higher education, business, and law at first because other contemplative organizations were not operating in those fields and their members were knowledgeable about those areas.

During the fall of 1994, in Pocantico, New York, Kabat-Zinn produced a white paper for the CCMS working group that laid out their strategy of how meditation should be brought into various professional fields with the support of central contemplative organizations. By 1994, Kabat-Zinn was already a central leader in the nascent contemplative movement. He had founded the Stress Reduction Clinic at the University of Massachusetts, which in 1995 became the CfM. He was also an active member of MLI, the other foundational organization in the contemplative movement. Kabat-Zinn's white paper (1994b), which Bush shared with me and had posted on the CCMS website, reads like a blueprint for how the contemplative movement would develop over the next several decades. For the inchoate small group of contemplative organizations of the 1990s, the document outlined a collective strategy to develop a collaborative effort to bring meditation into American's most powerful institutions:[4]

> Moreover, strange as it may sound, such a movement needs to avoid the human impulse to let this come about through the emergence of one particular person, who takes on the role of avatar, savior, messiah, charismatic leader, spokesperson, tempting as this is for many people. This has been the historical pathway by which the mega-emergences of the path of the sacred have manifested, through the major world religions and various cults. But the framing of a single person as the encapsulation of our understanding takes it out of the domain of direct experience and inevitably introduces a dualism and a lack of personal responsibility and engagement which create more problems than they solve. The same is true for the predominance of a single idea, ideal, belief system, or view of truth, or an us/them, enlightened/unenlightened, meditator/non-meditator mentality.

This statement urged the early contemplative movement not to attract members through a single charismatic leader or ideology, as religious movements have done. In the spirit of Buddhist non-dualism, Kabat-Zinn advised that the movement avoid distinctions between members of the movement and outsiders that privileged the former. He hoped to keep the structure of the movement flat and grounded in practitioners' experiences, rather than too institutionalized into a single organizational status hierarchy. Thus he hoped for a movement comprising collaborations between the contemplative movement and sympathizers in various institutional fields; he hoped the latter would become integrated into the movement and would serve as leaders of new mindfulness programs in their own right over time.

Kabat-Zinn's plan was based in part on his experience founding the MBSR program and CfM. As he wrote in 2011 (286–287), he had "pondered" for years prior to founding his program what his "karmic assignment" was. He had worked both as a biology faculty member at Brandeis and as director and "dharma teacher in training" at the Cambridge Zen Center. During a two-week *vipassana* meditation retreat at the Insight Meditation Society in Barre, Massachusetts, he had a ten-second "vision" on adapting meditation into a training program that could fit within the medical community.

As an MIT Ph.D. who had studied under a Nobel laureate, Kabat-Zinn had enough scientific legitimacy within the University of Massachusetts Medical School to undertake what he viewed as a risky new project. He has also credited his marginal location in the organization for his ability to bring mindfulness into healthcare: "There was a blessing of being in the basement and nobody knowing what I was doing for a very long time. No one knew. No one cared. A benign neglect" (Stiles 2011: 1).

Based on his experience, Kabat-Zinn (1994b) advocated that meditation programs should be developed through various pathways based on contemplatives' professional expertise and contemplative experiences:

> It is important to point out that there should and can be no fixed form for this to happen. Meditative pathways, teachers, and programs cannot be cloned, although effective models might be adapted and modified, as has been the case in medical and educational settings with mindfulness-based stress reduction. Appropriate forms and vehicles need to develop out of the personal contemplative experiences, meditation practices, and visions for what might be possible of the individuals who undertake to bring the contemplative dimension into mainstream life in society. These forms will have to interface in appropriate ways with the social terrain and be sensitive to professional, institutional, generational, and ethnic cultures and their values.

Kabat-Zinn's strategic plan for CCMS reveals how early contemplative leaders discussed that the contemplative movement should develop through different brokers who adapted and "seeded" contemplative culture in their workplaces. This prescient document predicted how the contemplatives mobilized to develop a new multi-institutional field over the following several decades through professional insiders (although of all the contemplative leaders I spoke with, only Bush mentioned the document). Kabat-Zinn (1994b) advised that:

> This work would be well served by establishing a small number of national centers for the in-depth training of a new breed of inventive and creative meditation teachers: for the most part, people who are already professionals in a particular area, hold other jobs, and who wish to introduce the meditative/contemplative dimension into their work and into their places of work. An understanding of the role of orthogonal consciousness and orthogonal institutions in this process is essential. Of course, the deeper their grounding and commitment to mindfulness practice before they undergo such specialized training, the better. Such centers will also conduct research and offer programs of various kinds, depending on their contexts and missions. Individuals who have received adequate training in such centers, and others who appear spontaneously, will establish second generation (F2) foci from which programs, scholarship, and diverse applications of the contemplative perspective to the lives of real people will emanate and spread further. These F2 centers need to be located for the most part within existing mainstream institutions such as universities, hospitals, clinics, medical schools, retirement and nursing homes (a very large and growing, receptive and in-need portion of our population), primary and secondary schools, college campuses, work environments (particularly large corporations and factories), prisons, shelters, and churches of denominations that are receptive to this message. These foci will be "seeded" through spontaneous and chaotic pathways, and this process will take care of itself in important ways, I believe, if the proper conditions are met.

The contemplative field developed as Kabat-Zinn and the CCMS working group hoped it would, by spreading an "orthogonal consciousness" rooted in individual transformation through contemplative practice to secular professional institutions. When the first contemplative centers—CfM, MLI, and CCMS—were established in the 1980s and 1990s, they focused mainly on their own separate field-building initiatives. As noted in Kabat-Zinn's (1994b) paper, contemplative leaders viewed their initiatives as having a shared underlying purpose to spread meditation practices to secular institutions, but their organizations strategically targeted different professional areas. Based on this strategy, founders of the movement established the foundations of multiple nascent contemplative fields that collaborated with each other and shared information and resources. These early strategies and habits created a collaborative base for a larger contemplative field to grow upon.

Early contemplative leaders developed dialogues, programs, and centers that convened professionals who meditated by professional sector. As centers formed and brought in new circles of professionals, new generations of leaders emerged. Building upon first-generation contemplative organizations (CfM, MLI, CCMS), which were most successful in developing meditation programs in healthcare, science, and higher education respectively, a second generation of contemplative programs has been founded since 2000 by people trained by CfM, MLI, and CCMS. Second-generation programs have spread rapidly across healthcare, science, higher education, business, and K-12 education. In addition, programs have been developed for veterans, the military, and athletes.[5]

Entering Organizations Unobtrusively Through Insiders

The CCMS working group, Bush recalled, began exploring where to place pilot programs by looking around and making a "chart of all the different sectors we might work in. But then we really kind of went where there was an opening, because by this time it was '95 and, you know, there weren't that many openings still."

What was an opening? "In each case," Bush said, "we found somebody inside who was a friend of a friend or something like that. It was very informal or 'opportunistic,' although that has a kind of negative implication."

The importance of support from insiders in institutions into which contemplatives brought meditation cannot be overstated. Of the eighty contemplative leaders I interviewed, 86% used insider capital to get contemplative programs into their targeted institutions. Two-thirds of contemplative leaders (fifty-three people) were insiders in the institution into which they brought meditation. An additional 11% of leaders (nine people) had previously worked in the targeted professional institution, and another 9% (seven leaders) relied on personal ties or positions to get their programs into their targeted organization.

Leaders of contemplative organizations found insider-collaborators with whom they could build contemplative subfields in new institutions through one of several main pathways. As Bush mentioned, contemplative leaders used their networks, and those of their friends, to identify and reach out to insiders at organizations where they wanted to bring mindfulness. As contemplative organizations established mindfulness programs in a professional field, interested insiders from other organizations, conversely, heard about contemplative organizations and sought help in creating mindfulness programs in their workplaces. Contemplative organizations also fostered the creation of mindful subfields in new areas by using money from foundations or private donors to provide financial incentives to motivate interested professionals to create their own contemplative programs. Through her work at CCMS, Bush used all of the above pathways to establish contemplative programs in new institutions.

Entering Organizations Through Familiar Insiders: Meditation at Monsanto

In 1996, through board member Robert Shapiro, who was CEO of the controversial industrial agriculture company Monsanto, the CCMS working group decided to bring meditation into business. It was the first program in the country to bring in-depth Buddhist insight meditation into a large corporation.[6] Shapiro, who had met CCMS co-founder Halpern in graduate school, had read a book on Zen and gone on to develop quite a serious meditation practice in the 1990s, Bush told me. When he became CEO of Monsanto, he wanted to get his executive team to think more creatively through contemplative practice.

Despite her initial abhorrence of the idea of collaborating with Monsanto (based on the adverse economic and health effects of their pesticides, which she had witnessed firsthand in her former work as an activist in Guatemala), eventually the others in the working group won her over. "I got talked into it," she said, laughing.

Why did Bush ultimately cave in and support the collaboration with Monsanto? Despite the ethical questions working with Monsanto raised for Bush, CCMS, and other meditators given the company's ethically questionable track record, she ultimately decided it was a good opportunity because the corporate giant was undergoing large-scale organizational change, had far-reaching effects on the world, and had a CEO interested in bringing in a contemplative intervention for its leaders. Although Shapiro had "been on a fast track to become CEO at Monsanto, once he slowed down enough to see what was there, he began to realize what mattered to him," Bush recalled. Monsanto had "just spun off their bad, manufactured chemicals so they had this opportunity to start a whole new emphasis." Bush said Shapiro wanted to change the direction of the company: "He had these really very ambitious, but wholesome, plans for Monsanto to go into agriculture." Although "he didn't really know anything about agriculture, . . . they had studied the population statistics for the twenty-first century and they saw that there wasn't gonna be enough food for everybody . . . and they decided agriculture would be a good place to work. They had all these scientists on board and so in the beginning they really genuinely thought that they were going to make a big contribution to feeding the world for the twenty-first century."

Like Shapiro, Bush came to believe that there was a real opportunity to change Monsanto, and more importantly to have a positive effect on broader society, by teaching the company's executives Buddhist meditation. In 2001 Bush told Helen Twekov, a writer for the Buddhist magazine *Tricycle*, that she was "persuaded to work with Monsanto because so many people work inside corporations, and because of the increasing power of corporations, not just economically but culturally, worldwide. I concluded that it could be very beneficial to change consciousness inside a corporation."

CCMS's choice to collaborate with high-profile businessmen like Shapiro did not go unnoticed by Bush's friends and colleagues. "People accused us of selling out, of sleeping with the enemy," Bush said. Both Buddhists and non-Buddhists thought that by "teaching stress reduction," they were "making it easier for them to do what they are already doing" and allowing employees "to feel better about it."[7] In recent years, the choice made by Bush and her organization to work with Monsanto has been subject to further critique. In fact, Bush acknowledged to me in 2016 that she "barely mentions" working with Monsanto "anymore because it closes down people's minds . . . I mean, it's like there's certain things that people just can't hear anymore. And they can't hear after 'Monsanto' is spoken."

Regardless, Bush held firm about her decision: "We did it and we learned a lot from it," she told me. The collaboration with Monsanto taught her a great deal about implementing social reform via collaborations between CCMS and targeted institutional insiders. She said that CCMS had to:

> make decisions about where to put our resources. Is it better to work with environmentalists who are already trying to save the planet than to work with those we think are destroying the planet? One thing I learned from working closely with scientists at Monsanto is that scientists and others who are working at the cutting edge of something as new and complex as, say, biotechnology, are making decisions every day in their labs that activists and other social change workers don't even hear about until they are on an unstoppable trajectory.

> I saw that the discussions about what these things mean for our society and for the planet need to begin in the labs, among scientists. What better place to apply some of the techniques that good scientists already know, of

looking carefully at things without judgment, exactly as they are? In business, for a long time the only considerations were science and the bottom line. We now know that that's just not enough—that there are huge social and moral implications. (Twerkov 2001 interview)

In addition, she said that it was "very helpful to have people on the board who have been part of these mainstream organizations. It helps us understand in what ways the dharma might be able to be there" (Twerkov 2001). Not only did Shapiro and the rest of the board help Bush understand how Buddhist teachings could be brought into business to influence organizations from within, but Shapiro granted Bush and CCMS access to teach company leaders and other employees insight meditation.

CCMS first facilitated an insight meditation program for the top eighteen Monsanto executives offsite at the Fetzer Institute. "And they all came," Bush told me, "and I'm sure they came because he [Shapiro] invited them . . . We did a three-day silent meditation practice, morning till night, [with] one-on-one interviews. It was very moving; they really got into it." The retreat was taught by Steve Smith, an insight meditation teacher who taught a standard *vipassana* retreat. Bush explained:

> Because we were working directly with the CEO, we didn't have to repackage it in any way. By the last evening, Steve began to teach *metta* practice, loving-kindness practice. You begin with lovingkindness for yourself. Then you take the energy of lovingkindness out in expanding circles to include many other beings: humans and mammals and birds and fish and insects and all beings everywhere. And after three days of practice by people who had a lot of concentration, bringing awareness to lovingkindness was very profound. We hadn't talked about sustainable agriculture or product mix; the executives hadn't explained why they thought Round-Up was good for the planet. I opened my eyes in the middle of the *metta* meditation as Steve was talking about these different species, and I looked around the room and saw tears rolling down the cheeks of many people there.
>
> That was a real turning point for me. I did not forget what I saw as negative about chemicals and monocropping. There's no way I was going to forget that. But at the same time I realized that these were basically good people who believed that they were contributing to help feed the world.[8]

Afterward, CCMS began voluntarily offering meditation sessions for all employees, and held talks on contemplative practice at the company. They additionally offered day-long retreats and scholarships to the closest Buddhist dharma center. Most participants were stressed, heard positive things about the program from friends, and decided to give it a try, Bush said. Most employees had no prior meditation experience.

Thus, through the company's CEO, CCMS had gotten meditation into a corporation that symbolized the best and worst of American capitalism. It had a great deal of economic and instrumental power, but the initiative was also complicated by the ethical quagmires. This case shows that even as early as the late 1990s, contemplative leaders faced the choice of working with elites who could help move meditation fairly easily into powerful new spaces. But in collaborating with elites, contemplatives had to consider the ethical implications of working in powerful organizations with spotted histories. Could bringing meditation to corporate America help business leaders and other employees to more deeply consider the long-term effects of their work, as Bush hoped? Or was meditation at risk of being coopted by an ethically suspect company to increase the creativity and productivity of its employees?[9]

Bush recognized that as she worked with people in business, to her, the boundaries between "us" moral meditators and "them"—profit-seeking corporate employees—withered. An unintended consequence of working with Monsanto's employees was that it forced her to face her previous stereotypes of Monsanto employees as terrible people. Instead of seeing them as a horrible "other" she was fighting against, in working with them one on one, she became more open and sympathetic to them. She began to see them as individuals "whose intentions were good." She took on their perspective in part, realizing that they were trying to feed the world. She learned about their lives and became sympathetic to the challenges they faced.

"They had kids in college. They had car payments. They were in St. Louis where there weren't any other jobs. They were the first in their families to have gone to college," she told me. "Once I got to start knowing people," she learned, "they thought they were gonna do a good thing for the world."

The question remains if her more moderate, empathetic position, which she gained from working directly with Monsanto's employees, leads to a susceptibility to being coopted over time. Do activists who work with oppositional forces to bring a new culture in gradually adapt to the opposition's goals and lose loyalty to their own?[10] We will revisit this question in the chapters that follow.

Regardless of the ethical implications, working with Monsanto set CCMS on the path to bring mindful meditation to other large companies, such as Hoffmann-La Roche, Inc., Hearst Publications, National Grid, Plantronics, and Google.[11]

Helping Google

As one of the original engineers at Google, when the company went public, Chade-Meng Tan earned a lot of money and was given the opportunity to "do whatever you want," Bush told me, as long as it was related to the company's mission.[12] In light of this opportunity, "Meng thought, 'This is the time.' He could bring meditation in. So he invited somebody to do an MBSR class and he promoted it. They wrote an online billboard where they post all these different things that are going on. And nobody signed up."

Meng was surprised Googlers were not interested in his mindfulness program. "He didn't know what to do next," Bush told me. Based on the referral of a friend, Tan contacted Bush in 2007. By working together, they would make the Google mindfulness program one of the most successful and publicly recognized contemplative interventions in business.

"So I went out there and we started looking at why people didn't sign up," Bush recalled. It turned out that they did not sign up because "they thought they weren't stressed. Or else they thought they were stressed, but they thought that it was stress that had gotten them to the top of their classes at Stanford or MIT, so stress was actually a good thing. Or they thought they were stressed but they didn't want anybody to know that they were stressed 'cause it wasn't cool to be stressed at Google." In short, there was a stigma about being stressed at Google, so no one would sign up for a stress relief program.

Tan and Bush decided to find a way to "offer the same practices, basically, but frame it in a different way. And so then we thought about what is it that this group needs and wants and, even though they probably needed stress reduction, they didn't perceive that they needed it." Tan and Bush realized that "They're all really young; they're really smart; they're mostly all nerd technical types; they've been in front of their screens since they were kids" However, "the place where they were weakest was in self-awareness and awareness of others. So we thought," Bush said, "If we could frame it as emotional intelligence then they'd recognize that they need that, 'cause they all know that, and it's kind of well known that the techies aren't good at communicating." So if they advertised the program as helping emotional intelligence, which is the ability to perceive, access, understand, and reflexively regulate emotions (Mayer and Salovey 1997), "they could sign up for that."

Bush and Tan thought that cultivating emotional intelligence would appeal to Googlers because "they have to work together" in teams "and there's been all that work done in emotional intelligence showing that people work better and they're more successful if they have the components of emotional intelligence." Consequently, rather than pitch meditation as a coping skill for stress, they developed components of the program that taught mindfulness as a means of fostering compassion, lovingkindness, and communication.

"And then," Bush said, "we called Danny Goleman in." Harvard-trained Ph.D. psychologist and best-selling author on emotional intelligence, Goleman was an old friend who lives in the same town as Bush. When she asked him to give a talk at Google, he told her, "I don't give talks in business anymore." He had, she said, grown tired of them. In response, Bush told him, "You HAVE to give this one," she recounted, chuckling. Goleman gave the talk at Google. There, she said, "for the first time," Goleman "did say that contemplative practices, meditation and so on, are a direct path to emotional intelligence. Before that he had intentionally never said that, although he's been meditating for forty years." She said that he had never before publicly disclosed his belief in the efficacy of meditation "because he didn't want anything to get in the way of the social science message of emotional intelligence. So for the first time he connected the two. And then we posted 'Search Inside Yourself,' which was a great title for the research engineers, and 140 people signed up in four hours."

In his 2012 bestselling book on the Search Inside Yourself program, Tan attributed the success of his program to the fact that he had credibility based on being one of the early engineers at Google. As a respected engineer, he was in a position to argue that doing the job well necessitated emotional intelligence. Tan believed that by explaining that mindfulness could help engineers develop needed social and emotional skills, he translated the language of contemplative traditions "into a language even compulsively pragmatic people like me can process" (2012: 4–5). Bush thought the adaptions they made to pitch mindfulness to the Googlers helped them better "relate to" the program there. "They don't think it's something brought in from outside . . . Basically it feels like a Google program, so it works for them."

On one hand, for the Google meditation programs, as well as in many other contemplative programs, having respected, often high-status, insiders on board was crucial to getting the practices in. They not only helped get organizational approval but could access organizational resources like funding and convening spaces. In addition, organizational insiders helped translate the importance of meditation to new audiences. On the other hand, the Search Inside Yourself program may not have gotten off the ground without outside support from central members of the contemplative movement who had experience bringing mindfulness into secular professional sectors such as business. Contemplative leaders had adapted meditation practices to appeal to pragmatic, hardworking, non-Buddhist professionals before. They knew how to tailor the marketing of the program to get it in. Bush additionally could call in favors from high-profile friends such as Goleman to support the initiative, when he otherwise might not have come. His talk, Bush recounted, was important in drumming up support for the program before signups were made available for the second iteration of the program.

Using Grants to Bring Contemplative Practice to Higher Education

Beginning in 1997, CCMS brought contemplative practice into higher education by offering Contemplative Practice Fellowships. The grants, funded by the Fetzer Institute, provided financial support to professors willing to integrate contemplative practice into their curricula. The fellowships encouraged professors interested in contemplative practice to "be willing to come out of the closet and design and teach courses when no one was doing it," Bush said during a panel on contemplative education at an MLI conference in 2012.

Like business leaders, professors were ideal vectors of contemplative practice. They had credibility and social legitimacy: people trusted and believed them. Furthermore, because professors had "a lot of freedom to develop their courses," Bush said, contemplative practice in higher education "just took off." Although CCMS required Contemplative Practice Fellows to get their dean or department chair to officially approve contemplative courses, Bush knew "the truth is that people integrate stuff into their courses all the time." CCMS wanted administrators' approval so they did not appear to be sneaking mindfulness in, but they knew that ultimately the professoriate was a promising population to work with because of the autonomy they had in designing their curricula.

CCMS gained further legitimacy for meditation in higher education by building a partnership with a reputable professional association, the American Council of Learned Societies (ACLS), which administered their Fellowships. Although Bush expected "there would be tremendous resistance to offering practices from the religious traditions to students in secular institutions," ultimately "there was much less resistance than we imagined" due to their partnership with the ACLS.

Hal Roth, a professor of religious studies at Brown University, founder of Brown's Contemplative Studies Initiative, and CCMS Fellow, agreed. Roth, who began his meditation practicum for his Brown students earlier than most others, said that in his case, "Having the ACLS stamp of approval gave it a legitimacy it would not have had ordinarily." He said this was especially true, and important, with regard to colleagues in his department who were wary of teaching meditation in the classroom. Interviews with past Fellows for a 2011 CCMS report on the impact of the Contemplative Fellowships suggested Roth's experience was shared by others. The Fellowship's support provided other contemplative educators with legitimacy for teaching meditation within their institution, as evident in one Fellow's comment that "The Fellowship gave my work additional legitimacy within my school which has helped expand the work and connect me with other faculty."

CCMS's network of Fellows brought contemplative practice into their colleges and universities with little opposition, despite their expectations to the contrary. Contemplative Fellows' success was due to their academic credibility, pre-established relationships with administrators, and autonomy to teach and research what they wanted, as well as the ACLS's "stamp of approval," which was tied to their grant award.

Assimilating Benchmark Programs into Organizations' Institutional Legitimacy

For the three CCMS initiatives discussed above, as well as for dozens of other Buddhist-inspired contemplative programs, building partnerships with institutional insiders was a crucial means through which contemplative leaders got their programs into new institutions without provoking opposition. Once established, the contemplative programs and centers in esteemed organizations, like Google or Brown University, served as "benchmark" programs in their respective professional fields. These benchmark programs were intended to assimilate into the legitimacy of their host organizations. In particular, this strategy was used to secure *institutional legitimacy*, or professional acceptance of meditation, within science, higher education, business, the military, and healthcare. Once established, pioneering programs offered a beacon of acceptability to potential sympathizers in each domain. Thereafter, others in targeted fields could emulate them without the concern that they were breaching secular, rational, institutional norms and logics.[13]

In science and higher education, for example, contemplative leaders from various organizations deliberately embedded their programs and research agendas in the most respected academic institutions in the country to gain legitimacy from them. CCMS incorporated their meditation programs into elite academic institutions so that the schools' approval and sponsorship would grant legitimacy to the programs. "Part of our strategy is to create legitimacy, so we chose some highly visible institutions," Bush told *Tricycle* magazine in 2001. "We started the law program at Yale, and now there are a number of law schools—Columbia, New York University—who are interested. Yale legitimized it." Similarly, Roth said that "Essentially . . . what we're trying to do here is build an entirely new academic field [of Contemplative Studies] to bootstrap it from the ground up at an Ivy League institution."

Like members of CCMS, MLI founders, and philanthropic organizations were also more likely to recruit and support reputable meditation scholars housed in prestigious universities. A program officer at a foundation that funded contemplative science before meditation became popular said that they "realized, because this is cutting-edge research, it needs to be done at the best institutions. So that's one of our strategies—to work with exemplary partners."

In business, contemplative leaders strategically created benchmark programs through collaborations between movement leaders and high-status institutional insiders in targeted organizations as well. Janice Marturano, founder and executive director of the Institute for Mindful Leadership, emphasized the importance of beginning her mindful leadership program at General Mills, where she worked. General Mills is internationally recognized by popular business magazines such as *Forbes* and *Fortune* as a particularly good place to work, with high-quality leadership training. When Marturano, the deputy general counsel at General Mills, began her mindful leadership course in collaboration with Saki Santorelli, the executive director of CfM, she said to Santorelli that it would be "very hard for it to be successful at General Mills because we're used to the best in terms of developing our leaders, and we have some extraordinary people here. But," she thought, "if you can make it happen here, it would say a lot." Her strategy worked: her program at General Mills led to other opportunities to bring contemplative programs into other firms. Shortly before I spoke with her, for example, she had completed a special retreat for Target's corporate leaders. "And I know that the reason they did it in large measure," she said, "was because I taught at General Mills, and they recognize General Mills as a place that . . . is known for training leaders."

A similar process occurred with contemplative programs in other esteemed businesses, such as with the Search Inside Yourself program at Google. In addition to maintaining its popularity at Google for nearly a decade, the founders of the program established the Search Inside Yourself Leadership Institute, which brings the program to other people and companies beyond Google.

Google's public steps embracing mindfulness have been noticed by other tech companies. Several leaders of smaller technology companies in

Silicon Valley and beyond told me that, because Google has a meditation program, it is more acceptable for them to have one as well. One technology company founder, for example, told me that Google's program has "set a tone where it's not extreme to do some of these [practices] because you can point to Google or Facebook and say 'Hey, the rules are changing.'" Top tech companies, he said, were redefining what is acceptable in business. The experimental, playful cultures of companies like Google, are what now "constitutes business rather than following some very strict set of cultural norms and support," he said. Younger tech founders I spoke with wanted to create similar innovative, positive company cultures by creating mindful workplaces. They suggested that contemplatives' tactics to legitimize meditation by establishing benchmark programs in esteemed organizations in secular fields were working.

Gaining Public Legitimacy

Legitimacy for meditation expanded beyond the bounds of the esteemed organizations contemplatives inhabited with the help of international media coverage about the programs. Newspapers and magazines such as the *New York Times* and *Time* magazine raved about contemplatives' innovative programs and practices. For example, when Google engineer Chade-Meng Tan, or Huffington Post founder Ariana Huffington, promoted meditation as beneficial for company employees and others, the international news media publicized their talks and books. With support from successful professionals in tech and the media, meditation became more popular among other engineers, techies, and entrepreneurs, as well as among the more general public. Celebrity sponsorship and media attention not only gave mindful meditation visibility, but it helped mindful intervention programs to build a base of supporters and to accrue resources to develop and scientifically study the effects of the programs.

As reputable and highly visible organizations ranging from Brown University to Google incorporated meditation programs, audiences in outside fields and among the public began to view meditation differently because of its perceived endorsement by organizations held as staples of mainstream society and epitomes of success. Mindfulness practitioner and U.S. Congressman Tim Ryan told me that popular acceptance of meditation is "accelerating now because it has made its way into institutions that have a lot of good brand recognition, a lot of credibility with the average American citizen. I mean, who's gonna argue with the Marines doing this?

It's tough to pigeonhole mindfulness as some kind of far-out endeavor when the United States Marine Corps is doing it." He went on talk about how K-12 mindfulness education programs are expanding in his home state of Ohio, and how they are increasingly accepted because companies like Google, Procter & Gamble, General Mills, and Target have adopted meditation programs for their employees. In addition, he noted the importance of some top athletes' support for meditation. Former mindfulness teacher at CfM George Mumford has brought meditation to professional basketball teams, including the Bulls, the Lakers, and the Knicks, since the 1990s. Ryan noted the broader impact of Mumford's work with Phil Jackson's basketball teams:

> There is obviously an appreciation for high-performing athletes in America, and you have the winningest basketball coach in the history of the NBA, Phil Jackson, taught it to the Bulls when he was there, and won a number of championships. Taught it to the Lakers when he went out there. They won a number of championships. So when you have that kind of credibility, as you're presenting this to the average citizen in Ohio, people are sayin', "And this will reduce my own personal stress, too?" And you tie all that together, and they're like, "Okay, I'll try it."

Congressman Ryan's statements allude to how getting meditation into organizations with good brand-names, such as Google and the Chicago Bulls, provided a more generalized *public legitimacy* and credibility to the practice among broader audiences. In addition, bringing meditation into organizations characterized by masculinity, strength, and fortitude, such as the Marine Corps and the Bulls, as well as successful corporations such as General Mills, Proctor & Gamble, and Target, cultivated new images of meditation. This new "branding" of meditation associated the practices with endurance, success, and mainstream American culture rather than the cultural associations from the 1970s and 1980s which portrayed meditators as part of a marginal, "soft," "woo-woo," or "flaky" New Age counterculture.

Congressman Ryan was not the only high-status public figure to extol the meditation programs to the public through interviews with the media and in his 2012 book, *A Mindful Nation*. Celebrities such as Goldie Hawn (founder of the MindUP program for kids), Ariana Huffington, and Evan Williams (co-founder of Twitter) have endorsed the benefits of meditation to national and international media such as the *New York Times*, the *Huffington Post*, *The Economist*, and *Time* magazine. Such endorsements further extend the legitimacy of meditation to the public by connecting the practice to the cultural legitimacy of its proponents' organizations, as well as adding another layer of public legitimacy from being supported by popular mainstream celebrities and public figures in government, the media, commerce and technology, and sports. These created a juggernaut of increasing legitimacy as different cultural authorities added to the intrigue and acclaim of contemplative practice.

Adding on Scientific Legitimacy

In addition to institutional and public legitimacy, the establishment of scientific credibility greatly bolstered the contemplative cause within secular professional institutions and to the public. Because the contemplative movement started largely in and contingent to academia, with Kabat-Zinn's MBSR program at the CfM, MLI, and CCMS, one would assume this movement was successful largely because these spiritual activists mobilized scientific legitimacy for meditation. After all, "'science' often stands metonymically for credibility, for legitimate knowledge, for reliable and useful predictions, for a trustable reality; it commands assent in public debate. If 'science' says so, we are more often than not inclined to believe it or act on it—and prefer it over claims lacking this epistemic seal of approval" (Gieryn 1999: 1).

However, developing a new scientific intellectual field is a slow process. Research on meditation was, by and large, not acknowledged and respected by scientists when the roots of the contemplative movement were being laid in the late 1970s with the CfM and in the late 1980s with MLI. The perception among scientists that little scientific evidence on the effects of meditation existed continued well into the 2000s; this perception was held by scholar-practitioners in the mindfulness community as well as scientists outside of it. The structural foundations of the movement were in formation for several decades before most of the research on meditation and mindfulness was published and publicized among wider audiences.

Contemplative scientists conducted their early studies as they were creating the movement's central organizations and developing their programs. After the organizational groundwork of their field was laid, much of the research began to be published. Basic neuroscientific research and clinical studies on meditation began accruing and gaining momentum after 2004 based on the work of scientists who were, by and large, affiliated with central contemplative organizations. Research on mindfulness and meditation was then passed through the social networks and organizations in the contemplative movement. Even then, the spread of the meditation programs into secular organizations outpaced the research. Contemplative programs in education and business were established before research on the beneficial effects of meditation for children or employees was conducted. It was these programs that called for studies to support their programs and provided the initial pilot programs that could be studied. Thus, scientific legitimacy and credibility supporting the beneficial effects of meditation occurred largely in step with, or after, the base structure of the field had already been established.

Before the scientific research was published, contemplative programs grew mainly through personal ties based on program participants' testimonials that "it worked." After the meditation research was published, contemplatives could build upon the scientific credibility of the studies by referencing them in conversations with potential new adopters, in their programs, on their websites, in their teaching manuals, and in the media. Founders and facilitators of contemplative meditation programs in occupational fields such as business, healthcare, education, and the military told me that in recent years they have increasingly referenced scientific research on meditation to lend credibility to the mindfulness components of their programs. They use findings from neuroscience, psychology, and clinical research on meditation and mindfulness to support their claims that contemplative practices promote health, help people cope with stress, teach emotional intelligence, hone attention skills, and have a host of other benefits. In addition to providing scientific credibility in support of the positive effects of their programs, contemplative founders said that talking about science "put people at ease" and provided cultural legitimacy. "On a base level," one contemplative teacher told me, "Americans believe in science. No matter what they say they don't believe, it's the subconscious authority. And so when you can bring stuff from that authority place, it's very helpful. They feel like they're on solid ground."

In 2014, when I coded all contemplative organizations' websites in my sample, about 45% of the programs with websites (twenty-three out of fifty-one organizations' websites) raised awareness of the scientific research on meditation conducted by contemplative neuroscientists, psychologists, educators, and clinical researchers by including links to their centers, laboratories, and research on their organizational websites.[14] Six contemplative organizations additionally posted peer-reviewed research findings on the benefits of their specific program. On the website of MindUP, the K-12 mindfulness program developed by Goldie Hawn, for example, a summary of research on the program suggests that it improves students' sense of optimism and self-concept, neuroendocrine regulation, executive function, and academic achievement.

The scientific legitimacy for meditation also spilled into other institutional fields because scientists and contemplative experts physically moved around, visiting each other's programs and centers.[15] Their talks gave scientific credibility to contemplative programs in other fields. For example, Bush not only brought in her long-time friend Goleman to speak at Google; she also brought other friends such as MLI neuroscientists Cliff Saron and Richard Davidson to give a talk on mindfulness and to help her brainstorm how to bring mindfulness into the U.S. Army. Having access to these scientists as epistemic authorities provided scientific legitimacy and credibility to claims of the beneficial effects of meditation. This helped CCMS and other contemplative organizations to establish their initiatives bringing meditation into new fields.

As science on the benefits of meditation was passed along by contemplatives working in different occupational fields, the credibility of scientific results was amplified by the credibility of the individuals and organizations it passed through. Social movement scholar Bert Klandermans (1988) theorized that "a diversion of credibility" occurs when a movement's sources of information, such as thought leaders, organizations, or the media, adopt parts of the message of the movement organization. Individual spokespersons from credible exemplar organizations can publicize and popularize contemplative beliefs more broadly than a movement organization can on its own. As new professional and public audiences, who followed the "out of the closet" meditator-professionals, adopted parts of the message, the contemplative movement gained more legitimacy for meditation, and over time, traction among broader circles of people.[16]

The Reverberating Effects of Insiders' Power

With the support of contemplative networks and organizations, institutional insiders brought mindful meditation programs into targeted organizations in academia, healthcare, business, education, and the military. These insiders had a great deal of autonomy over their work as professors, business leaders, K-12 educators, doctors, and psychologists. Before bringing meditation in, many of them already had considerable "symbolic power" (Hallett 2003: 133), or the power to define the situation in which interactions took place in their organizations. They used their symbolic institutional power to rebrand meditation and bring it in. Contemplative professionals strategically reclaimed meditation, altering its associations with flighty hippies, mystics, or Asian immigrants' ritualistic religious practices (e.g., chanting, bowing, and guru worship). Instead, mindfulness leaders and professional elites collaborated to market meditation as a scientifically supported practice used by successful, rational professionals, athletes, and celebrities. This process made meditation appeal to people who might be interested in spirituality or curious about meditation but had not considered trying it before. Professionals' legitimation of meditation (through their assimilation into reputable organizations, their support from public figures, esteemed professional leaders, and celebrities and through scientific research) fostered a disinhibition process. As meditation was increasingly popularized and legitimated over time, professionals with private meditation practices could "come out" and identify with or join the movement to bring personal meditation practices and their associated spiritual philosophies into professional workplaces, with less concern about negative stigmas attached to their practices.[17]

A positive feedback loop ensued. As more professionals in top "name-brand" institutions came out in support of meditation, the practice gained further institutional legitimacy and was more likely to gain support from other institutional insiders open to the practices. Getting into socially legitimate mainstream organizations gave the contemplative movement a toehold into further expanding among broader, mainstream audiences. Esteemed secular organizations became vehicles through which the movement's message was spread to specific professional audiences and to the larger public. Media outlets were fascinated by the spread of meditation in powerful social institutions and reported on this burgeoning trend in reputable presses syndicated across the United States and the world.

Even though scientific results on the benefits of meditation became available only after the primary contemplative organizations' interventions had already been established, when produced, these results bolstered the subsequent spread of the movement in several ways. Contemplatives incorporated scientific research on meditation into their mindfulness training programs to strengthen and legitimize them, making them more interesting, resonant, and credible to targeted professional audiences. This process was supported by positive media attention, which communicated the beneficial effects of meditation, as "proven" by science, to the public.

It is clear that insider involvement contributed to the contemplative movement's spread and legitimation of meditation in so many professional sectors. However, it is important to reflect upon the tradeoffs that come with relying upon insider access and influence in moving meditation into corporate and institutional America. As Bush discussed, the CCMS's work with Monsanto and Google raised ethical questions. Was the cost of success, and getting meditation and contemplative values into powerful organizations, worth potential drawbacks such as the risk of being coopted or reducing the length and intensity of intervention programs? In working with insiders, would contemplative educators come to view the companies in a more favorable light and be desensitized over time to their prior commitments? Might those working inside the system become more sympathetic to the corporate valuation of elite status, power, and profit-seeking? Would meditation programs cease to be an anti-materialistic, oppositional consciousness within powerful secular institutions—as contemplative organizational founders such as Engle and Kabat-Zinn hoped—and start to become a productivity tool for corporate elites in the service of increasing company profit? Or could meditation programs truly transform corporate insiders into more thoughtful, ethical leaders? Could institutional cultures become kinder and more supportive of their members through interventions with small groups of insiders?

Other outcomes might result as well, which combine the above possibilities. At a systemic level, corporate power could continue to increase at the cost of democracy and others' voices, as some political economists suggest (e.g., Reich 2015), yet insiders could become more thoughtful and ethical in their decisions. Or, influenced by contemplative practice, leaders could choose to leave their corporate positions; in that case, the system would continue grinding on. While I cannot decisively answer these questions with the data in this study, it is necessary to raise and consider these questions in light of the ethical conundrums CCMS and other contemplative organizations faced in developing collaborations with elite insiders—and which they continue to wrestle with in their contemporary work.

It is also important to note that while having high-status insiders in esteemed organizations, celebrities, and scientific research supporting meditation was important to the success of this movement, it was not sufficient to guarantee meditation would make it into new institutional spaces, such as in education, business, and the government. Contemporary research on elites and insider support documents how having elite insider access is often not enough to guarantee that movements will be able to establish themselves in new fields (Binder 2002; Duffy et al. 2010; Lindsay 2008). Various cultural processes were crucial to the success of the contemplative movement. In addition to building upon spiritual and Buddhist modernist antecedents in American history, and fostering an impressive network of advocates across professional fields, the contemplatives strategically adapted Buddhism to appeal to their targeted professional audiences, as shown in the next chapter.

CHAPTER 5

Making Mindfulness Appealing

IN 2009, MICHAEL TAYLOR,[1] a fit, energetic veteran in his mid-forties, began introducing meditation to other veterans after witnessing their rising mental health issues from the war in Afghanistan. Taylor had first tried to bring Buddhist-inspired meditation to the chaplains at a local Army base but had failed due to their strong evangelical bent. Next he connected with leaders of a Mindfulness-Based Mind Fitness Training program for military servicemen, which was developed by two Mind and Life Institute (MLI) members—Amishi Jha, a professor of psychology at the University of Miami, and Elizabeth Stanley, a professor of security studies at Georgetown University. Taylor worked with them on their program for a while and then struck out on his own.

Like other contemplative leaders and educators, Taylor's program adapted Buddhist language to make meditation accessible to the people he wanted to reach. Taylor first began experimenting with how to describe Buddhist meditation to military colleagues while studying at Naropa University, a Buddhist-inspired institution, after he completed his military service. To appeal to veterans and law enforcement, he translated Buddhist concepts into the secular, masculine, sports vernacular:

I put together a curriculum that was aimed at taking this stuff out into the world in a very particular languaging way . . . And so it was, "Okay, can I use that type of languaging to really communicate the mind training to this particular demographic," and the demographic is blue collar, git-'er-done kind of guys. And so then I designed a curriculum that comes from a very operational perspective . . . It's very mission-oriented in terms of my experiences in combat . . . We basically designed a curriculum that would speak to these kinds of folks. And, not talking about meditation, not doin' anything that they would consider weird or unusual, you know what I'm sayin'? . . . Don't ever use the word *meditation*. Don't even use the word *mindfulness*. It's all couched in science, in terms of the neuroscience and the nervous system regulation . . . It's all under the rubric of peak performance to some degree, in terms of what we present to 'em.

Despite the secular language Taylor used to describe his program, "all of our techniques are pulled from the pantheon of Tibetan Buddhist practice techniques," Taylor told me. "All of it." Naropa University, where he studied, came from a Kagyu lineage of Tibetan Buddhism, he said, and their program was "very much" based in that tradition. For *shamatha* breathing practices, "we call it 'riding the breath,' and then the *vipassana*, we call it 'the zone'."

In his program, Taylor changed the name, motivations, practices, and interactional context of Buddhist meditation into a secular "mind training" exercise in order to bring Tibetan Buddhist–inspired practices to veterans and law enforcement officers to help fortify their mental health. He coupled his program closely with military and law enforcement culture—through the language of "peak performance" and using military training techniques—and removed suspicious elements of Buddhism, such as Buddhist cosmology, guru worship, or other rituals or language deemed too religious or "weird." In doing so, Taylor added more instrumental goals to the meditation practices he was teaching; in addition to improving the mental health of his clients, he promised to improve their job performance. Like other mindfulness programs building upon the contemplative movement, he situated the program in scientific language to provide credibility and put "people at ease," he said. Ultimately, with its masculine, militarized culture grounded in scientific discourse, his program succeeded in bringing meditation to new audiences that might not otherwise be interested.

The practice of meditation itself was transformed when brought to the military, veterans, and law enforcement officers. After they learned the program's basic contemplative techniques, participants were taught to use the techniques in close combat simulations that involved multiple assailants and guns. There was the "whole shootin' match," he said. The program had the following sequence of events:

. . . we first let them feel that parasympathetic response when they do belly breathing—that's the dopamine. That's what you guys want. You have the ability to feel good inside without taking any medication. Watch this. Breathe . . . And, then later on that day, we teach 'em the basics of *shamatha*: "Come back to your breath."

And, then the next day, we start running through simulations . . . "So, imagine you have a bunch of mats, like in a gymnastic tournament . . ." Then, we have a partner of ours who does what he calls adrenal stress training. So, he gets people in an activated sympathetic state. Where adrenalin and cortisol are really falling, you know, screamin' at people and just getting in their face. And cops and those people don't like that stuff. So, they get totally activated . . . And each person goes through this, and everybody's watching. As they're going through it, we're coaching on the sidelines, going, "Okay, belly breath if you start feeling yourself getting very activated." And, typically, they watch and they get activated this is what they do for a living. And, then it's like, "Okay, if you feel your mind running off in terms of fear or thoughts about, you know, whatever the case may be, bring it back home."

. . . we run 'em through a simulation, put 'em back in the classroom, and we run 'em back through the meditations and go, "This is the state that you want to be noticing." So, what we basically do is amplify it really loudly so that you can go, "See this? This is what you want. See that? That is what you want." Notice the difference. And, they can, and [finger snap] and it really clicks for them that way.

For many Buddhists, who may balk at killing an ant or a spider, the use of combat practice to teach contemplative practice may come as an affront, as it fails to support Buddhist treatises not to kill or incite harm to others. Taylor admitted that his program was "somewhat off the reservation in terms of normal meditation instruction. We don't really, necessarily, consider it normal. It's not normal," he said, laughing. Their combat simulations, he said, chuckling, would give "ordinary meditation teachers and a lot of therapists a conniption fit."

Yet, from Taylor's perspective, his mind training program was an important practical aid that taught those suffering from anxiety and posttraumatic stress disorder that they could find an internal state of mindful equanimity, even in their most stressful moments. This outcome of relieving suffering and teaching others to foster equanimity aligns with Buddhism. He believed these outcomes were worth letting go of other ideological parts of Buddhism and worth adding elements of masculine militarized culture, such as the goal of attaining peak performance during potentially violent interactions, to contemplative practices.

How did we get here—to the point where Buddhist meditation has become a form of mind training that would be problematic to many devout Buddhists, and virtually unrecognizable to the men attending the course? How was Buddhist practice altered from its original purpose of pointing practitioners toward enlightenment to a means of attaining instrumental aims such as stress reduction and peak performance? How has Buddhist mindfulness been transformed to get into other institutions? Were the tradeoffs that attenuated Buddhism so that it would appeal to new audiences worth making?

In this chapter I show how contemplative leaders adapted the content of Buddhist contemplative practices to spread it into new institutions. In many ways, Jon Kabat-Zinn's Mindfulness-Based Stress Reduction (MBSR) program provided the initial model of how to get Buddhist-inspired mindfulness into secular institutions. Research on the effects of Kabat-Zinn's program, as well as the MLI's research on adept meditators in the 1990s and early 2000s, then brought credibility to claims that Buddhist meditation was good for you.

Next I trace how contemplative interventions were brought into other powerful secular institutions, such as education and business, during the first decade of the twenty-first century. Many of these programs were the second-generation programs Kabat-Zinn so presciently predicted in his Center for Contemplative Mind in Society (CCMS) report (1994b). As the military example above shows, contemplatives took care to adapt meditation to make it appeal to new audiences when they first broke into new institutions. Once they were in, they walked a tightrope between different institutional loyalties. They respected the majority of the dominant host institutions' structures and rules, yet strove to include elements of Buddhism and American spirituality in contemplative subcultures. This careful dance to please many audiences led to further cultural differentiation of contemplative culture across sectors.

As predicted by Kabat-Zinn's (1994b) report, although nearly all the founders of mindfulness programs I spoke with were connected to the original contemplative organizations and their networks, they had a wide latitude in how they altered mindfulness to fit where they sought to bring it. Based on their own religious and spiritual backgrounds, contemplative leaders each decided which traditional Buddhist elements were necessary and which were unnecessary cultural baggage. Even though most of the early contemplatives I spoke with took seriously their contemplative practices and their Buddhist roots, they largely rationalized the many alterations they made to Buddhism to fit in their institutions as well worth it.

The Mindful Model's Adaptations in Healthcare

Contemplative programs are located in a precarious social space between private spiritual/religious fields and secular institutions. Early leaders of the contemplative movement in the 1970s through the 1990s were acutely aware of how foreign Buddhist culture was to most Americans, and to professionals in particular. To get Buddhist practices into powerful secular institutions, contemplative leaders designed their programs to align with targeted institutional structures, professional norms, and professional goals. As exhibited above, to make his program resonate with the men he trained, Taylor added the goals of peak performance during stressful, violent encounters to the more ostensibly Buddhist goal of relieving the posttraumatic suffering of military veterans; this coupled his program to the work cultures of his clientele. In doing so, like other contemplative leaders, he decoupled his program from elements of Buddhist culture that might be off-putting to the audience he hoped to appeal to. He removed explicit religious references and did not discuss Buddhist tenets of nonviolence.

In organizational studies, the term *loose coupling* is used to describe organizations in which local practices and interactional culture deviate from formal, macro-level organizational cultures (Hallett 2010; Meyer and Rowan 1977). Given loose coupling, movements can target organizational change in local on-the-ground cultures. To do so, contemplative leaders established educational "intervention" programs to teach interested members of an organization meditation practices. Programs conducted within or contingent to workplaces socialized participants to approach their work and their daily interactions with others in new ways, which deviated from and could challenge dominant secular cultures at their workplaces.

However, contemplatives rarely thoughtfully assessed the potentially negative consequences of their integration into powerful established institutions. In coupling their programs to their targeted institutions' cultures, they decoupled from Buddhism and entered spaces that had their own set operating procedures and norms. This put the contemplatives at risk of being unintentionally coopted into the dominant professional cultures and structures of the organizations they moved into.

The MBSR program is an important case to consider because of its success within the movement and in expanding mindfulness in the United States and internationally. MBSR served as the foundation stone of the contemplative movement; it was the pioneering mindfulness program and influenced nearly all of the programs that followed it. To date, more than 24,000 people have completed the course.[2] MBSR is taught in every state and in more than thirty countries.[3] MBSR programs are offered at more than 250 hospitals throughout the United States (Baum 2010).

According to Kabat-Zinn (1994b), he established the program at the University of Massachusetts Medical Center in 1979 as:

> a conscious attempt to introduce the essence of Buddhist mindfulness meditation practice and hatha yoga to patients with chronic medical problems in a

university medical center within the mainstream of medicine and healthcare. We chose to position it as a part of "clinical behavioral medicine" and to structure it as a clinic in the form of a course designed to train patients in mindfulness and its applications in everyday life, including coping with stress, pain, and chronic illness. However, *its basic mission was orthogonal from the start, in that we saw it as operating within an entirely different paradigm and consciousness from the larger institution within which it was embedded. From the outside, it looks like a clinic, bills like a clinic, operates like a clinic, but once inside, one gradually discovers that it is "rotated in consciousness" and operates out of very different principles and values from the overall mission of the institution* (perhaps truer to the fundamental mission of the institution). For instance, its paradigm includes a model for the sacred quality of the encounter between a person as patient and his/her physician and health care team. Thus arises the principle that all patients referred to the clinic are encountered as full human beings and are listened to and spoken to from the heart by the interviewer. In other words, the encounter itself is held in mindfulness and part of the work of the staff is to make their work part of their meditation practice and their meditation practice part of their work. (Italics added for emphasis)

In creating the Stress Reduction Clinic at the University of Massachusetts Medical School, Kabat-Zinn had dual allegiances. To make his program seem legitimate, he strategically coupled his center's work to the structure and standard operating procedures of a medical clinic at an academic institution, making it look and operate normally, like any other medical clinic. Yet his ultimate purpose was to bring an alternative sacred cultural "consciousness" based on principles from humanistic strains of American spirituality, religious liberalism, and Buddhist modernism into everyday work in his center and into the larger field of healthcare. This, he thought, radically diverged from mainstream Western medicine at the time.

As Jeff Wilson, a religious and Asian studies professor, described in his 2014 book *Mindful America,* mindfulness advocates initiated a process of "mystifying" Buddhist culture: they hid overt references to Buddhism so that it would appeal to a wide range of secular audiences and further other agendas (44). Through this process, contemplative leaders established what Wilson called a "pragmatic legitimacy" based on the "practical application of their message" (50). To get his program into a medical school, Kabat-Zinn nominally reduced Buddhism to an attention tool to aid the chronically ill with his MBSR program. Like other contemplatives, Kabat-Zinn deliberately removed telltale "religious" Buddhism elements that would alienate or upset secular professionals, such as references to Buddhist gods, enlightenment, or other facets of Buddhism that did not seem rational or scientifically testable.

Neither Kabat-Zinn nor his staff believed these changes posed a problem or lost anything essential to Buddhism. In fact, Saki Santorelli, director of the Center for Mindfulness in Medicine, Health Care, and Society (CfM), thought that in a medical center, their program benefited from being "freed from cultural constraints, familiar jargon and underlying assumptions of traditional centers for contemplative practice" (2011: 215). By moving Buddhist meditation into secular institutions, contemplative leaders were no longer accountable to traditional Buddhist languages, normative restrictions, and practices common in Buddhist temples and dharma centers. Mindfulness practitioners could remove religious "jargon" and "underlying assumptions" to reach more people and more tightly couple their adapted Buddhist-inspired practices and ideas into practitioners' everyday lives, which were largely spent in secular institutions, like schools and their places of employment. Santorelli thought that being embedded in secular institutions forced "one to skillfully translate, transmit, and embody, in a secular manner, the essential reality of interconnectedness, mind-heart training, wholesome ethics and economies and universal responsibility in a manner that is non-alienating and inclusive, welcoming and highly participatory" (2011: 215). Furthermore, he thought the tension between adapting Buddhism to fit in secular institutions and the desire to "authentically" transmit the "essence" of Buddhism fostered the creative production of powerful new forms of contemplative culture:

> Through these years, we have used this unique position as a laboratory—an experimental ground for testing ways to remain absolutely and unequivocally true to the foundational roots of the work while interfacing with and living fully in the world of people not particularly interested in traditional practice centers . . . While saddled with our own set of constraints and procedures, working within a large, mainstream institution creates a friction that, if used wisely, can provide an incredibly rich ground in which to realize first-hand the interconnectedness of the world, and to develop a host of approaches and methods that express the potential of the trained mind and cultivated heart. (2011: 215)

During the first decade of the twenty-first century, other contemplative practitioners established mindful intervention programs in education, business, the military/law enforcement, and other sectors. Like CfM, over sixty other contemplative organizations I spoke with translated and adapted Buddhism in specific ways, which reflected their host institutions' structures, motives, and cultures, to get it into their workplaces. All of the organizations (1) coupled their programs explicitly to targeted institutional structures, cultures, and missions, (2) explicitly decoupled their programs from certain aspects of Buddhism, yet (3) brought elements of Buddhism into their programs in various, often covert, ways. Buddhist elements were disguised deliberately by founding members of the contemplative movement. The degree of Buddhism brought into contemplative programs varied by sector and by individual leaders and practitioners. This initiated a process of cultural differentiation with benefits and drawbacks to the contemplative movement.

Compromises on the Buddhist Side: Meditation as an Object of Scientific Investigation

Even from the outset, Kabat-Zinn was aware that he needed scientific evidence to legitimize his MBSR program among medical professionals and broader audiences. He began collecting data from the very beginning. His first article on MBSR was published in an academic journal in 1982. While Kabat-Zinn inspired substantial interest in mindfulness meditation among clinical researchers, MLI began researching adept meditators in 1992 in an effort to bring contemplative studies into the fields of psychology and neuroscience.

It was not easy to legitimize meditation in a field as critical as that of scientific research. Several neuroscientists trained at top research institutions, such as Harvard, remembered being warned by advisors in the 1970s not to do research on meditation if they aspired to have reputable academic careers. Other scholars' colleagues have remained skeptical of their interest in meditation and their inclusion of it in their courses. One Ivy League professor's colleagues even threatened to report his inclusion of meditation practice in a course to the administration. Hence, scholar-practitioners bringing meditation into their work exercised caution in how they presented their commitments to contemplative practice and meditation research. They were careful not to explicitly or overzealously proselytize Buddhist meditation at work.

When Buddhism and science were brought together, the rigidity of science required compromises—at Buddhism's expense. A scientist who had been involved with MLI since the early 1990s suggested that in the dialogues between scientists and the Dalai Lama, Buddhists compromised their perspectives more than the scientists. "To understand each other, certain kinds of compromises or choices have to be made," he said, "and they tend to be made on the Buddhist side. The Buddhists tend to adapt, and reframe, and edit more than the scientists do. And, that speaks to a kind of power asymmetry between the two."

Despite the best of intentions to bring Buddhist meditation into science because of the scholars' commitments to the Dalai Lama and their own meditation practices, to get meditation into science and healthcare, contemplatives circumscribed Buddhist motivations, goals, philosophy, and cosmology to fit within the epistemological and normative paradigm of science, especially at the outset. Parts of Buddhism appropriate for science were cherry-picked out of the religious canon. The practice of meditation, and its effects on health, could be empirically studied using the scientific method and new technology such as functional magnetic resonance imaging (fMRI). As another MLI leader noted,

> Techniques within Buddhism are not designed to just investigate what's so about the mind. They're designed to have you get off the wheel of birth and death. There is a thing called enlightenment within Buddhism. There is Buddhahood. There is a method for a RESULT. There is no RESULT in science except the self-limiting, asymptotic convergence on the way we can know nature. Period. Wherever that takes us. There is no end point. And, there is no goal except provisional goals. And, the provisional goals always fall, either because they're achieved or because they're proven to be the wrong goal to begin with. So, when you say, *"Okay, these things are useful because of their side effects,"* then *you're in interesting territory because, because this is fine. It's . . . an empirical question.* (Caps note speaker's emphasis; italicized emphasis added)

Buddhist motivations, such as the quest for Enlightenment, were sidelined by meditation researchers because they cannot be empirically studied using the scientific method; instead meditation researchers focused on the instrumental outcomes of meditation that they *could* validate. Thus, Buddhism was cut down to fit into what could be credibly investigated under the purview of science.

Why were the contemplative leaders so deferential to science? Contemplatives deliberately distanced themselves from Buddhist religious elements to avoid accusations their work was illegitimate in science. They were aware of prior similar religiously tainted intellectual movements, such as scholarship on Transcendental Meditation (TM) in the 1970s. Contemplative scientists, like many of their colleagues in psychology and neuroscience, viewed TM research from that period as pseudoscience (Tøllefsen 2014). This, they believed, was due to using weaker research methods and technological equipment, generalizing results beyond empirical evidence, and basing interpretations on religious epistemological claims rather than science's more limited focus. To ensure they produced credible, reputable science on meditation, the contemplatives were careful

(1) to use academic language and a scientific epistemological framework, (2) to publish their results in respectable peer-reviewed journals, (3) to associate with other esteemed professionals, and (4) to distance themselves from spiritual or New Age believers who would not be perceived as credible in science. In adopting all these strategies, early contemplative scientists first and foremost sought for their work to uphold the standards set by their scientific field, rather than prioritizing Buddhism. They thought this was the only way to gain scientific credibility and legitimacy for Buddhist meditation practice.

John Dunne, MLI participant and a professor of contemplative humanities at the University of Wisconsin - Madison, said that from the very beginning, MLI scientists carefully focused their research on empirical rather than metaphysical questions in order to avoid the accusations of overgeneralization that plagued TM researchers in the 1970s:

> The methodological problem that many TM studies seem to fall into, or the framework in which caused the problem, is that the purpose of the studies was to prove the metaphysical truth behind the tradition. So that the efficacy, or just whatever effects the meditation practice might have—if the meditation practice enables you to, you know, sleep better—then somehow that must mean that the metaphysics, the philosophical or theological position behind or informing it was also true. Right? So that's a very dangerous framework in which to be conducting research. And I think we've been very effective at avoiding that . . . and if one tries to operate in that fashion, then one is actually confusing epistemologies.

MLI scientists learned from the failed attempt of TM researchers to legitimize meditation based on their research two decades earlier. TM research lost credibility as "rigorous science" and was instead relegated to the suspect realm of "pseudoscience" because it did not follow the cardinal scientific rule of prioritizing scientific logic above all. As philosopher of science Karl Popper postulated, proper science must have falsifiable research questions that can be proven or disproven. Consequently, as Dunne explained, MLI researchers took care to adhere to scientific standards by posing tractable, testable, empirical questions in a scientific framework. They made a great effort not to overgeneralize their interpretations of their findings to reduce accusations that they were trying to "prove" that Buddhism was true because they were meditators.

MLI scientists further distanced themselves from prior TM research by describing their work using secular, scientific language, striving for the utmost scientific rigor, and publishing in the most respected venues possible. University of Wisconsin at Madison neuroscientist Richard Davidson told me in 2011 that "By and large, we really haven't gotten much negative backlash." He attributed this to how MLI scientists have "attempted to do this work in a way that's different than in the seventies with the TM people." In contrast to TM researchers, he said:

> We are doing it in a way where the description of the work is quite secular. We are publishing in the best journals in science . . . there's an unswerving commitment to do it really rigorously. And we've gotten papers into places where they've never had papers on meditation before. And, we had the very first paper on meditation in the *Proceedings of the National Academy of Sciences.* We had the very first paper on meditation, ever, in the *Journal of Neuroscience.* We had the very first paper on meditation, ever, in *PLoS Biology.* All of them are super-high-profile places. And I think that's made a huge difference. (Italics added for emphasis)

Not only did MLI scientists take care to describe their work in a secular way that aligned with scientific norms and standards, but their work has received peer approval by being accepted through the standard scientific vetting process—the peer-review process— into competitive, highly respected journals. Thus, their scholarship has been validated by credible academic standards in their particular disciplines. In so doing, they leveraged the legitimacy of science to legitimize select Buddhist practices, even if their stated goals were instrumental rather than religious.

While contemplatives distanced themselves from stigmatized religious movements like TM, they likened themselves to other highly regarded professional groups. For example, when others questioned whether his meditation practice affected his "objectivity" as a scientist, Davidson compared his status as a meditation researcher who practices meditation to a cardiologist who exercises. Claims he was not an objective scientist because he meditated were, he argued, the equivalent of "telling a cardiologist that they can't study the effects of physical exercise on the heart if they are exercising themselves."

Like Davidson, other contemplative leaders compared their work to secular professional groups held in high social esteem and distanced themselves from stigmatized religious, spiritual, or countercultural groups. They were quick to separate themselves from "New Age" or other seemingly "flaky" spiritual believers. This was evident on June 20, 2012, at a session of the MLI's Summer Research Institute, an annual academic summer retreat for contemplative professors and graduate students. Brown University professor Catherine Kerr was giving a presentation on the benefits of tai chi when the following episode occurred:

> One middle-aged woman with long brown hair asked a long question about how chi is really a pervasive field of energy. "We're swimming in it," she said. Her language was florid and sounded spiritual. Several graduate students sitting behind me snickered and laughed.
>
> Kerr responded with a deadpan face, "I'm agnostic in any public talk. In my practice I talk in one way, but in practice [with regards to work] I talk another way. The stuff I talk about is all measurable."
>
> The woman asking the question replied, saying, "This is a place where we can do this. If we can't talk about it here, where can we talk about it?" She mentioned Zen Roshi Joan Halifax's earlier meditation on sending out love to others. "What are we sending out?" she asked. "I don't think it's several different things. I think it's one thing." . . .
>
> Later, Roshi Joan Halifax responded, explaining, "What we are sending is not about sending it to a person at a distance. It's about deconstructing the self and intrapsychic work on the self."

Contemplatives carefully guarded and policed the boundary between spiritual or religious belief and scientific analysis of contemplative practices. The contemplative scientists I spoke with clearly distinguished themselves from New Age spiritual practitioners who believe in astrology, crystals, mystical energy fields, and other elements of spirituality not supported by science. When confronted with that kind of spirituality, their academic role-identities came out.

The careful distinction between which contemplative elements were empirically testable and which were spiritual elements beyond the purview of contemporary science (with the latter held at arm's length) was crucial to this movement's success in spreading contemplative beliefs and practices into secular fields. Even though the retreat was primarily for professors and graduate students, and included daily meditation and yoga practice, optional seating on Asian *zafu* cushions, and informal dress, all of the MLI representatives were careful to articulate perspectives that did not challenge scientific beliefs and norms. To graduate students and new members of the movement, members of the MLI "old guard" continually articulated the necessity to conduct research with the utmost scientific rigor. They modeled this by producing first-rate research themselves published in highly selective, peer-reviewed journals. And when confronted with more explicitly spiritual or religious views, leaders of the contemplative movement were quick to shift to careful answers, while graduate students snickered in the background.

Above all, the contemplatives did not want to jeopardize their scientific credibility and legitimacy by professing belief in an ethereal field of energy they could not empirically validate.

To get meditation into new secular spaces, contemplative leaders and educators walked a tightrope between the various institutions and audiences they were in conversation with. In this cultural dance, they made considerable alterations to Buddhist meditation so that it would appeal to professional audiences. They translated Buddhism into local professional vernacular languages, tailored meditation to fit within each institutional sector, and created new hybrid mindful work practices.[4] They eliminated religious elements that were less likely to resonate with targeted professional audiences. Goals of meditation were altered from Buddhist enlightenment or personal spiritual liberation to align with more pragmatic institutional aims, such as cultivating employees' social skill, attention, or creativity. Through this process of adaptation, they strategically coupled contemplative culture to secular institutions' structures, norms, and purposes.[5] Consequently, over time and across institutional space, a cultural differentiation process occurred in which Buddhist-inspired contemplative practices were translated into a number of institution-specific, subcultural forms. These new hybrid cultural forms were by and large received favorably by the institutions they moved into.[6]

The Differentiation of Mindfulness Interventions Across Sectors

Building on the success of MBSR in healthcare and advances in scientific understanding of contemplative practice, other meditators began to explore ways to bring meditation into their professional domains in the first decade of the twenty-first century. They did not attempt to alter the structures or missions of the institutions they worked in. Program leaders like Kabat-Zinn, MLI scientists, and Mirabai Bush of CCMS made mindfulness fit within their institutional landscapes. They adapted descriptions of contemplative culture and its practices to resonate with new secular, institutional audiences. Table 5.1 shows how contemplative culture was differentiated into many subcultural forms through these adaptation processes. The many cultural forms of this movement stand in marked contrast to past scholarship on social movements which has tended to portray movement culture as a relatively uniform, homogenous resource that binds members together (Platt and Williams 2002; Williams 2006).

TABLE 5.1. Cultural Differentiation in Contemplative Culture

CONTEMPLATIVE CULTURE	INSTITUTIONAL SECTOR	LANGUAGE USED	EXAMPLES OF INSTITUTION-SPECIFIC PRACTICES	STATED PURPOSES
Mindfulness	Healthcare	mind–body, consciousness, mind–heart, dharma	Mindfulness-based stress reduction (MBSR); mindfulness-based cognitive therapy	Advancing medicine; cultivating compassion and empathy; resilience; individual mental and physical health and well-being; attention training; stress management; inclusion
Mindfulness and Contemplative Practice	Science, higher education	rigor, empirical questions, measurable, evidence, subject to criticism, subject to discussion, no dogma, meditation labs	Meditation as the object of scientific investigation; meditation; mindfulness; silent reflection; contemplative listening	Advancing science; individual mental and physical health and well-being; attention training (reduces "default mode network"); stress management
Mindfulness, Brain Training, Social-Emotional Learning	K-12 education	kindness, caring, from the heart, listening, focus, impulse control, brain break, neuroscience, amygdala, stress response, liberation, empowering to respond consciously to systemic problems	Reading mindfulness books; listening practices (e.g., wand exercise); attention practices focusing on toys as objects of attention; "golden moments of silence"	Academic performance; social-emotional competencies; individual health and well-being; stress management; caring; self-control

Mind Training	The military, veterans, law enforcement	breathing techniques, riding the breath, nervous system regulation, adrenal stress training, the zone, operational, situational awareness	Mindfulness talks; mindful combat training	Peak performance; resilience; posttraumatic stress disorder; mental and physical health
Mindfulness and Mind Training	Business and technology	being present, stillness practices, humanistic values, being centered	Mindfulness meditation; mindfulness talks; mindful conversations; mindful emailing; mindful meetings; mindful leadership	Cultivating personal excellence; focus; clarity; performance; productivity; creativity and innovation; leadership skills; emotional intelligence; useful mental habits; mental and physical health and well-being

In what follows, I provide examples of how mindfulness program founders and facilitators adapted Buddhist meditation to fit in education and business in a manner similar to how it was adapted in healthcare and science.

Mindfulness in Education

In contrast to how the foundation of the contemplative movement began through the efforts of central organizations such as Kabat-Zinn's CfM, MLI, and CCMS, contemplative programs in schools for children and adolescents first arose in a grassroots manner across the United States. Most of the early K-12 mindfulness programs were established between 2000 and 2004. Their founders were largely unaware of others doing similar work. After individually beginning their programs, word of other mindfulness programs began trickling in. Mindfulness educators learned about the MBSR program and others from the internet, meetings, and conferences facilitated by MLI, CCMS, the Association for Mindfulness in Education, and the Garrison Institute, a philanthropic nonprofit that took on the project of developing a field of contemplative education in 2004. Thereafter, mindfulness education programs grew rapidly. Many contemplative educators incorporated elements of Kabat-Zinn's program, borrowed from each other's work, and incorporated ideas from other sources such as the internet. Grants also became available through the major contemplative organizations and their networks of private donors to support pilot programs and research on mindfulness in education. Today mindfulness education programs have reached millions of children and teens in over a hundred countries on five continents.[7]

Buddhist meditation was adapted a great deal to get it into K-12 schools. Mindfulness for young people was made to fit within the bounds of the public education system. Because the Establishment Clause of the First Amendment to the Constitution prohibits government institutions, such as public schools, from supporting a particular religion, it was critical that K-12 mindfulness education program founders secularize mindfulness practices. Rather than teaching Buddhism or meditation, programs explicitly taught "mindfulness," "social-emotional learning," and "brain training," which promised to help young people improve their academic and social aptitudes. An anonymous educator, whom I will call Julia Martin, discussed how she took care to frame contemplative lessons in secular language so they would not provoke any opposition. "*Meditation* . . . really triggers people," she said. "So I don't usually say *meditation*. I usually say *mindfulness practice*. And then the other is *lovingkindness*, because that sounds really religious. And what I say is *caring practice*." That being said, a number of educators I spoke with said that the children they taught knew exactly what they were learning; the kids were quick to call contemplative practices "meditation."

Like CfM and MLI, mindfulness educators couched their programs in science rather than Buddhism to get it past educational gatekeepers such as parents, administrators, and teachers. A member of Goldie Hawn's MindUP program explained to me how their program was deliberately pitched as a neuroscientific brain training and social-emotional learning program to avoid opposition. In bringing mindfulness into a public school system, their team brainstormed about:

> How do you get people to buy into it? How do you get teachers who maybe started off typical like me and administrators who are worried about complaints of church/state parents, worried about parents complaining, and so on ? . . . in any of this kind of work in schools, you constantly have to be aware of that and think about, ok, what is the languaging you use and how do you present that? So that led—Goldie right from the start has always been fascinated by the neuroscience, and so she then said, "Why don't we just bring in a part that's all about your brain and teach kids how their brain works and what happens when they do this quieting of their mind and teach them about their amygdala and the stress response, and about your prefrontal cortex and hippocampus?" And that really was her brilliance, I have to say. That is how the program then is presented.

As they developed their programs, contemplative educators continually refined how they described their programs, as well as justifications for adopting them, to various specific audiences, such as educators, academics, other mindfulness leaders, and the social-emotional learning community. Megan Cowan, the director of Mindful Schools in Oakland, California, explained:

> You start to find out what resonates with educators, and you start to find out—I don't mean sound bites in the sense of, like, news media sensationalism, but I mean in the sense of, how can I explain this very simply in a short period of time that will be meaningful to them? And that just came from talking about it over and over and over again, and then also learning how to present in a way that was appealing and academic in a sense.

In creating a mindfulness program for kids, Cowan and her team developed justifications and motivations for bringing mindfulness into the classroom that aligned with the goals of education. She emphasized that the program taught a skillset that students need in order to succeed in their academic work:

> ... if the idea of what we're teaching is to improve focus and improve impulse control, then the experiences that are relevant to them are things like: you get an assignment and you are reading the paper and you get to the bottom and you realize you didn't really pay attention to what you are reading. Or you're sitting in class and you get kind of distracted by what's happening outside and you're watching or you're thinking, and the teacher says, "Do you know the answer?"—and you know how that makes you feel. You get kind of nervous or scared or frustrated with yourself that you weren't paying attention. So asking them about those experiences, and asking them how they feel when those things happen, and telling them that mindfulness helps have more choice around where our attention is.
>
> And then the impulse control things are questions like: Have you ever been so mad at somebody that you said something, but immediately wished you didn't say it? Like, you feel bad, or they got hurt, or you got in trouble, so you wish that you hadn't done it? And everybody has had that experience. It's universal, so they [say]—"Yeah, I've noticed that," and then you get to explain to them that mindfulness helps us notice our emotions so that we can make choices around our actions.

Cowan's framing of mindfulness as an effective tool to help students develop attention skills and control their emotions resonated with students because it could help them improve their grades and relationships. It also appealed to teachers because students' increased attentiveness made classroom management easier. These examples showed how the language and purpose of contemplative practice were adapted in education to cohere with the instrumental aims of the American education system.

Mindfulness educators additionally inserted mindfulness into public and private schools in ways that did not take up too much time or compete with the school's core curriculum. Instead of using the relatively long sitting meditations that many Buddhist centers have, educators created much shorter lessons. Some programs offered fifteen-minute class visits, while others introduced afterschool programs. Practices themselves were shortened as well, with some activities, such as mindful breathing or sitting practices, lasting only thirty seconds, or five minutes.[8]

Leaders of contemplative K-12 education programs created kid-friendly versions of meditation based on Western conceptions of childhood to appeal to young people. Buddhist traditions do not typically teach lay schoolchildren to meditate. Most leaders of mindful K-12 education programs revised their own contemplative practice to make it fun and age-appropriate. They incorporated toys such as stuffed animals or candy as objects of attention for meditation exercises so that they would be playful and interesting for kids. Mindfulness educators also changed solitary traditional forms of meditation into interactive contemplative exercises by using a trial-and-error process with the kids.

Julia Martin's program used fun, interactive, age-appropriate lessons to teach students mindfulness and elements of Buddhist philosophy. For example, with small children, she used an activity with "kindness wands" to teach them how to practice kindness and forgiveness. In pairs, students communicated using a wand with a star and a wand with a heart. "If you're holding the heart wand, you're speaking from the heart about what happened to you," she told me. "And the person who has the star wand is a star listener. And so they listen and then tell back to the person who just said to them what they heard them say. And then they switch wands."

Like many other contemplative educators, Martin's mindfulness education program drew from Kabat-Zinn's MBSR program, Buddhist modernism, and her life experiences. MBSR components of her program included Buddhist-inspired states and tools "that cultivate mindfulness," such as "beginner's mind, non-judgment, non-striving," and "bringing awareness to three things basically: to sensations in the body, thoughts, and emotions," she said. A prominent Buddhist *vipassana* teacher connected to the center she worked at also helped her develop curriculum on Buddhist lovingkindness practices and theories of interdependence:

> That's a traditional practice in Buddhism that when you offer love and kindness, first you offer it to self, then to others. So it's kind of a building out, building community, and along with that, although it's not stressed particularly in MBSR, an aspect of it is the interconnectedness that we have with people in our environment. And that's a part of the curriculum with the preschoolers, . . . with the fifth graders and the teachers, but in different ways because of the different cognitive levels.

Although some critics suggest that mindfulness variants, like Martin's mindfulness education program, are increasingly separated from Buddhism, her case shows it is not so simple. Martin deliberately brought elements of Buddhist modernism into her curriculum at all levels. Not only did she work with a Buddhist teacher to develop her program, she also picked up parts of the program through other sources, like popular media. For example, she incorporated a contemplative practice she found on the *Huffington Post*, into her fifth-grade curriculum. For this "just like me" exercise, which I have seen used in Buddhist modernist temples and in other mindfulness education programs, she has students sit in pairs with others they do not normally interact with, close their eyes, and imagine their partner's face. Martin reads statements such as, "So notice that this person has a body and a mind just like me." And they see that. "Notice that this person has hopes and wishes and dreams just like me. Notice that this person has suffering in their life, in their families, in their school, in their community." Martin also adapted the above "just like me" practice for different groups of teachers. For one particular group, she knew from prior interactions how hard the teachers were on themselves. Consequently, instead of doing the typical practice, she had the teachers focus on receiving rather than sending love.

Mindfulness education program teachers walked a fine line to bring contemplative practices into secular schools. They adapted their programs around the structures and requirements of K-12 schools by continually revising their programs to better appeal to their various stakeholders. Yet as Martin's program shows, despite mindfulness educators' public assertions to the contrary, many of them wove Buddhist elements into their curricula—carefully.

Mindful Business

Mindfulness in business became popular after a few well-known, respected companies, such as General Mills and Google, gained publicity for their mindfulness training programs (which were established in 2006 and 2008, respectively). Awareness of mindful business practices then expanded based on the Wisdom 2.0 conferences, which were founded in 2010 by Soren Gordhamer to convene technology elites in Silicon Valley.

Especially during the first years of my study in 2011 and 2012, when mindful business was a relatively new phenomenon, I encountered business executives who expressed reservations about sharing an interest in meditation with their colleagues. For example, one high-profile venture capitalist worried that potential clients would see it as a "religious or New Age thing not founded on reality," which would undermine confidence in his ability to do his job well. He said there was a "suspicion of things that are not rational" in his industry, and likened the idea of bringing meditation into the Silicon Valley tech sector to the case of Joseph Firmage. Firmage was an entrepreneur who in 1999 announced he had had a mystical experience in a dream and was convinced aliens had visited him. "Here was a guy who founded a multimillion-dollar company at the age of 21. People were worried to put their eggs in that bucket and were wondering if he'd gone insane or been doing drugs or something like that."

Various contemplative leaders thought that business was a particularly difficult realm for meditators to break into. As a result, leaders of programs in business experimented with different ways of getting meditation in. A wide range of mindfulness programs were created in business. Some of the business-minded intervention leaders I met with were willing to make considerable alterations to get contemplative culture in the door in business. A few business coaches made no explicit references to Buddhism, mindfulness, or meditation. Instead, they described contemplative practice as "stillness practices," "centering practices," or ways to be present through pausing and perceiving. One Buddhist teacher even said that in working with businesspeople, he takes out all references to the dharma and meditation and teaches only communication skills. Other mindful business programs tried harder to maintain the integrity of Buddhist modernist practices, bringing in some meditation instructions directly from Buddhist dharma centers.

With such variation, critics have argued that some advocates of mindfulness in business have gone too far in making it appeal to executives as a tool to increase profits and better control employees. Of all the contemplative leaders I spoke with across different professional areas, the language of mindful business leaders deviated the farthest from core Buddhist values—such as nonattachment to self, achievement, and material objects.

eBay: Getting Mindfulness in the Door to Foster Excellence

As a senior director of learning and organizational development at eBay, Rich Fernandez began bringing mindfulness speakers there in the spring of 2010. Using language appropriate for a secular business context was important in bringing meditation to his company:

> When George Mumford came—who is the mindfulness and Zen teacher of Phil Jackson and Michael Jordan, and all these famous athletes—we framed the event as cultivating personal excellence. Right? So, now that's something that's really resonant to the business. Like who doesn't want to be personally excellent?
>
> And, then, we also framed it as a question. What do championship NBA teams, premier league soccer players, and blah, blah, blah, utilize . . . to achieve high and sustained performance? It's not what you think. Come find out at this compelling talk by sports psychologist . . . So everything was like performance, productivity, excellence metaphors, which is slightly ironic because, as you know, the mindfulness practices are about being rather than achieving.

And that any attainment—it comes from being present and centered. But such was what we needed to do to help foster the adoption.[9]

Fernandez was careful not to challenge the status quo of his organization. In his mind, mere exposure to the potential benefits of contemplative practice was better than no exposure at all. In deliberately altering Buddhist motivations from cultivating a state of being in the present to justifying meditation as a tool for attaining greater personal excellence and achievement, he changed the purpose of mindfulness meditation. Changes like this aligned meditation with a self-interested, capitalist business culture rather than emphasizing Buddhist nonattachment to self, success, status, and material objects. Using an achievement-oriented culture in mindfulness programs served to propel, rather than question, capitalist firms' goals of increased worker productivity and profit.

Google: Emotional Intelligence for Tech Nerds

In contrast to eBay's initial mindfulness programming, Chade-Meng Tan's Search Inside Yourself program drew heavily from Buddhist practices and created some new mindfulness exercises for businesspeople, such as "mindful emailing." Tan's mindfulness program for Google employees has been described upfront as cultivating skills that are important to being successful at the company, such as emotional intelligence, fostering attention, and cultivating self-knowledge and mastery (Tan 2012: 7). Although these skills seem practical and secular at the outset, much of Tan's 2012 book on the program refers to various Buddhist teachers and contemplative leaders who have influenced him. His recommended exercises could easily fit into most American Buddhist dharma centers. He includes instructions on the traditional Buddhist seven-point meditation sitting posture (40) and provides instructions for several kinds of mindfulness meditations (45, 55–56, 73) as well as meditations on destructive emotions (118–120) and lovingkindness (169–170) that I have seen used in traditional Buddhist centers. In addition, Tan branches out and includes other forms of mindfulness practice not taught in traditional Buddhist centers, such as mindful listening exercises (58–59) and mindful conversation (62–64).

After bringing the Search Inside Yourself program into Google in 2007, Tan wrote in his 2012 book that two of the primary reasons his program was so successful was because he could translate contemplative traditions "into a language even compulsively pragmatic people like me can process" (4–5) and because they incorporated scientific findings and justifications for mindfulness.

Mirabai Bush also attested to the importance of adapting the language of mindfulness to appeal to Googlers and of couching the practices in science. For example, she told me that at the outset of the program, Stanford neuroscientist Phillippe Goldin taught a Buddhist *tonglen* altruism practice in which meditators visualize taking in others' suffering on the in-breath and releasing compassion and aid to others on their out-breath. This commonly used Buddhist modernist practice, Bush thought, was "very intense with people you work with and maybe don't know, and I thought that was pretty risky." Instead, they changed the practice to the "just like me" practice Julia Martin used in her mindfulness program for kids. Search Inside Yourself participants would "look at the other person" in the eye and think, "This person is a human being just like me, and this person has suffered just like me, and this person has done things she regrets in her life just like me, she's suffered physical pain," Bush told me. The practice is "very powerful," she said, "but it's not quite as weirdly spiritual. And it's not quite as intense, but the basic practices of mindfulness, of doing free writing in a journal, of walking meditation, sitting, walking, lovingkindness—they're all the same."

Although Buddhist mindfulness practices were adapted, shaped, and transformed in a number of ways in the Search Inside Yourself program, Bush told me several times throughout different interviews that the course uses "the same practices" she and CCMS have taught in other spiritual and secular settings. Search Inside Yourself's founders and teachers have worked merely to "focus" the content they teach to resonate with and aid Google employees, she explained. To do so, they incorporated more content "on emotional intelligence so there's more emphasis on compassion, lovingkindness, interactive practices, like mindful listening, communicating."

Over the years, Search Inside Yourself leaders have continued to get feedback from Googlers, Buddhist leaders (such as Zen teacher Norman Fischer), and scientists (such as Stanford neuroscientist Phillippe Goldin) to improve and update the program. Due to the amount of days many Googlers travel and work offsite, program leaders have played around with adding and subtracting the number of days in the course over the years to respond to the needs of attendees. Now they offer a short introduction to the neuroscience on meditation, meditation practice, and what the full course entails. Offering a standalone introduction "helped us—it helped people make better decisions about whether they could be there for the whole time or not," Bush said. Program leaders have also continually added and updated the scientific component of the program. "Anything measureable—anything that is data-driven—they love," Bush said. "As a result, I think it's had . . . a big influence, impact on the culture at Google," Bush told me in 2016.

Making Sense of and Justifying Alterations to Buddhism

In developing the science on meditation and bringing the practices into their workplaces, contemplatives struggled to maintain allegiance both to the institutions they worked in and to what they viewed as authentic, essential contemplative practices. Ultimately, contemplatives navigated this conceptual quagmire in different ways based on the sector they worked in and their own life experiences and spiritual backgrounds.[10] Contemplative leaders across sectors justified changes they made to Buddhism as done by necessity to get it in, and by emphasizing the transformative potential of their mindfulness subcultures.

Justifying Alterations by Necessity

Like many contemplatives, Kabat-Zinn justified transforming Buddhist meditation into a secularized mindfulness program by necessity. At an MLI conference in Denver in 2012 he said that, "If I took *abhidharma* terminology [from Buddhist literature] people would be running."[11] Instead, contemplative leaders like him deliberately used vague multivalent language to get mindfulness meditation through the door into esteemed secular institutions, such as medicine, while fully aware that the practices carried deeper spiritual significance. With the increasing public legitimacy of mindfulness, leaders like Kabat-Zinn have become more comfortable acknowledging how carefully they crafted their program descriptions to partially reveal and partially conceal their programs' Buddhist roots:

> Because naming is very important in how things are understood and either accepted or not, . . . the entire undertaking needed to be held by an umbrella term broad enough to contain the multiplicity of key elements that seem essential to field a successful clinical programme in the cultural climate of 1979 . . . Naming what we were doing in the clinic *mindfulness-based stress reduction* raises a number of questions. One is the wisdom of using the umbrella term to describe our work and to link it explicitly with what I have always considered to be a universal dharma that is coextensive, if not identical, with the teachings of the Buddha, the Buddha dharma. *By "umbrella term" I mean that it is used in certain contexts as a place-holder for the entire dharma, that it is meant to carry multiple meanings and traditions simultaneously not in the service of finessing and confounding real differences, but as a potentially skillful means for bringing the streams of alive, embodied dharma understanding and of clinical medicine together.* It was always felt the details concerning the use of the word *mindfulness* in the various contexts in which we were deploying it could be worked out later by scholars and researchers who were knowledgeable in this area and

interested in making distinctions and resolving important issues that have been confounded and compounded by the early but intentionally ignoring or glossing over of potentially important historical, philosophical, and cultural nuances. (Kabat-Zinn 2011: 288–290, emphasis in italics added)

Kabat-Zinn drew from two institutional cultures at the same time— Western clinical medicine and Buddhist modernism—through the use of verbal gymnastics, vague word choice, and multivalent language that held different meanings for different audiences. Mindfulness's ambiguous language and ideology can be exploited by its advocates in ways not available to adherents of traditional religions or legally trademarked practices such as TM. While secular potential audiences will approach mindfulness in an unassuming, open way because it seems to be a secular, scientifically approved, healthy practice, Buddhist and Hindu audiences will hear descriptions of mindfulness and connect it to Asian religious philosophy and practices. Buddhists in particular can point to Kabat-Zinn's training in Zen Buddhism and the fact that he grounded his program in mindfulness because it is sufficiently vague and could serve as "a place-holder for the entire dharma." Like Kabat-Zinn, Western Buddhist sympathizers and converts may believe that he authentically translated concepts from Buddhism into a language palatable to the clinical medical community by necessity. Naming his program "Mindfulness-Based Stress Reduction" was a skillful, wise decision, they will argue. Had he not done so, they believe, meditation would not have been allowed into medicine and academia in the late 1970s and 1980s. Because of the flexibility of mindfulness discourse, it could be used to bridge quite different secular, spiritual, and Buddhist audiences.

However, advancing such adaptive versions of contemplative culture came at a price, which at times was coherency. It is not easy to speak from multiple traditions to varied audiences at the same time. At times, Kabat-Zinn ensured confusion about mindfulness by filling his talks with seemingly contradictory statements. For example, he defined *dharma* as "both the teachings of the Buddha and also the way things are, the fundamental lawfulness of the universe. So although the Buddha articulated the Dharma, the Dharma itself can't be Buddhist any more than the law of gravity is English because of Newton or Italian because of Galileo" (Boyce 2011: 57; c.f. Wilson 2014: 86). Thus, Kabat-Zinn appealed to both a Buddhist and a secular audience—if they were not trying too hard to rationally understand what he was saying. Here he collapsed the Buddha's teaching and immanent laws of the universe (which are typically identified through reason and the scientific method). Yet, the Buddha's teachings included religious cosmological ideas, such as reincarnation and the possibility of attaining enlightenment, which could not be tested through science.

Critics versed in Buddhist traditions wonder if, with their creative constructions of a secularized Buddhism, contemplatives lost important elements of Buddhist traditions and ideology. After all, how could contemplative leaders be sure that they kept the true essences of Buddhism and did not, through direct or subtle influences from the institutions they worked in, inadvertently remove important elements of Buddhism? As Kabat-Zinn has acknowledged, he is not a Buddhist scholar or historian.

Justifying Changes by Incorporating Select Buddhist Elements

Contemplatives justified making alterations to Buddhism by claiming that, despite the changes, contemplative culture retained the transformative essential elements of Buddhist practice and philosophy. Contemplatives from all sectors referred to the importance of retaining the transformative nature of contemplative meditation in their programs.

For example, Rohan Gunatillake, mindfulness entrepreneur and creator of the smartphone app Buddhify, said he cared most about mindfulness's ability to transform its practitioners. He said it was important "that we don't ignore more transformative elements of contemplative practice, 'cause that's the whole point, really." He continued:

> And, so talking about Buddhism particularly, Buddhism is only really defined by the transformative elements of it . . . What's different is the understanding and the insights around identity and suffering, and the scale in which those are experienced. And . . . there's a risk that contemplative practice is a shallow pool, like a paddling pool, rather than it being a proper swimming pool with a deep end and a shallow part. Not a kiddy pool, not a wave machine . . . we need to maintain that full swimming pool ability, I think.

Like Kabat-Zinn and his colleagues, Gunatillake made a distinction between the organizational structures contemplatives bring their programs into, and the separate, transformative potential of the alternative culture they bring in. He did not think using for-profit business models to promote Buddhist meditation was problematic. "Commercialization is fine," he told me. "Commercialization itself—in the broader sense—is not a bad thing . . . I don't care, whether you do it commercially or non-commercially—that's just business model choice." He viewed his business model as a mere structural container for the important practices he spread. He believed that by exposing people to the practices, some would naturally seek to learn more about Buddhism, and this would improve the lives of a lot of people.

Contemplative educator Aidan Keller[12] explained, for his mindfulness program for kids, that:

> I think there's what I want them to get out of it, and then there's also this whole thing, what do the schools want them to get out of it, which have a lot of crossover, but are not exactly the same. So the crossover of what the schools want out of it and what I want out of it is they are building attention skills, they are emotion regulation, they are building empathy—caring skills, understanding of difficult emotions, which is kind of emotional regulation.
>
> And then there's this much deeper aspect, which I think the schools don't think about as much, or it isn't the reason they're excited about it. But I think some teachers are. But it's this really—the deepest level is around liberation . . .
>
> Sometimes I think teachers just want the kids to be calm and be regulated more so they can pass tests, and that's not my intention. My intention is to give them this deep sense of inner awareness and stillness, but from that to be able to empower them to be able to maybe react in a conscious way to things that are happening in this system that aren't actually good.

Keller suggested that even though contemplative programs are cloaked in secular language, some teachers, like him, have continued to be motivated by underlying spiritual and activist-minded concerns. Although schools and contemplative educators both wanted students to benefit from the "side effects" of meditation, some contemplative teachers' deeper underlying motives were closer to that of American religious liberalism, spirituality, and Buddhist modernism; they sought to teach the students how to attain personal liberation. Contemplatives wanted students to gain liberation through self-awareness, inner peace, and self-empowerment. Many contemplatives hoped that students would act upon their newfound perspectives and challenge parts of the system that need reform. (Interestingly, this reflected the longstanding American cultural commitment to individual development, democracy, and social reform, rather than a reference to traditional Buddhist enlightenment.)

How could mindful dharma, which cuts out inconvenient religious parts of Buddhist cosmology, be the same as Buddha dharma? After all, this is the claim that Kabat-Zinn and other mindfulness leaders have made. Mindfulness practitioners remained unfazed by others' critiques that their adaptations lost core elements of Buddhism by hearkening to a modernist interpretation of Buddhist ideology, which justified adapting to contemporary contexts to appeal to new audiences based on Buddhist precedent and elements of Buddhist philosophy. Kabat-Zinn has explained contemplative Buddhist modernist ideology on various occasions. At MLI's first International Symposium for Contemplative Studies in Denver in April 2012, for example, he distinguished between Buddhist practice and the concept of mindfulness: "Buddha wasn't a Buddhist. His insights were about being human and capacities we can cultivate. A lot of people think Jon Kabat-Zinn invented it [mindfulness] in 1979. My nightmare is that people think it's a concept. We need to maintain the practice that underlies transformative aspects of dharma."

What did Kabat-Zinn mean here? How is it possible to separate Buddhist practice from the concept of mindfulness? To understand what he meant, it is necessary to delve deeper into Buddhist modernist ideology. As he explained at the Denver conference, Kabat-Zinn viewed his work on mindfulness like a Zen Buddhist koan. Many koans metaphorically allude to the appearances of duality and underlying intrinsic wholeness (Hori 2000). To Kabat-Zinn, in a similar way, there are appearances and an underlying, nonconceptual reality that one can discover through meditation. In the world of appearances, people reify and become unconsciously attached to concepts and objects. Contemplative practitioners believe such a way of living is based on inhabiting an illusory world. Attachment to names and concepts thereby reveals a practitioner's lack of contemplative understanding and ability to see through it. As a result, Kabat-Zinn carefully avoided using and reinforcing explicit forms of Buddhist *ideology*. What mattered most to him was an emphasis on contemplative *practice*. Contemplative practice is meant to foster tools to see through this world and reveal an underlying reality of interdependence and wholeness. Thus, it was acceptable for Kabat-Zinn and others to alter the language, practices, and philosophy of Buddhist meditation in order to spread the dharma among new audiences.

While to outsiders this distinction between Buddhist practice, which applies the Buddha's teachings, and Buddhist ideology, which contemplatives would view as the reification of Buddhist teachings, may seem flimsy and opportunistic, to contemplatives this was a crucial distinction and litmus test of one's true understanding of contemplative practice, and thus of one's authenticity. Because they believed in an ideology of nonduality, early contemplatives could legitimize and justify their alterations to Buddhism to make it appeal to new audiences.

Challenges of Lingering Ideologies

Of course, savvy readers will see that contemplative culture, and the professional cultural "containers" they moved meditation into, contained their own ideologies. Each ideological tradition had its own blind spots. Moreover, the different religious and secular ideologies could be at odds with each other.

Contemplatives drew on Buddhist ideas of nonduality and nonattachment, as well as upon cultural strains of American spirituality, even if leaders and their followers argued against relying upon ideology. Although this nondualistic ideology was quite convenient for contemplatives seeking to make mindfulness appeal to other groups of people, it also came with unrecognized drawbacks. Contemplatives often suggested that changing Buddhism was okay if it was done by experienced meditators with a sufficient contemplative awareness. However, when you asked contemplatives what the most important elements of contemplative practice were, many did not know. They said their work was grounded in the practice, but, as this chapter discusses, contemplative "practice," like Buddhist practice, includes a wide array of behaviors and their associated motivations and beliefs (shown in Table 5.1). Surely not all of these diverse manifestations of contemplative culture produce the same outcomes?

Given how much is unknown about the specific outcomes of different contemplative practices, some leaders' failure to fully consider what they could be losing in their simplifications and adaptations of Buddhism could be interpreted as arrogance (which is antithetical to Buddhism) at worst. They often assumed that they were changing Buddhist culture in appropriate ways, without fully recognizing how the Western secular culture they lived in changed them in ways that might detract from Buddhist practices. At best, contemplatives exhibited a considerable amount of faith in Buddhist ideology and the authenticity of their contemplative experiences on the cushion (which is antithetical to their arguments that mindfulness is grounded in reason and science). In theory, it seems, it is not as easy to seamlessly adapt Buddhism to contemporary life as contemplative leaders claim.

Despite some contemplatives' claims to the contrary, in practice, challenges arose when contemplatives' commitments to their work and to their meditation practice pointed them in diverging directions. Ethical quandaries over the appropriate limits of adapting Buddhism to align with particular professional workplaces, or of how much Buddhism to bring in, continually surfaced. Mindfulness leaders and their clients varied in their awareness of when these discrepancies occurred. I suspect many mindfulness facilitators do not notice value conflicts between Buddhism and their work when they arise; when such conflicts arise unbeknownst to mindfulness practitioners, they are likely to defer to what is professionally comfortable.

Even when contemplative leaders were well versed in Buddhism and sought to remain loyal to both Buddhist and their professional obligations, managing the two at times led them to fall short in one or both respects. For example, Lisa Miller, an administrator for a contemplative center at a prestigious university, revealed the complex nature of sacred and secular commitments in the center's programs.[13] First, she said that her work adapting Buddhism for secular students was acceptable from a Buddhist perspective. "To make Buddhism work in this context we have to adapt it to here. That's part of practicing skillful means. This has always been a part of Buddhism," she said. "It has always been adopted as it was brought to new places like China. And to use skillful means in transmitting is a basic element in the Buddhist teachings." She added, "We have to meet people where they are."

But Miller then quickly clarified, "This is my personal background history and I'm not speaking for [the center]. I do this for work in my foundation, but at our center, our work is explicitly a SECULAR program. Its aim is not to promote Buddhism, but it is rooted in Tibetan Buddhism, psychology, and science" (capital letters indicate the speaker's emphasis).

Miller then described how her center's founder had a commitment to compassion. As an organization, they wanted to teach about compassion through Buddhist philosophy and psychology. Their educators used secular language to teach about scholarship on empathy and compassion. In their classes, she said, "We teach self-compassion. This is non-Buddhist. Of the people taking the classes, most are in service professions. There are a small percentage of Buddhist practitioners. Some people feel isolated. Some have heard about meditation and want to learn more about it but are nervous to go to a dharma center." She then told me that Thupten Jinpa, the Dalai Lama's translator, created the program. She quickly clarified that, "Jinpa is not a Buddhist teacher and he'll say that." Yet, Jinpa's curriculum was "drawing from [Buddhist] teachings he knows, such as *bodhicitta*, lojang, and the thirty-seven practices of a bodhisattva," she said. "He is boiling it down and drawing on where it dovetails with psychology."

Miller's explanation of her center's work reveals the Buddhist and secular professional forces that are simultaneously at play in contemplative organizations. On the one hand, personally, many contemplative leaders want to share the Buddhist dharma with nonreligious audiences. They want it to survive by modernizing it. On the other hand, to avoid religious/spiritual stigmas, to maintain legitimacy and credibility with non-Buddhist audiences, and to avoid potential legal issues, mindfulness educators clearly state that their programs are completely secular. Yet, the particular program discussed above incorporates Buddhist ideas, practices, and texts that overlap with psychology. With regard to their program's content, contemplatives like the center's administrator are careful to describe these Buddhist elements in secular ways and as objects of scientific investigation, to avoid accusations they are directly promoting religious ideology. This, of course, raises questions of whether teaching religious ideas, values, and practices in a secularized, scientifically grounded way is promoting religion or not.

To further protect themselves from potential opposition, several education programs, including the program at hand, refused to accredit overzealous Buddhist practitioners as teachers of their programs if these practitioners would not teach meditation in a completely secularized way. Despite these precautions, it is clear that many mindfulness education programs ultimately teach Buddhist values and align with Buddhist goals of promoting compassion and seeking to reduce suffering.

The center's mindfulness program described above and other mindfulness education programs contain a mixture of secular and religious Buddhist influences. They contain Buddhist teachings and have been shaped by people personally committed to Buddhism. Yet mindfulness education is taught through secular language and under the cover of organizations with ostensibly secular missions. Speaking with contemplative leaders revealed that Buddhist influences, secular language, and personal and organizational missions can be integrated in complex ways that do not always appear to be consistent or to make sense. But ultimately, whether such programs are religious, spiritual, or secular depend on the eye of the beholder, the definition of religion used, and the unit of analysis (whether they focus on individuals, groups, organizations, movements, etc.). Social scientists, religious scholars, and average Americans by no means agree on the definitions of *secular, spiritual*, and *religion*. This conceptual murkiness and the porous boundaries of the edges of the contemplative movement leave room for meditators to play with contemplative culture, adapt it, "language it," and identify it as secular in complex and sometimes convoluted ways.

Although ethical quandaries arose in all sectors, they seemed most challenging in bringing Buddhism to business. Mirabai Bush, who has worked for nearly two decades bringing meditation into businesses, has thought at length about the challenges and opportunities of teaching contemplative practice within corporate climates in a capitalistic economic system. In a conversation with me in 2016, she acknowledged that the movement of Buddhist-inspired culture into business breaks with how meditation was taught in the past, which inevitably impacts the Buddhist teachings:

> BUSH: Once you set it in a corporate climate, the whole climate is based on the capitalistic profit motive . . . But once you get into the corporate

environment, there are all these people who want to be consultants and coaches and they feel like they have something to offer and so then they offer it and want to be paid for it. And for people to do this work, they have to be compensated for sure.I didn't understand that well enough early enough (chuckling), or I wouldn't still be working so much. But when I first learned meditation, nobody paid for meditation. You might make a contribution to the monastery when you left, but you did it very quietly, like you slipped the money under something. It was connecting.These are the priceless teachings that have been passed on for 2,500 years and the idea of charging—like when Meng, the engineer at Google, said, "And when we get this all put together, because we're Google, we're gonna make it open source." I said, "Meng, these practices have been open source for 2,500 years" (laughing). The open source branded by Google (laughing again). God. So even there—and he's had a lot of practice and it's a great program—but it's just part of the culture. So that's part of it—that doing it because you want to make some money from it and thinking of it as a commodity, something that can be sold—that all affects it.

KUCINSKAS: How does it affect it?

BUSH: It affects it because it keeps you from appreciating and understanding that this is not a commodity; this is a way that for thousands of years people have been learning to look at their own hearts and minds and consciousness. These are human practices and they really can't be sold. We all have that capacity within us. Now it's true that I needed a teacher to let me know. One time someone asked [Shambhala founder] Chögyam Trungpa, "If it's all within you, what do you need a guru for?" He said, "You need a guru to tell you that it's all within you" (laughing). And there's a lot of truth in that. But it's delicate, that whole part of it.

And then the other comes out of the nature of mindfulness meditation, which is that it's simple, but it's not easy. It's really simple, and lots of people think, "Oh, I could do that. I could tell people to close their eyes and watch their breath. That's easy." What isn't easy is right then understanding what happens when all this stuff begins to arise. Once you do develop this focus—What to do with that? How to use that in order to wake up?

As Bush attests, at times the differences between the two ideologies of contemplative religious practice and capitalism are jarring, even comical. Bush realized that something is lost when contemplative coaches and educators operate in a capitalistic context and have to charge for their dharma teachings. Rather than view the teachings as priceless lessons "which can't be sold" and are taught on a donation basis, in which the donation can be "connecting" and signify gratitude, honor the teacher, and thus signify sacred Buddhist values, in a capitalist context, meditation teachings are easily, and sometimes unintentionally, commodified. By translating meditation instruction to fit in capitalist models of exchange, suddenly programs become not only a product to be sold, but subject to the institutional logics and frames of the market. They become "branded," "marketed," and "sold." Capitalism becomes a formative piece of what mindfulness programs are.

As commodities, the sellers can stand to benefit. Cases of coaches charging exorbitant prices to companies, such as hundreds of dollars for an hour of meditation instruction, abound. However, not all central members of the contemplative movement have financially profited from their work. As Bush said, at the age of seventy-seven, she still works full-time out of necessity. Other prominent Ph.D. trained scholars chose to leave academia or have yet to secure stable, tenure-track academic positions; they reflected that this was partly a cost of their commitment to their contemplative work.

It is also clear that many of the early contemplative leaders and educators, like Bush, remain deeply committed to the longstanding Buddhist and Hindu roots of contemplative practice, which are intended to teach people to "wake up," become empowered, and more fully realize their potential. Bush stood by how contemplative programs like Search Inside Yourself provide space and tools for employees to think about their personal values. "In a contemplative environment . . . you allow those values to come forward . . . Lots of times people haven't really focused on them. Everybody knows what they care about, what's most important to them, but they haven't made it really clear." To foster more self-awareness about their values, in teaching contemplative practice, Bush said she sometimes facilitates "indirect exercises like . . . talking in pairs or journaling" on topics such as "I feel most alive when," "I feel most at home when," or "I feel best about my work when." Bush thought that fostering more self-awareness and personal value commitments led participants in her trainings to "see that when they work together in a more wise and compassionate way that their own work is more successful—they enjoy it more. And then the group work is more successful. And," she clarified, "you don't cultivate those things just for a level of corporate success, but the truth is as you become more fully who you are and more fully in your work, then inevitably—It's not always winning, sometimes you just realize you're in the wrong work and then you have to change. But at least you're doing it consciously—that's the thing."

Like other contemplative leaders, Bush thought despite the ethical quandaries and ways in which Buddhism had to be delimited and morphed to fit into secular professional institutions, in the end it was worth it. She held that the contemplative practices taught still contained transformational kernels that made other cultural compromises worthwhile. Yet, contemplative leaders did not always fully see how the time they spent in professional organizations shaped them and their programs in ways that led them to sometimes quite radically alter Buddhist practices over time.

At worst, the integration of mindfulness into workplaces could lead to the cooptation of the practices so that they became a tool to control and manipulate workers or to ignore workplace discrimination and other problems. As a middle-aged black woman discussed on a *Humans of New York* episode:

> Wellness is being commodified, and everyone's looking in and doing all of this inward reflection. If you're unhappy, it's because of you. Your unhappiness isn't a reflection of any systemic imbalance that we could address together. It's a "you" problem. I worked the most shit job when I moved back to New York last year. I was told instead of me becoming upset, because someone's spoken to me in a way that's horrifically disrespectful, unprofessional, and above all probably illegal, I was told, "Just take a few deep breaths. Maybe you should get the Mindful app, the meditation app."

She looked upset and incredulous. "Are you serious?" she asked. She continued:

> The things you are saying are not, one, only not relevant to the job. Why are you commenting on my body? Why are you commenting on my weight? Why are you commenting on my hair? Don't tell me to meditate my frustration away because my frustration is valid and it's real and it's coming from a genuine place. I wouldn't be frustrated if it didn't matter.[14]

This woman brought attention to how mindfulness meditation could be manipulated by employers and managers who use contemplative practices as a way to blame employees who tried to push back against exploitative or discriminatory workplace practices, rather than as a way to guide employees toward personal and professional liberation. This could all too easily occur when managers knew little about contemplative practices or did not care to uphold the spirit of the practices taught by spiritual or Buddhist meditation practitioners. Such misuse of the practices is inevitable when contemplative programs across institutions are not regulated, or when contemplative practices become used by managers and corporate leaders outside of controlled contemplative courses. Experiences such as that of the woman discussed above could not be farther from contemplative founders' aims when establishing their programs, but they are now unfortunately becoming commonplace.

The Proliferation of Mindfulness Adaptations Across Fields

In moving Buddhist meditation into secular organizations, contemplative leaders and educators engaged in a cultural dance among many audiences, fields, and loyalties. In their dance, they catered to some interests more than others. The founders of, leaders of, and participants in contemplative programs—mostly American converts to meditation—did not feel compelled to protect most parts of Buddhist culture based on loyalty to their ethnic heritage or an ascribed religion. On the contrary, they wanted to modernize meditation and make it relevant to broader portions of contemporary Western society.

Contemplative leaders and educators largely took up the opportunities that arose and accommodated to their host institutions' preferences in forming their mindfulness programs. They did not try to make substantial changes to the way their host organizations functioned. For the most part, contemplative leaders accepted and affirmed the traditional institutional structures, professional norms, and standards of evaluation in the institutional fields they targeted. They strategically coupled their programs to key institutional logics, norms, structures, and practices in host organizations by integrating elements of local and professional institutional cultures into their programs. This, they suggested, helped them gain cultural resonance and normative legitimacy among new professional audiences. Through these processes, programs in the movement refashioned nearly every element of meditation and eliminated any potentially threatening or stigmatized religious elements. They created a variety of new forms of contemplative culture, which were differentiated across sectors and programs.

Contemplatives justified the alterations they made to Buddhism in several ways. They said that the changes were necessary and that they were using Buddhist "skillful means" to meet new audiences where they are. Committed contemplatives suggested that they were merely changing the "window dressing," or the superficial labels and appearances of their practices, rather than altering their fundamental transformative nature. These justifications made sense to contemplatives, because, as a movement, they were *most committed to contemplative practice as a vehicle to a particular kind of personally transformative experience.* In the face of secular legal, structural, and normative constraints, this commitment allowed the movement's founders and leaders to adapt and translate various components of contemplative culture to bring it to others without provoking opposition—or feeling as if they were losing their practices' essence or authenticity.

The cultural differentiation of Buddhist contemplative practices likely helped their programs to avoid conflict with other secular and religious groups. Due to the program leaders' strategies of culturally camouflaging the religious roots of their programs and the care they took to publicly present secular, target-audience-appropriate curricula, many programs had diverse names, frames, and forms of contemplative practice. The variety of forms of contemplative practice, and the vague, multivalent language used to describe them—which could be coterminous with or inclusive of secular, spiritual, and religious approaches to meditation—made it difficult for potential opposition to track which religious elements they retained. Because of this, it would be extremely difficult to build a case that the groups were proselytizing, as protesters have done with other religious intellectual movements. It would be equally difficult to clearly identify which groups used Buddhist-inspired forms of meditation, which used secularized forms of Buddhist-inspired meditation, and which facilitated other similar kinds of programs supporting humanistic psychology, social-emotional learning, and other recent scientifically based programs for pro-social behavior.

The ability to differentiate and adapt contemplative programming by institutional sector enabled contemplative culture to spread rapidly and broadly. However, ease of expansion came at the cost of quality control. As Buddhists, scholars, and journalists alike wonder, did this lead mindfulness to become "so vague and elastic that it serves almost as if a cipher into which one can read virtually anything we want?" (Bodhi 2011: 22; c.f. Purser, Forbes, and Burke 2016: v). The lack of regulations around mindfulness programming has led to the wide variation in program content and quality. On the one hand, some contemplative programs, such as the Google Search Inside Yourself program and several mindfulness education programs for kids I researched (which were created by collaborative efforts between program founders with longstanding meditation practices and adept Buddhist teachers), included substantial Buddhist elements. On the other hand, other institutional efforts, such as Fernandez's mindfulness talks at eBay, set a lower bar; they merely sought to expose members of their organization to the possibility that meditation practice might aid them in their pursuit of professional success. Rather than support Buddhist aims of cultivating nonattachment to worldly objects and success, the eBay initiative used professional aspirations to encourage employees to meditate. Furthermore, contemplative leaders and their organizations had even less control over what happened to mindfulness rhetoric outside of their intervention programs. After introducing mindfulness as a means of addressing emotional problems and other workplace stressors, it could be referenced by middle- and upper-level managers as a means of shifting grievances about company problems onto employees' backs through suggestions that it was their individual responsibility to find inner peace and make themselves happy.

Furthermore, even with regard to programs in which Buddhism is clearly evident, or in which educators explicitly espoused an oppositional consciousness that challenged normative parts of the workplace status quo, critiques remain about how much change the people in their classes learning to meditate can individually effect in their workplaces without more focused, strategic, collective action. It is still largely unknown if and how much changes in new meditators' attitudes or actions reverberate within their work environments. It remains to be seen over the long term whether such interventions are enough. Critics argue they are not. In Chapter 6, I share, largely in their own words, the impact that contemplative educators perceive they are having through their intervention programs.

| Interventions' Transformation from
the Inside Out

INSTRUMENTAL ELECTRONIC INDIAN MUSIC blared from an Apple computer as we entered the UCLA classroom. Leaders of a student group who the prior year had taken a class with Marvin Belzer, the associate director of the campus's Mindful Awareness Research Center (MARC), had asked him to teach a mindfulness lesson at their first meeting. Belzer was a quiet man whose eyes lit up as he discussed things he was passionate about, such as teaching mindfulness to young people. He had short gray hair and dark glasses, and wore business causal with a buttoned shirt, khaki slacks, and black sneakers to the meeting. Belzer had been practicing Theravada Buddhist meditation for over thirty years. He had learned the practices from books and various retreats with Burmese Buddhist and Tibetan monks, as well as from *vipassana* insight meditation teachers.

About thirty students trickled in and sat in a rough circle, several students deep. Like the student leaders, Belzer took his shoes off. As he did this and sat down, the room went quiet. After the girls described how the group would do various kinds of sitting, walking, eating, and dance meditations, they turned it over to Belzer. Belzer introduced himself as a former philosophy professor at Bowling Green State University. He was recruited to work at MARC out of the UCLA medical school. "It's my job to come teach people about mindfulness, which science now supports," he said. He asked if anyone had questions. No one did.

Belzer began a twenty-minute sitting meditation. "Sit with a straight back," he instructed. "Your eyes can be open or closed. Most people are more comfortable with closed eyes . . . For this sitting meditation," he said, "we will focus on neutral things. Experiences are like a pendulum. Our attention will wander and we should gently bring it back to the neutral object."

He had the students focus on something they were grateful for. Then he had everyone listen to the sounds in the room. He noted the quiet whirling of air, sounds in the next room, and his voice. Next he had us focus on our breathing. "Focus on how it fills your stomach," he said. "Notice your nostrils opening." Then he led a silent portion, telling the students to pick one thing to focus on. When the meditation was over, he rang a bell.

After students shared their experiences from the sitting meditation, Belzer pulled out a bag of raisins the student leaders had brought. He said they knew about this exercise from his class the prior summer. Everyone took a few raisins and passed the bag around the room. As students passed the bag, he spoke of waiting and the eagerness to get the bag of raisins. Then he noted the impatience students felt as they held a raisin in their hand, waiting for the bag to finish circulating the room. Finally the bag got around the room. "Put one raisin in your hand and feel it," he instructed. "Look at it. Put it to your lips." Even though I do not particularly like raisins, I found myself salivating, eager to eat the raisin.

Belzer next facilitated a standing meditation. He told us to slowly shift the weight from one foot to the other, noting the difference in where the tension was in our bodies. He said we could extend this into a walking meditation but we didn't have the time.

For the last portion of the lesson, Belzer modeled an interactive exercise with an assistant from MARC. For the exercise he had us think of someone we care a lot about.

Then one person asked a partner, "What do you like about them?"

The second person responded.

The first then answered, "Thank you," and the exercise was repeated for the partner. The exercise was powerful because after hearing someone lovingly discuss a person they cared deeply about, a strong urge arose to ask the person more—yet the exercise prohibited this. After the exercise was over, communication in the room spontaneously changed from a relatively quiet murmur into lively conversations between partners, who were all eager to get to know each other better.

At the end of the session, Belzer had everyone stand a bit farther apart and close their eyes. We wished the person we had thought of peace, happiness, and safety. Then we wished it toward our partner's person. Next we wished it for our partner. Lastly, we wished it onto ourselves. He noted this could be quite difficult.

Through meditation practice, contemplative leaders thought people would gain insights into their values, their cognitive and behavioral habits and the emotions they elicit, and their relationships with others. On a deeper level, contemplative leaders believed meditators would learn to see through their own cultural and personal illusions about the world. They would thereby gain agency, realize that people are interconnected, and commit to a moral responsibility to take care of each other. This, they thought, would generate long-term humanistic social reform.

In this chapter I discuss what happens in mindfulness intervention programs. Contemplative leaders conscientiously modeled mindfulness and other Buddhist-inspired values, offered a graduated exposure to contemplative culture, and taught new practitioners embodied practices so that they could self-monitor their own experiences and incorporate contemplative values more deliberately into their lives. Although they believed that their programs would have lasting positive reverberations within the larger organizations they were a part of, this claim was largely not substantiated by the organizations I connected with. Like other alterative movements, the contemplatives' greatest impact seemed to be on the individuals they taught meditation to, rather than on the structural foundations of the institutions they wanted to change.

Socialization to Initiate Social Change

Sociologists have long acknowledged the powerful nature of group socialization processes. Organized trainings that initiate new members into a culture or movement are important in religious conversions and in training committed, competent social movement activists (Isaac et al. 2012; forthcoming). When the causes, values, and tactics of certain movements do not resonate with conventional lifestyles of potential adopters, movements have to produce a *frame transformation* for their new participants. In a frame transformation, prior meanings and beliefs are replaced with those of the movement (Snow et al. 1986). Sociologist Erving Goffman (1974: 43–44) referred to this kind of frame transformation as occurring through a "keying" process that redefines people's interpretations of their activities, events, and biography according to a new framework. Yet, few studies have examined how these processes occur in movements (Benford and Snow 2000).

Sociologist Larry Isaac and his colleagues (2012: 167–175; forthcoming) identified *movement schools* in the civil rights movement, for example, as sites where movement members were educated and socialized mentally, emotionally, and morally. Civil rights movement activists were taught self-discipline and emotional regulation through embodied practices in safe places, such as basements and backrooms of black churches, so they could successfully carry out nonviolent tactics in their protests such as the Freedom Rides.

First, the trainings were intended to transform participants' shame, anger, and self-doubt, which had been inculcated from years of racist experiences, into personal pride, strength, and the determination to initiate change. Second, the Nashville workshops taught participants that because their cause was consequential and just, others would follow their lead. Third, the movement schools argued that nonviolence was the most viable tactic for a powerless group to achieve their aims, given that with the movement's limited resources, civil rights activists could not compete with the violence of their antagonists. Participants were taught about the history and philosophy of nonviolence, drawing on sources as varied as the Bible, Thoreau, and Gandhi. Students were also trained through "sociodramas" in which they acted out roles of activists and the opposition. They practiced regulating their emotions when antagonized and learned how to protect their bodies when attacked.

Unlike these movement schools in the civil rights movement, contemplative programs used "interventions" to teach mindful practice, philosophy, and action. Contemplative participants were not being trained for a particular movement event, but rather to change the way they thought about and executed their work and carried themselves in interactions with others.

Buddhist meditation training teaches practitioners to experience Buddhist tenets on a bodily level, which can lead them to realize new truths. In a study of a *vipassana* meditation retreat, sociologist Michal Pagis (2010) documented how group meditation retreats in *vipassana* meditation centers foster new embodied experiences and teach practitioners to connect such experiences with abstract Buddhist concepts like impermanence; this creates new phenomenological realities for meditators. With their use of related practices, which were often rooted directly in Buddhist *vipassana* traditions, the contemplatives I spoke with experienced a similar process of personal transformation through their group retreats and personal contemplative practices. However, instead of teaching meditation in Buddhist meditation centers such as the ones Pagis attended, contemplatives deliberately brought meditation into secular institutions to spread the transformative potential of meditation practice more broadly.

When meditators leave a retreat, they try to fortify the embodied experiences and ideology they learned in the retreat in their everyday lives by doing daily meditation practice. Pagis (2010) likened daily meditation sessions outside of Buddhist retreat centers to Kohler's (2002) "labscapes," defined as a lab situated in nature that bridges science and nature. Daily meditation sessions at home or in other everyday locations create:

> semi-sterile environments in which one can renounce social interaction and resurrect Buddhist wisdom. The semi-sterile environment is based on an imitation of the conditions of the meditation center: a temporal and spatial renunciation from daily life through sitting in an isolated corner, turning off the phone, dimming the lights, and concentrating on sensations . . . This daily shift back to ultimate reality enables practitioners to maintain a fresh embodied understanding of Buddhist wisdom. (Pagis 2010: 485)

Likewise, contemplatives carved out new spaces for resurrecting Buddhist understandings and lifeworlds within the organizations they inhabited. Mindfulness educators also created a battery of ways to encourage program participants to practice "off the cushion" in their everyday lives. In Kohler's words, they helped novice meditators create mindful labscapes, or places of retreat, in the midst of their everyday lives at work and at home.

Socialization in Mindfulness Interventions

Like the movement schools used to train civil rights activists, contemplative programs sought to transform participants' personal and interpersonal habits, norms, and beliefs. Contemplative leaders did this by creating safe, contained spaces within targeted organizations where they taught meditation by modeling contemplative practice and by guiding new adopters on how to embody contemplative values and tenets. Contemplatives like Marvin Belzer instructed trainees to center their attention on the embodied awareness they practiced during meditation. Then, mindfulness teachers taught the new meditators in their programs to deconstruct the social knowledge they had accumulated over the years.

Meditation practices, and their associated ideology taught in contemplative intervention programs, often contrasted in explicit and subtle ways with the secular, instrumental institutional cultures they were embedded in. Not only did mindfulness programs arrange for new adopters and seasoned practitioners to sit in meditation together, which broke the typical fast-paced environment common in many high-stress professions, but they also encouraged practitioners to reflect on an alternative set of Buddhist-inspired values and commitments that could differ from the instrumental rational aims of targeted institutions.[1] The contemplative perspective that new practitioners gained was intended to help them operate with more agency and in a kinder, more compassionate way in their daily lives at work and at home. In addition,

contemplative programs were attractive to professionals because they promised to help them develop self-awareness, attention, and emotional intelligence,
which would arguably help them not only in their work and relationships but
in further spreading meditation practice among their own networks.

Modeling Embodied Contemplative Practice

To teach meditation to new adopters across institutional sectors, contemplative educators modeled contemplative practice, values, and philosophical
beliefs. "Spiritual life is a lot about imitation. It's about role modeling," Rob
Roeser, a professor of psychology and human development at Portland State
University, told me. Modeling contemplative behaviors and values served
various purposes for meditators. It was a subtle, nonthreatening way to teach
new adopters about mindful practice and to remind clients and students to
practice mindfulness when they forgot. By enacting contemplative values,
beliefs, and practices, teachers also embodied and reinforced their own
commitment to meditation. Embodying contemplative culture simultaneously affirmed contemplatives' sense of authenticity and commitment to the
practices they preached.

Many contemplative educators used modeling strategically as well to prevent accusations of proselytizing. Diana Winston, director of mindfulness
education at MARC, told me that modeling was the most appropriate tactic
in teaching Buddhist-derived cultural content in secular institutions. In
contrast with how she taught Buddhism to meditators at Buddhist dharma
centers, at UCLA she instead taught mindfulness and its associated Buddhist
values and philosophy by subtly embodying it:

> When I teach in a Buddhist context it's really different than what I do here be-
> cause there's a more, I guess you could call it, "religious" aspect of it, although
> I don't think of myself as a religious teacher. But I bring in the cosmology
> and the ritual, and the, perhaps, more explicit ethical teachings—things like
> that—within a Buddhist context . . . But when I'm teaching in a secular con-
> text, what it requires me to do is take some of the principles and embody those
> principles, and share it in that way. So *I may not be explicitly be teaching ethics,*
> *although I might talk about how it makes you kinder to practice mindfulness—but*
> *I'm also trying to embody that kindness, and embody the compassion when it's not*
> *my explicit topic.* (Italics added for emphasis)

Because of normative, and sometimes legal, restrictions to bringing Buddhist
religion into many secular spaces, contemplatives like Winston thought
it was more appropriate to teach Buddhist ideology and values in implicit

ways, such as through modeling, rather than through explicitly discussing religious components of Buddhism.

Similarly, the founder of Inner Kids, Susan Kaiser Greenland, emphasized the importance of modeling mindfulness. In a 2011 interview for the Buddhist magazine *Tricycle*, she argued that modeling was an effective pedagogical practice for kids:

> I hate to sound like a broken record, but mindfulness with children begins and ends with our own practice; it's all about embodiment. Kids learn by example. So if you model a kind, compassionate, attuned, and less reactive stance, they'll internalize that stance themselves in a way that's, in many respects, more powerful than if we just talk to our kids about being mindful, kind, compassionate and attentive.[2]

Although many contemplatives expressed the importance of modeling contemplative practice, it was not always easy to do because it often contradicted normative practices and values in targeted institutions. For example, business coach and former Burmese Theravada monk Greg Burdulis encountered two kinds of reactions from his business clients when he acted mindfully in their workplaces. "Some people," he said, "are gonna be repelled by what you model and . . . make fun of you. Humiliate you. I mean, it may not be to your face, but . . . I can feel it when there are people who just go, 'Oh my God, would you, like, get real? I mean, you don't have a Porsche.'"

In modeling mindfulness in corporate settings, at times Burdulis bumped up against its profit-driven, materialistic culture, which was antithetical to the Buddhist value system he embodied. This at times made for uncomfortable, antagonistic relationships and being treated with derision. In this face of these experiences, he said he would "let them go 'cause they're not open. They're not ready. They're not interested, and to proselytize would be the worst." Then he would continue in his effort to embody contemplative values, such as kindness, to them and everyone else.

Others intuitively resonated with mindfulness, even if "they don't have such a strong grasp or connection" with what it actually is. "But," he explained, "they see you doing it and so they move closer . . . some people are much more willing to say, 'You have something for me to learn.'" For these people, Burdulis thought modeling was an effective strategy. By simply embodying mindful awareness and practice, contemplatives presented an alternative way of being and acting in secular institutions. While not everyone in their targeted audiences was interested in this alternative mode of action, some were, and these new adopters attended contemplative programs and were likely to become practitioners.

Modeling was also used by contemplative field organizers to structure their conferences and trainings for educators as they developed and expanded the field of mindfulness education. Susan Fountain, the field development manager for contemplation and education at the Garrison Institute, explained, "It's interesting to organize events here, 'cause the idea is we want to advance the field. Well, to advance the field," she wondered, "how can we embody it? Because it's not just about how can we get people who have really good things to say so that we can all sit there scribbling notes for the whole time . . . How do we drop into our bodies and really experience what we are talking about as well?" To build mindful practice into their conferences, Fountain adapted a typical conference format. For an upcoming symposium, she planned to "slow it down to have a lot of time for contemplative practice, but also to have our sessions run in a contemplative way. So it's not just, 'let's timetable fifteen minutes of meditation in our schedule,' but 'let's see if we can really embody a more contemplative approach to having a conference.'"

By trying to foster mindful presence throughout the conference, Fountain saw her work at the Garrison Institute as strategically pushing back against the privileging of academic knowledge and skills such as "linguistic, logical, and mathematical" skills in K-12 education. With the preeminent focus in American K-12 education on imparting cognitive knowledge and skills, Fountain thought other ways of knowing were neglected. "We don't have to acknowledge these other ways" of learning in school, she said, "and they [traditional subjects of academic learning] can all be approached in a contemplative way. It's a contemplative process just to stop and slow down and take in those other ways," such as embodied, reflective awareness. To incorporate contemplative ways of learning and knowing, in addition to contemplative practice periods at the beginning of every session and hosting contemplative expert speakers, Garrison gave participants multiple ways to reflect on what they learned. During their conferences, Garrison provided "quiet time to write, reflect, journal, meditate—digest" individually, as well as through discussions in pairs.

Modeling was also used as a means of exhibiting an alternative way of working in and running organizations. In the white paper he wrote for the Center for Contemplative Mind in Society (CCMS) working group (1994b), Jon Kabat-Zinn reflected that at his center at the University of Massachusetts at Worcester, "most importantly, we are learning to work together as a team and to embody the principles and practices of mindfulness in all aspects of our work and in our interfaces with the medical center and the medical community." Thus, from the time his center was being established, Kabat-Zinn hoped it would serve as an mindful organizational model that would represent an alternative to the ways professionals typically did their work and ran their organizations.

Graduated Exposure to Religious Ideology

In another attempt not to alienate potential new adopters, many contemplatives strategically did not disclose the depth of their relationship with Buddhism to beginning meditators. Some contemplative leaders confided in confidence to me that they or their peers in the movement were practicing Buddhists. Others were clear they were not Buddhists, but over the course of interviews it would emerge that they attended Buddhist retreats, had taken some Buddhist vows, and read texts by eminent Buddhist leaders like the Dalai Lama.

Contemplatives were careful to state that participants in their programs were not required to profess any kind of ideological religious or spiritual belief. John Dunne, a contemplative humanities professor at the University of Wisconsin-Madison, suggested this movement was compelling because it did not seem to require that new adopters subscribe to the elaborate ideological systems that converts to more traditional religions typically commit to. "The advantage that a movement like that has," he said, "is that there's no proposition that anyone has to buy into." He spoke of how when Mindfulness-Based Stress Reduction (MBSR) was developed, "When you walked in the door there was nothing that you had to assent to in terms of belief or a statement other than 'I'm in pain' or 'I'm here because I have too much stress.' And even those statements would vary from person to person, so there was no particular position that anyone had to adopt." The way the contemplative movement seemed to pitch more of a "style" than an ideological "creed," he thought, resonated with a modern Western worldview:

> Especially in late modern North America . . . the assent to a creed or assent to a proposition carries with it a whole set of other different kinds of commitments, *whereas assent to a way of going through the day, or a style of life, or the use of certain techniques, doesn't seem to be carrying—it might in fact carry those other commitments, but it doesn't seem to.* So I think that's really one of the main differences between something like the Intelligent Design movement and something like Mind and Life, or if you wanted to be broader . . . the mindfulness movement . . . *So the mindfulness movement . . . spreads, or the way in which people can adopt it is similar to the way in which they can adopt style . . . And style doesn't carry with it . . . a creed.* It therefore had a way of spreading virally

that works in our society for some reason, whereas sort of more creedal-based movements have a much more difficult time. Right? The whole late modernist thing about suspicion of metanarratives—it kind of applies. (Italics added for emphasis)

In late modern American society, with its individualistic, consumer-based culture that privileges choice and reason, imposed ideologies necessitating "faith" can be anathema to many scientists and professionals. As Dunne argued, mindfulness was an appealing alternative among the educated middle and upper classes in the West who were suspicious of explicit faith-based metanarratives, because mindfulness appeared to be a set of stylized healthy practices. Yet, as Dunne also acknowledged, the practice of mindfulness was tied to the complex Buddhist-inspired ideologies advanced by the Center for Mindfulness in Medicine, Health Care, and Society (CfM) and other Buddhist modernists, who suggested that contemplative practices were time-tested, transformative, and therapeutic. Contemplative ideology suggested meditation practice would reveal a whole new world of understanding—a deeper underlying reality—to practitioners, despite contemplatives' claims they did not believe in an ideology. Clearly, an ideology was infused in contemplative practice; it was just not apparent to practitioners at the outset.

In accordance with Buddhist modernism and the Buddhist trope of teaching others through "skillful means" or "meeting people where they are," contemplatives used various metaphors to describe their strategy of gradually exposing new audiences through adapted, delimited, and secularized forms of meditation practice. These metaphors depicted the process of conversion or recruitment as a long-term strategy in which new adopters' commitment to contemplative practice and culture would naturally increase over time with meditation practice. Meditators had a faith that if people only tried it, many would learn that it worked. With regular meditation practice, contemplative leaders believed new adopters would enjoy an improved quality of life and would go on to investigate the practices and their underlying religious ideologies more deeply.

Drawing from the Buddhist metaphor of cultivating seeds of mindfulness or goodness, as opposed to cultivating tendencies that obscure true underlying nondual reality, many contemplatives were not concerned about teaching only some kinds of meditation practice or translated renditions of Buddhist ideology to new adopters. They thought exposure to meditation and Buddhist ideology operated like a planting a seed; although the seed might not germinate and grow immediately, it could be activated and nurtured to grow at some point in the future. One university educator likened this process to her own experience with mindfulness meditation. She first attended a mindfulness meditation retreat in 2000, but she didn't fully commit to the practice and do it regularly until four years later, when she realized it would be useful to her students.

Vincent Horn and Rohan Guntillake, who founded the popular Buddhist Geeks podcast for meditators in the tech industry, viewed the process of learning meditation like a funnel. They wanted to expose a wide range of non-practitioners to meditation, Buddhist philosophy, and values in a superficial way at first. They hoped that over time, some would become more interested and seek deeper knowledge of the traditions that underlaid them. Horn said that in his experience teaching meditation:

> I've seen that people come at it from whatever angle they come at it. But, when they start getting into it, if they really truly engage with their own minds and they start to understand what's happening on a subjective level, they start to notice things about themselves. Their motivation actually starts getting deeper . . . But I think it is fundamentally leading in a similar direction if you get into it. And there's a funnel, and there's probably multiple ways into the funnel, and I'm not saying it goes to the same exact place, but there's definitely a pattern or a trend in human development. When it comes to this contemplative stuff, it doesn't seem like it really matters if you came in because you wanted to be less stressed. If you start to realize the benefits of that, then there's gonna be another level oftentimes that comes up . . . and if you have support, and the proper conditions to go deeper with it, it'll go to another level. At least that's what I've noticed. But some people will stop . . . They won't go deeper and that's—I don't have a problem with that . . . from my perspective, I can only create conditions that that optimize the success rate of the journey.

Similarly, Gunatillake said his aim in creating Buddhify, a meditation app for smartphones, was to market Buddhism to broader audiences. By exposing more people to meditation and "working on the aesthetic" of Buddhist meditation, he thought that they could "really widen the funnel. And Buddhify is one way in which I'm trying to help that conversation [in] happening, of making more accessible but authentic ways of getting involved in meditation." He hoped that "in time people who really want to go down the rabbit hole further can then explore" (Buddhist Geeks Interview 217).

I heard this patient, long-term strategy in exposing new secular audiences to meditation from a number of people. For example, Hal Roth, a professor of religious studies at Brown University, told me that in teaching meditation to his students, "we're just introducing people here. If they're interested, they need to go and follow up in practice centers of any kind."

A business coach disclosed a similar patient, long-term strategy in diffusing contemplative culture when I told him that my preliminary research findings suggested Buddhist meditation was being secularized and attenuated as it diffused. He told me that although he did not explicitly mention Buddhist culture to his clients, as they practiced meditation and learned, he helped them navigate the process. As he said this, he made a sweeping gesture, swinging one arm open to reveal an invisible path behind him. This gesture indicated that although he did not typically teach about liberation or enlightenment, as new meditators developed their practice, if they came to him with their spiritual or religious experiences and questions, he showed them how much more there was on the path in a spiritual or religious direction. Then he verbally clarified that secular forms of personal liberation from personal habits, misery at work, or problems in other parts of one's life could occur. Thus, in bringing meditation to business clients, he found that the practice could lead them to secular forms of psychological liberation from daily struggles or to deeper interests in other spiritual or religious aspects of meditation practice. Regardless of the kind of transformations experienced, many of the contemplatives hoped that a feedback loop would ensue in which, through contemplative practice, meditators would experience personal breakthroughs and then delve deeper into meditation.

Embodied Contemplative Lessons in Self-Awareness and Self-Monitoring

What are the deeper lessons and skills committed meditators are supposed to learn? Figure 6.1 depicts skills that the contemplatives said they learned

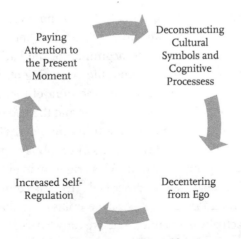

FIGURE 6.1. Embodied contemplative lessons in self-awareness and self-monitoring

from meditation and other mindfulness practices, and that they hoped to impart to others. Through mindfulness practice, they learned to pay greater attention to their minds, interactions, and social contexts. They said not to judge or take too seriously whatever was noticed during contemplative practices, such as paying attention to and controlling the breath, body scans (in which they focus on sensations in different parts of their body), and visualization practices in which practitioners imagined or recalled specific emotional states or experiences. Through these practices, meditators described learning to deconstruct mental habits, emotions, and cultural perspectives and to decenter themselves in their experiences. Meditators' reports and some contemplative neuroscientific research suggest that development of the preceding skills contributes to an enhanced self-regulatory ability among meditators over time.[3]

Paying Attention to the Present Moment

A key tenet of Buddhist meditation and mindfulness is paying attention in the moment. Contemplatives shared various stories of how they taught new practitioners how to pay attention in the moment. Professor Robert Roeser recalled a particularly lucid lesson Buddhist teacher Shinzen Young gave to one of his college classes. Young told the students to imagine they were putting their foot down mindfully. Then he started to count how many mind moments there were in the simple action of putting down your foot.

"For most people," Young said, "there's one, right? The foot goes down. But, imagine you could do the back of the foot, and then the middle of the foot, and the front of the foot, and then your footfall would actually have three mind moments."

Young went on to say to the class, "Okay, so now you're getting a little clearer on the way things are happening. It's not just one. It's actually three. And then imagine you can feel the beginning of the back of the foot, the middle of the back of the foot, the end, the beginning of the middle of the foot, the middle of the middle, and then the front of the middle. Then the beginning of the front of the foot, the middle, and the end of the front of the foot—now you have nine frames in one mind moment." Then Young kept going, breaking down the infinite moments in simply laying down one's foot.

"He just was taking the mind of the class right up to enlightenment with a mathematical formula," Roeser described. "He was commenting on what it means to become more real . . . And he was saying that has to do with clarity of what's actually happening. And we can understand that increasing in a nonlinear way through mindfulness practice, shooting off to infinity so that each mind moment has [an] infinite number—amount of information."

Young's lesson to Roeser's students taught them to pay close attention to their often taken-for-granted embodied experiences, encouraging them to examine their actions at a minute level of detail. His example also showed them that by paying attention, their perceptions and experiences changed, and they could have fuller embodied experiences in the world.

Other contemplative teachers taught meditators to pay more attention to their cognitive experiences by watching and noting their typically unnoticed thoughts. Kristen Gray, a pioneer in contemplative education, said that in teaching mindfulness, "the biggest thing is being real and not forcing them to do anything or believe anything—and still encouraging them to try it. And in a certain way challenging them on different beliefs, or at least naming—helping them to name—their thoughts."[4]

Gray then provided an example from a class she had recently taught:

> I was doing a thought-watching practice. And in general this is a pretty tough group of kids. And two girls were sitting, doing their nails and chatting while I am leading the practice. And instead of staying in the front of the room, I was walking up and down the aisle. And I stood by the girls' desk, which at least toned down the volume a little bit.

She continued on, saying to the class, "Just notice your thoughts, including why the F is *she* standing next to my chair?"

"And that was it, because I clearly got her attention at that point. And I didn't say the whole word cause I wasn't gonna do that either. This was a girl who had been pretty disengaged when I was in the front of the room."

At the end of the class, Gray asked the class how her lesson was for them, and if they had any questions.

In response, the troublesome student asked her, "Can you read minds?"

"And," Gray continued on, "I said, 'No. I can't read minds and I have a mind and you have a mind and our minds are pretty much the same . . . I have spent a lot of time watching my mind and I have a good idea what your mind might say.' And so this girl went from being totally checked out to like, 'What's going on here?'"

In reflecting on the story, Gray said how important it was in teaching mindfulness not to ask them "to be any different than they are," or try to be some stereotypical rendition of a mindful person who is seemingly nice, calm, collected, adept at paying attention, and so forth. Instead, she showed she was "willing to show them or make visible somehow their habits of thinking, feeling, reacting and living in the world," even when they were uncomfortable, disruptive, or acting in a deviant way from the situation at hand.

In this situation, Gray accomplished various things simultaneously. She accomplished her goal of staying "real" and authentic by practicing what she preached. She modeled paying attention without judgment in teaching her lesson on naming thoughts. And instead of acting upon a natural response to get upset with students who were blatantly not paying attention and disrupting the class by doing their nails and talking, she took an alternative mindful approach. Gray created a teachable moment in which she used the naming exercise to identify and make more visible uncomfortable, unstated parts of the classroom dynamic. In so doing, she brought uninterested students into the fold. Through her reaction and naming of the disturbance in the class, she taught the disruptive students there was value in paying greater attention to one's thoughts, and more reflexively taking into account their own experiences in the context of the larger classroom. Moreover, because of the way she handled the classroom, she gained their interest and respect.

Deconstructing Cultural Beliefs, Attitudes, and Actions

Developing greater attention to one's unconscious cognitive, emotional, and behavioral habits was a stepping stone to other contemplative practices, experiences, and skills. After teaching new practitioners to pay attention to their thoughts and actions, reactions, and social contexts, contemplatives trained their students how to further deconstruct social reality. One way they did this was through breathing techniques. By focusing on their breath, meditators were taught to realize that they are not their thoughts. As meditators tried to focus on their breath, they realized they continually stopped doing so when thoughts arose. Meditators learned their thoughts continued occurring independently of their volition and their conscious mind. This exercise was meant to teach them that they could identify their thoughts as separate from who they are. As former Buddhist monk and university educator Diana Winston described, meditation trained people not to be "swept away by fearful thoughts or anxious thoughts . . . One of the biggest things they learn," she said, "is to not believe everything they think . . . So their relationship to their thoughts changes."

Business coach and former monk Greg Burdulis explained that teaching clients breathing techniques helped them identify their thoughts as separate from everyday action or the "doingness" of their day. Instead, it allowed them to "enter into the being aspect of life, of me . . . and not be caught up with their thoughts." Burdulis said how they were "able to see a thought come and not— like if that thought were a bus—not get on that bus." Next, he taught them that they could train themselves through meditation practice to control whether they "get on the bus" and ride the thought's emotional ride, or instead identify a thought as just a thought, and watch it pass by. By learning this, contemplative leaders suggested that meditators would develop a greater capacity to shape their experiences, to question ideas and view them as illusory, transient, subjective concepts.

New adopters of meditation reported similar accounts. A computer engineer working for a large software company in Silicon Valley told me that since he began meditating regularly, "the biggest benefit," he said, was that it helped him "stay objective. It's like stepping back—looking at a bigger picture . . . You get a chance to look at yourself other than completely [being] engaged with your thoughts. Looking at my thoughts really has helped me. Before that, I was totally consumed by my thoughts."

After teaching new meditators to focus on neutral objects rather than get carried away by their thoughts, stories, and emotions, many mindfulness educators helped their clients to uncover their own underlying "purpose, their deeper intention for why they're there . . . at that ad agency" or their place of employment, Burdulis explained. He had clients identify and question taken-for-granted institutional roles, logics, and purposes. It is this part of the contemplative socialization process that had the most subversive potential from an institutional perspective. Many contemplative educators were teaching new adopters to think on their own rather than to unconsciously enact and affirm the dominant institutional culture.

Willoughby Britton, an assistant professor of psychiatry and human behavior at Brown University, described a similar process in which she learned from meditation practices to deconstruct social reality, to be skeptical of it, and to act instead based on her own personal commitments. "For whatever reason," she told me, "meditation practice deconstructs all that stuff. You come out of there and you're just like, 'I don't really know what's true anymore' and everyone else around you is so engrained in their belief system, and you're like, 'I don't really believe in that anymore.'" Brown believed that there were predictable stages of insight that occurred from meditation practice, and in one of the stages she has identified, "you become disenchanted by the value systems that you were brought up in. And there's a period where everything feels meaningless, because it is." She described how over time, meditators came to feel less constrained and burdened by social expectations. In her own case, she realized that her academic career was less important to her than her personal meditation practice and spiritual development. It became apparent to her that her curriculum vitae (the academic's equivalent of a résumé) was "just a pile of paper." Britton's self-reported experience, and the experiences of other meditators that she has tracked in her research, share commonalities with Burdulis's description of how meditation practice socializes practitioners by teaching them to identify and assess the cultural systems they are embedded in, and to more deliberately act in accordance with their own personal and/or spiritual motives, aims, and values.

As many of the committed meditators I spoke with developed their meditation practice, they became more conscious of, and often critical of, the work cultures they were a part of. They no longer took them for granted and unconsciously accepted them for what they were at face value. Moreover, after practicing meditation for extended periods of time, the contemplatives described their values in ways that aligned with or were coextensive with various facets of Buddhist ideology and its value system. It seemed that committed meditators' inner moral compasses became more sensitized to Buddhist worldviews and either more disaffected or even critical of their profession's constraints, norms, and typical motives.[5] This psychological keying process was a crucial part of contemplatives' attempt to change organizational culture from within.

No-Self Awareness

Central to Buddhism is the tenet of *anattā*, which is commonly translated as "not self" or "no self." Buddhists believe that the concept we call an "I" is an illusion that is composed of five impermanent aggregates: the body, sensations, perceptions, reactions, and consciousness. Although most people believe the five aggregates are real and are part of their own personal self, Buddhists argue to the contrary that each of these elements is impersonal, ephemeral, and subject to continual change (Pagis 2010). Buddhist meditation is meant to teach practitioners that these aggregates and the concept of an individual "I" or self are illusory.

Various contemplative teachers said they taught new meditators to decenter the individual sense of "I" or ego from their experience. Loosening meditators' attachment to their ego could be scary for some new adopters; business coaches in particular commented on how challenging this part was for some of their clients. Burdulis told me that he encouraged his clients gently to let go of the ego, telling them, "you can go back to being you, it's not like you disappear." Then he likened the loosening of the ego for clients to "the carapace or the shell of the crab or the insect." "There's a separation between the crab that is molted," he said, "and the shell. So it's OK to let that shell go." He said letting the shell of the individual ego go felt like "a small and limited personal notion release. Then there's a kind of a freshness, a newness that is no longer limited by that particular belief or thought. Then sooner or later what arises is a sense of joy, a sense of peace and freedom. But the peace is not bland or complacent, it's energized."

In a similar manner, psychotherapist and Buddhist meditation teacher Harvey Aronson (2004: 64) wrote that "Understanding that our sense of 'I' is not as solid, permanent, or substantial as we habitually hold it to be ultimately uproots clinging, attachment, and hostility. Understanding this burns up the fuel that runs our repetitive habits . . . Those who have understood this report a sense of spacious lightness and freedom. They exhibit deep concern and tenderness for others."

Contemplative neuroscientific research associates mindfulness and meditation with less time spent in the "Default Mode Network," which is the part of the brain that is associated with a "wandering mind" and "self-referential" processing (Brewer et al. 2011: 20254). Contemplative neuroscientists argue this mechanism is one of the central cognitive processes that leads to enhanced well-being among meditators (Brewer et al. 2011; Britton et al. 2013; Taylor et al. 2011). Some studies suggest that mindful meditation diverts attention in the brain from the ruminative cognitive processes in the Default Mode Network to areas in the brain related to embodiment, attention, and modulation of the limbic system, which regulates emotions, as one would expect (Farb et al. 2007, 2010; Taylor et al. 2011).

These neuroscientific research findings align with contemplative teachers' and practitioners' descriptions of how meditation is related to a decentering of the self in their experiences. As one contemplative educator described, meditation helps practitioners connect to the "bigger picture as their experience centered less around parts of their ego, such as their thoughts."

Rather than attaching to their egos so steadfastly, many meditators I spoke with reported becoming more firmly committed to their values. The practical repercussions of this varied. With meditation practice, some people could better align their personal values and their aspirations at work. For example, a meditator working in a tech company said embodied meditation practices serve as anchors that help him to decenter from his ego and create his day: "My ritual is I meditate," and it "helps me be more selfless in a way. I'm not just thinking about myself; I'm thinking about how I can add value."

For others, their new commitments to meditation and contemplative values led them to leave their jobs. I saw this occurring in meditators who ranged from contemplative leaders to fairly new adopters of meditation who had only been practicing for several years. During interviews and contemplative conference presentations, I heard many accounts in which, with increased meditation practice, people's priorities and interests changed. Some left lucrative, high-status jobs as corporate leaders and managers at Google, Twitter, General Mills, and *O* magazine (Oprah's magazine) to pursue contemplative practice and teach it to others.

With their greater attention skills; an ability to deconstruct and analyze their minds, interactions, and the larger cultural systems they are a part of; and a reported psychological decentering away from egotistical impulses, it makes sense that people who practice mindfulness meditation might have an enhanced capacity to regulate their minds and actions. Meditators' descriptions of their experiences suggest this is the case. For example, mindfulness coach Greg Burdulis said that he learned to better regulate his mind in the following way:

> . . . it was in meditation that I realized for the first time that I could sense my own thoughts. Previous to that they were transparent to me, transparent like glass is transparent: you can see through it and you don't pay that much attention to the glass. But when I began to see how negative they were, I could see how much suffering I was creating through my mind through thoughts. That was the first understanding of why the Buddha said that the mind is so important, and it was the first glimpse of what freedom entailed. So as I continued to practice, I could see those negative thoughts coming up.

Using a metaphor from a parable in the Theravada texts of the Buddha, Burdulis said that being angry or planning vengeance was like holding a hot burning coal in your hand. When you recognized the hot coal was burning your hand, "you don't have to think about what to do." You drop it. "And the same is true," he continued, "when you see yourself creating pain and suffering in your own mind." This is what happened to him as he practiced meditation for prolonged periods of time:

> So really for months what was happening for me was a decrease in the suffering, in my suffering, because I simply wasn't perpetuating it. I was seeing it for the first time and dropping the coal again and again and again and again. Now neuroscientifically we understand that there is a neural pathway that's already established for negativity, so the meditation practice helped me to see, "Oh, I'm in that neural pathway. Step out." And I automatically strengthened the process of stepping out and at the same time weakened the neural pathway of negativity. Now I would not say that that neural pathway is completely gone, but it no longer dominates my mind, or my self-image . . . It's so touching and it's so freeing and it's so significant.

When Burdulis watched his negative thoughts, he realized that they led to experiences of suffering, so he gradually learned to step away from the thoughts and detached from them over time; this led to increased mental control over his experiences.

Contemplative programs systematically taught new adopters how to better regulate their minds. In his mind training program for veterans and law enforcement officers, Michael Taylor focused on the "somatic," embodied perspective, rather than on people's narratives. After leading clients through breathing techniques, Taylor and his co-teachers helped interpret what their clients experienced. "When people come into the classroom, we want to know what their experience was in terms of their practice. 'What came up for you?'" However, they were careful "about not doing that from a therapeutic perspective," like psychotherapeutic talk therapy. Course leaders guided "the conversation to less about the storyline and more about the actual physical feelings that are behind that. I'm not interested, frankly, in their stories," Taylor said. "I don't put myself in the role of the therapist guy for them. And so we teach them then to regulate that way, and learn to start cutting some of the stories in terms of their mind." Instead of paying attention to painful internal narratives and stories that triggered feelings of anxiety, fear, and other forms of discomfort, Taylor taught new practitioners to focus on neutral embodied sensations, such as their breath. From there, they learned there was a neutral place they could go when they were upset and they could start to control their mind and regulate when the stories arise.

At times, contemplative teachers had to give "tough love" to their clients. If new practitioners under their tutelage could not see patterns in their behavior that from a Buddhist standpoint were not useful and were causing suffering, teachers had to intervene. Burdulis told me that he sometimes acted according to an axiom he'd learned from a Zen teacher: "Compassion can be a slap in the face." "I mean," he said, "that can be a compassionate act." Accordingly, in working with clients, he tried to "distinguish what they are saying with their mouth," while also watching

> their tone of voice, their facial expressions, their posture, [which] can all be communicating something very different. And for me to be able to point out that incongruity or dissonance has been really important to help that person align their body, mind, and speech. So that it's unified as opposed to becoming diversified and . . . to unify their energy, it could be that simple.

When novice meditators could not see incongruities or dissonances in their speech, actions, or values, teachers like Burdulis, who coached or taught them regularly, stepped in and offered alternative perspectives so that they could better see themselves and improve their self-regulation.

Reinforcement and Integration Mechanisms: Connecting Practice with Work and Everyday Life

Mindfulness programs helped teach their clients and students how to carry contemplative practice into everyday life "off the cushion" and in the larger organizations the practitioners inhabited. Many program founders and facilitators deliberately adapted contemplative practices so that they would be useful in daily operations in the workplace. Google's Search Inside Yourself program, for example, taught participants skills such as mindful listening, mindful conversation, and even mindful emailing, which would be particularly useful for increasing emotional intelligence in Google's engineers' and other employees. Programs across social sectors gave new practitioners homework to work on outside of their courses as well, such as journaling; keeping training logs; listening to audio-recorded mindfulness exercises; practicing mindful listening, generosity, and lovingkindness in their interactions with others; and periodically internally noting their thoughts and experiences.

For example, when preschool teachers completing her center's training did not know how to bring mindfulness into their work, educator Julia Martin created practices that helped them. At first, she told them to focus on bringing mindfulness practice into their own experiences at school rather than teaching their students the practices, "just so they were starting to bring their practice into the school building." Then she gave the teachers cards to bring with them to school to remind them to incorporate contemplative practice into their daily routines. One card, for example, told teachers to "recognize bodily sensations within interactions" and to "bring that practice right now into your interaction with a student." Other exercises had teachers reflect on lovingkindness. When facing challenging students, teachers were instructed to offer lovingkindness to the students, recognizing mentally that the students "were in distress, that they weren't trying to be difficult. They were just having trouble. And so," Martin explained, the teachers were taught to reflect, "in their difficulty, in the midst of being caught up in it, can I offer them kindness?"

To get their students to begin practicing mindfulness during the school day, Martin's program had the students wear small contemplative cards on the lanyards that held their school identification cards. The cards encouraged students to do "drop-in" practices, reminding them to do breathing exercises throughout the day when they saw their peers' cards. Martin's program also had students do lovingkindness practices three times during the day: before school, during lunchtime, and toward the end of the day. For the lovingkindness practices, students repeated phrases such as, "May I be safe. May the children be safe. May all be safe in the school . . . May my presence help create a climate of safety within the school."

Michael Taylor took a very different tactic with the veterans and law enforcement officers he trained. Drawing on athletic culture, after every session he assigned homework in which clients had to fill out a training log. If they did not do their training exercise or training log, "we punk 'em," he said. "We call 'em out, we embarrass 'em a little bit." He explained that the masculine group of veterans and law enforcement officers he worked with "kind of expect that, and they're okay with it."

Across sectors and programs, contemplatives developed creative ways to help clients integrate meditation practice into their everyday lives. These additional practices helped their clients integrate contemplative culture into their thoughts, actions, and interactions with other people throughout the day at work and at home.

Changing Individuals or Institutions?

What, in fact, were contemplatives transforming? From contemplatives' perspectives, their programs had a tremendous impact on the people they served and on the teachers themselves. As discussed above, when asked about the effects of their programs, contemplatives discussed how they have experienced meditation as a personally empowering transformative practice, which taught them to deconstruct the cultural worlds they were a part of, decenter from self-centered perspectives and goals, better self-regulate their emotions and actions, and foster greater kindness and compassion toward others. They believed that the world would be a better place if everyone had this experience, so they inhabited institutions deliberately and taught others the practices leading to individual transformation. In working with elites, organizational leaders, and new audiences across various institutions, contemplative leaders hoped that the personal changes they initiated—such as greater self-awareness, consideration for others, and heightened pro-social values—would lead meditators to make more socially responsible decisions.

When I asked Mirabai Bush about the impact of these interventions on the organizations they were based in, she discussed individual-level outcomes she had seen contemplative educators in the prison system experience. Although Bush had previously assumed that teaching meditation in prisons was merely "good pastoral work, and great one-on-one," she did not expect it to lead to "any kind of systemic change." But, to her surprise, she noticed

> that pretty much everybody I came to know who did that work, they get so radicalized from being in the middle of it. And they weren't political types at all. They were meditation teachers. But they realized from being in there what was going on and then they found ways that they could work for change. And that really surprised me . . . One of the things the Buddha said, and certainly Christ said, is go where the suffering is. And once you get where the suffering is, you're both more motivated to relieve it and also you can see what's going on and what needs to be changed. And sometimes how to change it.

She said that it "is not to say the systemic change is not important," but then referred back to the impact of contemplative practice on individual activists, caretakers, and change-makers:

> It's that combination of the practices that can really help with insight into how to make that change and also personal sustainability . . . in the years when I was in Guatemala—10 years—working with so much suffering, I could not have made it probably through one of those years without having the refuge of practice, and remembering—just resting in loving awareness after a day with the Guatemalan army and just seeing the suffering of people. That's why I think that when we got to Guatemala in '86, all the aid agencies and development agencies had all left, 'cause their people were getting killed. They were burning out. And the people who remained were nuns and priests who were amazing, but they had that total faith that allowed them to be sustained through it all. And I saw that these contemplative practices, they were really important for me. We did lots of retreats for social justice activists and many people reported that.

Bush reverted back to her trust in her lived experiences that suggested that (1) contemplative practice could lead to radical changes in people, which could lead them into activism, and (2) contemplative practice generated healing that could help sustain people undergoing a lot of stress and hardship, such as caregivers, and those implementing changes, like activists.

Some evidence suggested that contemplative practice could deeply affect secular professionals, including high-powered corporate executives. However, in the face of the powerful profit-driven organizations, rather than creating structural reforms to improve the lives of workers or mitigate undesirable unintended consequences of company products, some transformed executives instead chose to leave their jobs. In this respect, the Monsanto case was telling.

"As things unfolded," Bush recalled, "clearly corporate values were at odds with the original vision, and I think [CEO] Bob [Shapiro] kept thinking he could steer it in a way." Shapiro thought he could reduce the company's deleterious effect on the environment but ultimately learned that "it was bigger than he thought. And finally he left."

Bush attributed part of this decision to his meditation practice during that period. At the time, he was seriously committed to contemplative practice. "I mean, he'd take not just the retreats that were at Monsanto but he'd do off-site retreats with us in different places, week-longs and so on. So he was seriously looking at all this," she remembered. He was "very smart," she said, and was taking into account contemplative perspectives and asking really "great questions." Shapiro realized he could not have the impact on Monsanto he wanted, Bush reported; as a result, he left Monsanto, and the meditation program there was eliminated.

Shapiro was not the only person to leave Monsanto after committing to serious, sustained contemplative practice. Bush said "a number of other people there" were deeply affected by the practices. "One person there . . . in marketing," for example, "started meditating more and then she went to Spirit Rock [an insight meditation center in Woodacre, California] and took teacher training, which is rigorous. Now she's got a whole dharma center in St. Louis where there never was one . . . But she's a really sincere and good teacher now—so that was a radical shift."

There was some evidence that, within the centers, laboratories, and organizations that they controlled, contemplatives practiced what they preached and enabled their employees to bring more of their values, contemplative practices, and personal lives into the workplace. At Richard Davidson's laboratories at the Waisman Center at the University of Wisconsin - Madison, which house over sixty scientists, for example, Davidson strove to create a hybrid social environment that integrated scientific and Buddhist practice. He attempted to adhere to high-quality practices according to both fields. As he discussed in his lecture at Stanford University in 2012, the people at his lab sought to "to cultivate an environment where we can actually practice science and practice dharma in a way which is seamless." They did this despite the fact that bringing Buddhist dharma into science challenged its dominant secular norms.

Davidson explained that he brought the dharma into the lab in three ways. First, as the leader of his lab, he tried to embody Buddhist virtues such as humility and nonattachment, which he thought aligned with scientific rigor: "One of the ways we practice humility is by being really honest about what we don't know, which far exceeds what we do know." He also thought the sense of nonattachment to objects and ideas learned from a regular meditation practice could help scientists be less biased and attached to particular parts of their data or outcomes in their results. Second, he incorporated a meditation space, "smack in the middle of our lab," to support meditation practice during the work day among his team. The meditation space was used both for research purposes and for several weekly group meditation practice sessions. Third, with the feedback from adept meditators, such as French Buddhist monk Matthieu Ricard, Davidson's research team has been at the forefront of advocating bringing "first-person" perspectives, based on peoples' self-described perceptions of their embodied experiences, into their research to complement "third-person" ways of collecting data about people, such as external biophysical tests.

Davidson acknowledged that by bringing meditation and associated Buddhist ideas into his lab, he pushed the envelope of science past its status quo. "Combining science and practice," he said, "is going to require entirely new training models, which I'm afraid groups like the NIH [National Institutes of Health] are not going to support, at least in the near future. And it means practice time in the lab, and what I mean by practice time here is time on the cushion, which is something that we don't think about typically in a high-powered scientific environment."

Davidson sought to change the way neuroscientific research is done by bringing his religious values and practices from Buddhism into scientific spaces. He challenged secular dominant institutional logics in science—but was careful not to challenge too much at once. Instead, he chose to implement changes in localized work cultures within the centers he oversees while adhering to all other formal rules, regulations, and standards within his field. As director of several laboratories, he created rules differently than those in other parts of his academic institution. He valued and supported meditation practice by allowing members of his center to bring contemplative beliefs and practices into the office and affirm and practice them during the work day. He also allowed and even encouraged employees and graduate students to take time off for meditation retreats. Although he was careful not to challenge the rational, empirical foundation of science, he built upon the scientific system in a new way by bringing greater attention to "first-person," subjective self-assessments, which, the contemplatives suggested, could be honed through meditation practice.[6]

There were also some examples that gave contemplative leaders hope that their work would indeed reverberate out and make an impact on the larger organizations they were a part of. At Robert W. Coleman Elementary School in Baltimore, Maryland, for example, where Ali and Atman Smith facilitated yoga and mindfulness instruction through the Holistic Life Foundation, mindfulness has not only improved kids' lives but has also been creatively integrated into the discipline process at the school. Instead of sending disruptive pre-K–5th grade students to detention, they are now sent to a "Mindful Moment Room," where they do breathing exercises and discuss with a counselor how to regulate their emotions. With this new approach to discipline, the school reported zero suspensions, versus four the previous year (Khorsandi 2016).[7]

Although the preceding examples suggest that mindfulness is having an impact on the organizations it inhabits, for the most part it seemed that the impact of contemplative programs was confined to improving the lives of the programs' teachers and students. I did not find much evidence demonstrating that mindful interventions affected the larger organizations they were a part of. Although I asked many contemplative leaders, few provided concrete examples that contemplative practice does, in fact, lead most practitioners to initiate deeper reform in their broader organizations or institutions. It is possible that, as they stand, the majority of mindfulness programs are too content-light to have the impact their founders hoped for; after all, most mindfulness programs only provided a thin introduction to Buddhist ideas and practices. Mirabai Bush acknowledged that many contemplative programs just taught the tip of the iceberg of contemplative practice:

> Just the very first part of mindfulness is taught, which is to focus on breath. And as you focus, your mind becomes more calm and clear and stable, and that usually reduces stress and reduces cortisol, which causes inflammation. And that's all good. But these practices have the potential of really transforming the way in which you see the world, to deepen the way in which you understand the interconnection of all life, all beings and all life. And to know that the appropriate way of being in the world then becomes compassionate action.

To truly transform, though, Bush said that "you have to do a lot more . . . You can't just watch your breath for ten minutes a day and then before a meeting take three deep breaths. I mean, that's all good and I do those things, but there's so much more and our institutions need so much transformation." She explained that she had learned meditation quite differently from the way it was taught in most mindfulness programs:

> My first teacher, who was Goenka, said, "You should never teach meditation in less than ten days; ten days all day and evening." And of course that doesn't

work in this country for most people. But I really appreciated what he meant because in that amount of time you can at least get a glimpse of what's possible. Without that, usually you don't. And then as he said, people think that they've learned to meditate, and when it doesn't do anything for them, then they never do learn to meditate. But you know, if some people never do learn to meditate, it's fine.

Based on her experience with S. N. Goenka, when CCMS first taught contemplative practice to people in business, Bush said they would "never did less than a full three-day retreat with a great teacher," which was conducted "mostly in silence." This, she said, initiated "radical enough changes for these folks that they get a little glimpse of a way of knowing and a way of being that was different from what they were already comfortable with."

However, many mindfulness programs today, including the Google Search Inside Yourself program that Bush helped develop, consist of shorter introductory training programs. Bush attributed the attenuated nature of contemplative training to the fact that lay practitioners in the West are very busy. She acknowledged that, unlike Asian monastic training or other dharma centers' retreats and sustained teacher training programs, what many contemplative interventions were doing was "not the passing on so much" of Buddhist meditation, but the "desire to create forms that work in secular settings and that work in this frantic life that we're all part of. People have tried to find ways that we can fit it in."

With this approach to spreading contemplative practice among professions, Bush reflected that "there's lots of good teaching going on," but there is some "danger" that the depth of contemplative practices' lessons will be missed: "I mean, it's fine if people get a little stress reduction or a little feeling good or they're a little more focused on their work. That's all good," she said. "It's just I am personally more interested—and the center's always more interested—in the really transformative potential of these practices for institutions as well as individuals." Despite her dual missions to transform individuals and institutions, in her work, like most other contemplative leaders, Bush mainly focused on transforming individuals. Contemplative programs' focus on the instrumental outcomes of their interventions is evident in their research. Most studies of contemplative programs focused on the instrumental outcomes individuals and institutions cared about, such as individual health and well-being, cognitive and emotional control, and grades or performance reviews (e.g., Jennings and Greenberg 2009; Meiklejohn et al. 2012; Schonert-Reichl et al. 2015). They failed to investigate and assess if and how practitioners used mindfulness to improve the organization as a whole or to address deeper institutional problems.

Critics should continue to question if contemplatives have failed to initiate the important structural changes needed to reform the underlying conditions causing employee suffering, such as lengthy work hours, diminished workers' pay and benefits, and the domineering power of the workplace over employee's lives. Is mindfulness training merely a Marxist "opiate" that subdues the proletariat and reduces the chances that workers will collectively revolt against the oppressive labor conditions they live under? In this light, have the contemplatives sponsored mindful intervention programs that are the equivalent of social "trickle down" efforts to change? Critics may note the similar logic of providing elites with cultural resources and training so that their decisions are more compassionate to the rest of society. Is this far too little reform to exact from capitalist leaders, given the many social problems we collectively face at work and in broader society?

The truth may lie in the eye of the beholder. Perspectives vary based on what evidence and theoretical frameworks analysts are considering. Examining short- versus long-term goals and individual versus structural organizational outcomes likely affects evaluations of the success of contemplatives' efforts at mobilizing meditation.

Based on their lived experiences teaching intervention programs, committed meditation teachers thought their work was successful and they were optimistic about the future. At the end of our meeting in 2016, Bush reflected on her contemplative work. As Buddhists do, she rooted her motivation in the Buddhist bodhisattva vow, committing to save others from suffering in this world by teaching the dharma. She reflected on the critiques that people like her, who led the contemplative charge to bring meditation to secular institutions, are changing the purpose of Buddhist meditation from a sacred pursuit to get off the wheel of suffering in Buddhist lifeworlds such as our own, to a reduced, secularized, anti-Buddhist pursuit of utilitarian professional goals. She considered all these ideas and concluded, based on her experience, that

> I did take the Bodhisattva vow to save all beings, relieve all suffering, but everybody has their own timing . . . Some people say you're teaching bad people to do bad things better. That's the argument against Monsanto and the Army. But that wasn't my experience, actually. I think if you have good teachers and a good program, that's not what happens. People get that it's not just about— most of those people have very good focus anyhow in the Army. That's not really what it's about for them. And if it is about relieving stress, that means that they have to look at their stress and they have to discover where it's coming from.

So I just think inasmuch as there is a lot of superficial teaching, it'll pass. The whole mindfulness fad will pass. And the better programs—which are really from which people are learning more—they won't pass because people will recognize that this is a really good way to learn deeper things.

Bush has worked with a lot of leaders across various fields, such as business, the military, and education. She has seen many individual transformations among contemplative leaders, educators, and new practitioners. Like many other contemplative leaders and educators, she could share numerous stories about how people's individual worldviews, self-regulation, and interactions with others have changed.[8] However, she also acknowledged at various points to me that her evidence was anecdotal.

There is not conclusive evidence suggesting that contemplative interventions have deep, lasting structural impacts on the organizations and institutional fields they are placed in. Both in speaking with contemplatives and in examining the effects of their programs, it becomes clear that their attention has primarily been on fostering individual transformations through their group trainings. They largely have lacked a broader sociological imagination about how they could address the underlying root problems—located at the organization and institutional levels—that systematically cause individual suffering. This sociological blind spot has left them open to the criticism that they are complicit rather than subversive activists railing against the capitalist system. If they are merely helping individuals cope with systemic stressors, rather than collectively initiating direct reforms to the system, then are they part of the problem or the solution? Marxists would argue that by reducing individual discomfort by teaching individualized coping mechanisms, they are dulling practitioners into complacency rather than cultivating a movement of activists. Contemplatives would respond that they are providing a means of relief to the suffering of millions of people, and in some cases (although it is unclear in how many of these cases), they are planting the seeds of insight that might lead to future social reform.

CHAPTER 7 | The Elite Circuit

AS I TRAVELED AROUND THE country tracking how mindfulness moved, every step of the way, the contemplatives went out of their way to help me. They invited me to their homes for meals, tea, and occasionally a place to stay. Others spoke to their "best contacts" about how important my work was, or sent emails to connect me with their colleagues in the places I was headed. I realized I had tapped into a strong community of trust. This community for the most part extended help to those who were like them and shared a path committed to similar values of kindness, compassion, and advancing a contemplative agenda. This community propelled me along my way throughout the several years I collected data. Although some people were more apprehensive than others about my role as a researcher, most placed their trust in me out of respect for doing a project trying to better understand their work bringing meditation to secular audiences.

At times their generosity was astounding. During the first Being Human conference at the Palace of Arts in San Francisco in 2012, I happened to sit down on the floor for lunch next to a very kind psychologist. I told him about my research and how I was getting tired of traveling around the country staying at friends' houses. On the spot he offered me his place, which he was not using at the time. Quite incredulous, I asked him if he was sure he trusted a stranger to stay at his home. He looked at me and said, "Jaime, if I'm wrong, it goes against everything I've learned about people from working as a psychologist." He then handed over his apartment keys as we left the event and let me stay at his three-room apartment on Divisadero Street with a paid parking space for the next several months. It was serendipitous events such as these that reaffirmed to members that the mindfulness community was a special and generous group of people. Lucky windfalls like this also affirmed

the contemplative logic that, if you devoted yourself to contemplative practice and its aspirational values of kindness, generosity, and compassion, you
could trust the universe that everything would work out. At the same time,
as a sociologist, I had a hard time believing everyone could access this kind
of generosity; this mentality contrasted with decades of sociological research
on growing economic inequality in America.[1]

If some disadvantaged groups of people encounter barriers at every
turn, in elite contemplative circles it felt like living in a "Choose Your Own
Adventure" book. There was a seeming abundance of promise, fun, meaningful opportunities, and optimism. If you hit it off with the right people, it
felt as if your life could change. In fact, for some people I met, it did. One
Ivy League neuroscientist, for example, came up with a startup idea over
lunch with a wealthy investor he had met through the mindful elite network. Several months later, with funding in hand from the investor, he was
building the company the two had brainstormed on a napkin during their
initial meeting.

The longer I was on the road and the more people and centers I visited
along the way, the more I realized I was on a well-traveled circuit. It was invisible to outsiders but obvious to those on the path. With other journalists,
funders, and entrepreneurs doing market research in 2012, I found myself
exploring a burgeoning meditation movement. How did we get on this path?
As we connected with contemplative leaders, many were eager to help and
raise awareness of their programs' successes. Some contemplative leaders
were quite generous in their willingness to help a curious graduate student,
which reinforced the values many attributed to meditation practice such as
generosity, kindness, and compassion.

Where did the meditation circuit go? Common stops included regular
conferences hosted by the Mind and Life Institute (MLI), the Center for
Mindfulness in Medicine, Health Care, and Society (CfM), and the Center for
Contemplative Mind in Society (CCMS) for professionals in science, healthcare, and higher education, as well as conferences for those in tech and business (e.g., Wisdom 2.0 and Buddhist Geeks) and for K-12 educators (e.g., the
Garrison Institute and the Omega Institute). It also took us on a whirlwind
tour of state-of-the-art neuroscientific labs at the University of Wisconsin
and CfM in Shrewsbury, Massachusetts, and to academic centers at the
University of California (at San Diego and Los Angeles), Brown University,
and Stanford University. The path took me to breathtaking vistas from the
offices and homes of philanthropists. I met with a venture capitalist in an
office overlooking Central Park in New York City, and another in the midst
of a private winery in Northern California. I visited others in their homes

with expansive windows overlooking the San Francisco Bay. The beauty, the affluence, and the prime real estate left me reeling. I connected with quirky adept Buddhist meditators who had spent years meditating in exotic, remote places in Asia like Myanmar and Nepal. I met with passionate educators in California, Colorado, Pennsylvania, Maryland, and New York who were eager to share heartwarming stories of how teaching meditation transformed the lives of their students and colleagues. Like everyone else on the circuit, I spoke with Congressman Tim Ryan (Democrat from Ohio), author of *A Mindful Nation* (2012), in Washington, D.C., and interviewed folks from Goldie Hawn's MindUP program. I met George Mumford, who taught meditation to basketball greats such as Michael Jordan and Kobe Bryant. What world was this I had entered where everyone seemed to know everyone else, and the network included access to wise charismatic religious leaders, celebrities, and committed advocates who worked hard every day to transform their workplaces in seemingly astounding, heartwarming ways? The circuit of such lofty, surreal experiences left one amazed and wanting to be a part of it all with a group of affluent, cutting-edge leaders committed to changing the world. After all, this is what the circuit is intended to do: it is a vehicle for fundraising and promoting the contemplative field.

However, this sunny world was not open to everyone. The cost to access this circuit was considerable. The Zen Brain retreat at longtime MLI leader Joan Halifax's Upaya Zen Center cost $475, plus lodging and the Buddhist *dana* donations to the teachers. A Wisdom 2.0 general ticket was $750; buying your ticket after the deadline increased the cost to $1,250—again, without lodging or transportation costs. Even the contemplative scientific conferences were expensive. I paid more than $400 to attend MLI's first International Symposium for Contemplative Studies in Denver in 2012 and $585 to attend CfM's *Meeting the World Conference* at their center in Shrewsbury, Massachusetts, in 2015.

And even if you purchased a ticket, there was no guarantee you could speak to leaders of the movement. Many conference attendees were there to seek funding or access to mindful celebrities to procure legitimacy for their mindfulness initiatives. This became apparent at a talk by one of the movement's most affluent supporters. In a sharp suit, yet using casual, informal language, former business executive and contemplative funder Thomas Butler gave a confident, passionate talk extolling the importance of collaboration in doing great things.[2] He talked of how, with about forty other people, he participated in a United Nations–sponsored program to prevent unnecessary deaths from disease in Africa. Their work was as effective as it was, he said, because they "built harmonization groups" and "stakeholder partnerships" with members of powerful organizations, including oil companies, the World Bank, USAID, Save the Children, World Vision, the Peace Corps, and even the popular television show *American Idol*. Above all, Butler concluded, what he had learned from such experiences was the importance of "passionate partnerships." Collaboration in doing projects you are passionate about is like playing jazz, he said. It is fun—and you need to find partners with different skillsets that you enjoy hanging out with.

During the question-and-answer session, an executive director of a mindfulness nonprofit organization for children brought up how, beneath all their attested openheartedness in the mindfulness space, there lay fear, attachment to material resources, and competition for scarce resources. "Here, can we just tell on ourselves?" she asked frankly. She continued:

> I really need funding. And I really have a great program . . . I went to Wisdom 2.0 [conference], and the guy at the front said, "I want you to think about why you're here." And I'm like, "Oh, God, I'm here because the funders are here." And then he said, "I want you to think about why really you're here." And I thought, "Oh, shit. I'm really here because I don't want to be left behind." And then the guy goes, "Now turn to your partner, and share."
>
> The executive director said she turned to the man sitting next to her and started to tell him about how she had started a sangha in Seattle. But then she burst into tears and decided to be honest. "I'm here because the funders are here and I'm so afraid of being left stepped over," she had said.
>
> "And he looked at me," the executive director told the crowd, said, "and he goes," "That's why I'm here."

In response, Butler, the rest of the panel on stage, and the entire room burst into laughter. "That's why we're here!" the executive director reiterated seriously over the applause.

Butler thanked her for sharing her vulnerability and acknowledged how everyone is in that place when they have an organization they are trying to get resources for. He said that from his perspective, the funders "are just as scared as you are." They don't want to "make a dumb decision as to what organization to back." Funders want to "find people I can hang with," he said. He suggested figuring out how to lower that fear and get to the state where you can have an open conversation. He said he has done it through "compassionate connection over joint cause. And when you start doing that, money calls. . . I've raised ridiculous amounts of money and," he said, waving his hands upward repeatedly, "money comes when you find these partners that they believe you are really a partner with them, and that you're really open to them. And your ideas will start being shared."

Although I knew Butler to be a kind man (who took the time to provide a thoughtful interview several years earlier), I did not believe that everyone in the audience could raise money as easily as he could. It is different asking for money from peers with shared credentials, friends, or philanthropic missions, than from an affluent keynote speaker who is surrounded by others asking him or her for things at a conference. It is worse when you feel desperately in need of funding or other forms of support from the speaker and are uncomfortable asking for help from strangers.

As a conference attendee who was constantly seeking interviews, I understood where Butler was coming from as well. I had already learned on my own to try to enact the advice he had given, finding counterintuitively that to succeed in this culture, it was best not to overtly ask for anything. You had to interact with ease and find genuine connections with people, trying to ignore their clearly apparent status and what you sought from them. This was incredibly difficult at times when you had paid thousands of dollars to attend their events in hopes of getting access to the speakers. It was also increasingly difficult over the years. I watched the conference circuit grow in scale from 2012 to 2017. More people were interested in mindfulness, more conferences were held, and some of the conferences had expanded in size. This made it more difficult to access the elite speakers.

But my experience also showed that if you befriended one of the insiders, then he or she might generously provide assistance. Once we had shared real, authentic conversations about things that we deeply cared about, or about personal experiences, many contemplative leaders did the networking for me. They laterally referred me to their colleagues and friends. Or, as sociologist Michael Lindsay (2008) put it after studying a movement of elite American evangelicals, it is possible to "leapfrog" up to elites by connecting with their lower-status contacts.

Like the well-heeled American evangelicals Lindsay studied, the contemplative movement was led by elites. The contemplative leaders I interviewed had far higher socioeconomic status on average than is typical in the United States. As shown in Table 7.1, contemplatives were well-educated, capable individuals. Nearly half of the leaders I spoke with had Ph.D. or M.D. degrees or other top credentials in their field, such as a J.D. or Psy.D. Almost 24% had a master's degree in the arts, science, education, or business administration. Only about 4% did not have a college degree, and those people founded and/or led successful multimillion-dollar businesses.

TABLE 7.1. Sociodemographics of My Sample of
Contemplative Leaders[8]

	TOTAL	%
Education		
Ph.D., J.D., Psy.D., and/or M.D.	39	48.8
M.A., M.S., M.Ed., M.P.H., or M.B.A.	19	23.8
B.A.	19	23.8
High school diploma	3	3.8
Professional Experience		
Professor or researcher	31	38.8
Executive (CEO, director, vice president, associate director)	52	65.0
Business founder	23	28.8
Nonprofit founder	12	15
K-12 teacher	5	6
Gender		
Male	50	62.5
Female	30	37.5
Race		
White	68	85.0
Asian	7	8.8
Black	2	2.5
Latino	2	2.5

Note: This is a subsample of 80 contemplative leaders from my larger interview sample of 108. In accordance with Ganz (2000: 1014), I define leaders as "persons authorized to make strategic decisions in an organization."

In addition to having more education on average than the typical American, contemplative leaders tended to be privileged in other respects, such as by occupation, gender, and race. Nearly 40% of the leaders I spoke with were professors or researchers at colleges and universities, and almost two-thirds had worked in the highest levels of their company or organization. I spoke with leaders at various Fortune 500 companies, as well as chairs of collegiate academic departments and directors of contemplative centers at prestigious universities.

In addition to having high-status positions, many contemplative leaders had a great deal of personal initiative and efficacy. Nearly 30% had founded a business and 15% had founded a nonprofit organization; many of the organizations they created were part of the contemplative movement. The leaders I spoke with were more likely to be men (nearly two-thirds) than women, and were mainly white (85%). Only 9% of the contemplative leaders in my sample were Asian, despite Buddhism's roots in Asia. Blacks and Latinos each composed less than 3% of the leaders I met with.

Unsurprisingly—given these sociodemographics—what I encountered at contemplative conferences was a culture of privilege. In his book *Privilege*, which examines elite culture at an esteemed private high school, Seamus Khan (2011) discusses how privilege in contemporary society is different than the stodgy aristocratic arrogance of " 'right' breeding, connections, and . . . refined tastes" (14) that characterized the entitlements of the mid-twentieth-century elite. Among elites today, privilege is instead characterized by a de-emphasis on refined taste and explicit name-dropping of who one knows. Instead, privilege is displayed by developing a strong sense of self and a sense of ease in interacting with all people, whether a person is your trash collector or a billionaire philanthropist. The new elite can climb the social hierarchy by mastering the tricky interactive skill of how to act with one's superiors (or inferiors) in a way that simultaneously respects the existing social hierarchy while creating a sense of intimacy in the interaction that pretends the social power difference is not there. The new elite know how to "extract value from everything and anything, always savvy to what's happening at the present moment" (14). They also learn to explain their success not by who they are, as the old elite would have done, but by what they have developed, cultivated, and accomplished. Or, as Butler explained above, they learn to successfully recruit people by sharing their passions and inspiring others to help them. They know how to make the funders and other elites feel good about investing in them.

Elites develop adept social skill. Sociologist Neil Fligstein describes people with social skill as having developed a "cognitive capacity for reading people and environments, framing lines of action, and mobilizing people" to do what they want or "in the service of broader conceptions of the world" (Fligstein and McAdam 2012: 17). By taking the role of the other, or envisioning themselves in other people's shoes, they empathically relate to others and can thereby secure their cooperation (Fligstein 2001; Mead 1934).

Hence, it appears that the new elite's accomplishments are personal and achieved through their hard work and social skill. Yet, social skill in comfortably interacting with elites is not distributed equally in the world. As education scholars such as Khan show, kids and teens from middle- and upper-class backgrounds are better prepared to succeed at top schools because they have learned upper-class *cultural capital*. Cultural capital provides the knowledge, language ability, and comfort that are key in interactions with people in positions of authority. Having a privileged racial and gendered position is also related to one's ability to speak with people in powerful positions with ease. Part of this ease comes from self-confidence and social skill learned from interacting with others in powerful, high-status positions in the past, such as from one's parents or well-credentialed teachers. Ease comes naturally to the self-assured who know they deserve to be in the room with those in more powerful positions—and that their success does not depend on making a chance connection at an expensive two-day conference when the elites of interest, such as funders and keynote speakers, are inundated with dozens of other people pestering them with questions and requests.[3] Moreover, it is easier to speak naturally and comfortably with people who are similar to you. Homophily—having shared experiences and conversational styles—makes it easier to connect with elites.[4]

The culture of privilege identified in Khan's research at an elite private boarding school is remarkably similar to the culture of the mindful elite. Contemplatives are supposed to navigate any situation with social skill and ease and not be ruffled by others' credentials, wealth, or celebrity. They are supposed to find shared passions and common interests with whoever they interact with. This is most likely to occur with other, often affluent, meditators—as many meditators have had the excess time and money to attend meditation sessions taught by respected, charismatic teachers. At these training sessions, the mindful are likely among other predominantly white, affluent people who, like them, have learned to connect over self-development, their deepest passions, and their own increased self-awareness.

Expert Legitimacy Building

At the contemplative conferences I attended, the leaders and invited speakers were incredibly polished (especially compared to the academic conferences I have attended). Chosen representatives of top contemplative organizations were, for the most part, composed, articulate, and heartfelt. The mindful elite seemed not only competent in their professions—as demonstrated through their scientific presentations, their prestigious institutional affiliations, their academic credentials, and their many accolades and accomplishments—but very passionate about doing meaningful work. The top leaders I met with were committed to improving themselves and developing a greater awareness of and compassion for other people—as taught by Buddhist forms of meditation practice. In short, they came off to an outsider, and even an outsider working on her own Ph.D., as quite an impressive group.

There were various ways contemplative events and conferences drew people in. Of course, the primary factor that attracted people to contemplative events was an interest in meditation and other mindful practices. However, there were other attractive reasons for people of all professional backgrounds to join the contemplative movement. By being with the contemplatives, there was a palpable sense of heightened possibility common to many burgeoning movements. It felt like if you found a way to become part of this community, you would be part of "the next big thing" and would be carried up with it. You could become not only wise and spiritually aware by being a part of this contemplative community and adhering to their meditation practices, but you could also be affluent, confident, rational, and professionally successful, just like them.

Where did this feeling come from? In addition to their elite social status discussed above, the contemplatives were constantly legitimating their work and, in quite a grandiose manner, suggesting it would address some of the most challenging social problems in the world. How did they convincingly do this? During conference presentations and in more informal conversations with contemplative movement members, various "legitimators" for movement involvement were provided by a number of "experts" with different areas of specialty. These legitimators for contemplative work were reaffirmed formally through conference presentations and informally through conversations with other attendees. Common justifications for people's involvement in the movement's events and agendas were based upon different mutually reinforcing kinds of legitimacy and access to opportunities the contemplative movement afforded. The interdependent forms of legitimacy drawn upon by the movement are displayed in Figure 7.1.

The movement was led by a network of respected scientists, charismatic religious leaders, esteemed wealthy and professional patrons, and on-the-ground program founders and facilitators. Each group brought a distinctive form of legitimacy to the table. Everyone looked to the scientists to confirm the legitimacy of meditation's beneficial effects. All could benefit from money from the philanthropists. People also could receive public acclaim by association with highly accomplished professionals and their reputable organizations. Respected professionals' support further legitimized meditation as a useful "tool" rather than a wonky New Age practice within the sectors the professionals worked in. Buddhist contemplative leaders gave a sense of moral and spiritual legitimacy and authenticity to the movement. Lastly, program educators showed that meditation is a useful tool on the ground in various settings. By showing it worked and helped people, they contributed a sense of pragmatic legitimacy to the movement, as well as institutional legitimacy in the institutions where they operated (Wilson 2014).

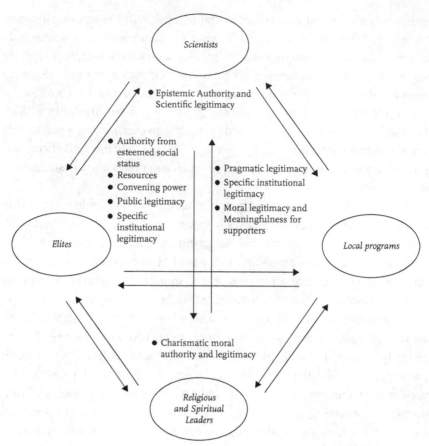

FIGURE 7.1. Mutually reinforcing legitimation and resources within the contemplative movement

Note: These categories are not mutually exclusive; some people were members of several categories. I include people in all of the above four categories as "leaders" of the contemplative movement.

The Scientists

Although the contemplative movement comprises a wide array of professionals, in its early years the two most important organizations, CfM and MLI, were dominated by accomplished scientists with impressive credentials. CfM founder Jon Kabat-Zinn earned his Ph.D. in molecular biology from MIT. While there, he studied under Nobel laureate Salvador Luria. All of MLI's founding members had advanced degrees from the best universities in the world, such as Harvard, Cambridge, and Oxford. Most had Ph.D. degrees, and founder Adam Engle had a J.D. Credentials and membership in prestigious academic institutions were two primary ways through which scientists

conferred epistemic and scientific legitimacy, as well as a generally high social status, to the mindfulness movement. Graduate education additionally
provided training in reason, as well as persuasive oratory and written skills.

Leaders of MLI, CCMS, and other early contemplative funders, such as
the Fetzer Institute, deliberately cultivated a contemplative academic elite.
Organizational founders, program managers, and conference coordinators
said that "of course" they sought colleagues who had "academic rigor,"
demonstrated by distinguished research records and associations with "high-
status institutions." In addition, MLI leaders invited academics they knew
and liked, who had social skill and good oratory skills, to take part in their
events. They looked for scholars with "managed egos" who did not "suck the
air out of the room," said Engle. They sought presenters who could explain
academic topics of interest to the Dalai Lama in lay terms that nonspecialists
could understand. As a result, MLI discussants were good extemporaneous
speakers who shared their opinions and research results clearly, unapologeti-
cally, and often with a dash of humor or self-deprecation. They bantered back
and forth in dialogues with ease, making inquiries across fields and pushing
their peers to think in new and different ways.

The scientists' most important contribution to the contemplative movement was their research. They produced credible peer-reviewed articles in
reputable journals and books that attested to the beneficial effects of contemplative practice. The findings from their research, and the thousands of
articles that built upon their foundational work, were important resources
for contemplative leaders trying to bring meditation into powerful secular
institutions. Research that "proved" the efficacy of meditation in promoting
mental and physical health, reducing the deleterious effects of stress, and
honing attention skills was used to promote the credibility and legitimacy
of mindfulness programs and to convince new practitioners to try mindfulness practices (as discussed in Chapter 4). Contemplative educators, nonprofit leaders, coaches, and funders appreciated the credible, sophisticated
justifications for meditation developed by "top scientists" at some of the best
research institutions in the world. They often discussed "facts" about meditation they had learned from the scientists' presentations and publications in
their own talks, on their websites, and in conversations.

The scientists in turn also got a lot out of being part of the contemplative elite. With their interest in both meditation and science, many MLI
participants felt isolated and believed their everyday work lacked spiritual
inspiration. They were eager to have the opportunity to spend time with,
learn from, and help the 14th Dalai Lama. They also appreciated being with
other academics interested in meditation, and contemplative leaders with

serious meditation practices. Over time, friendships developed among the scholar-practitioners, and between the scholars and contemplative leaders interested in science. Thus, from the burgeoning contemplative network, the academic mindful elite found spiritual inspiration, friendship, and social support from colleagues in other academic disciplines and adept meditators. Contemplative scientific leaders noted how they cherished their relationships with each other at contemplative retreats and conferences; they commented on how long they had known each other, and how much they valued time spent together. Such displays of mutual respect and affection exuded a sense of goodwill and camaraderie that publicly highlighted how personally important the movement was to its leaders.

The contemplative networks additionally provided scientists access to money, which scientists require to furnish their expensive laboratories and pay their researchers.[5] Ultra-wealthy philanthropists donated generously not only to the MLI itself but also to support the scientific and applied interventions of some MLI academics.

Charismatic Religious Leaders

The Dalai Lama played a key role in the formation of the contemplative movement and in the creation of the field of contemplative studies in particular. He inspired contemplative leaders and has served as a source of charismatic religious, spiritual, and moral authority to the movement. Various long-time MLI members told me the Dalai Lama had a pivotal influence on their lives, leading them to commit more deeply to working for the organization. A scientist at a top research institution, who had long been involved with MLI, confided to me during a conference that he joined MLI because he "was devoted to the Dalai Lama and wanted to help with his scientific skills." Other top contemplative leaders told me about their reticence in going public with their meditation practice before meeting the Dalai Lama for fear of losing professional credibility and legitimacy. After meeting "His Holiness," they changed their minds and publicly committed to helping MLI establish a field of contemplative science and mindfulness interventions. Like other central contemplative leaders and funders, they enjoyed their access to him and their ability to teach and help the world's most eminent Buddhist leader. Neuroscientist Richard Davidson, for example, said that meeting the Dalai Lama changed his life:

> I went to India to meet with him in 1992. And that was a meeting that, that
> I think it's fair to say, changed the course of my professional as well as personal

life. And I had been practicing all these years [since his first retreat in 1974 in India] up until then . . . And so I made a commitment to myself and to His Holiness that I was gonna come out of the closet with my interest in this area, and start doing research in this area, and speak about it publicly. I hadn't spoken about it at that time. So, that was really the beginning of this recent chapter.

The Dalai Lama supported the development of the contemplative movement in a number of ways. His books on secular ethics (2011) and his perspective on Buddhism and science (2005) have helped contemplatives justify their work on secular, ethical, spiritual, and religious grounds. He has not only been a source of inspiration for, an advisor to, and a participant in MLI events but has also been a key funder of the organization and its spinoff centers and programs, such as Richard Davidson's Center for Healthy Minds at the University of Wisconsin and Paul Ekman's Mapping Emotions Project.[6] The Dalai Lama is also the primary in-house celebrity and charismatic leader at MLI; where he goes, the media and the public follow. This attention, of course, was a tremendous boon to a fledgling organization and movement. The Dalai Lama's participation certainly helped draw interest to MLI's dialogues on science and Buddhism.

It is important to acknowledge that the Dalai Lama is not the only charismatic religious leader associated with the spread of mindfulness and other contemplative practices to secular audiences. At contemplative conferences, other spiritual and religious leaders have regularly been invited as speakers representing a religious locus of authority and moral fount of wisdom. Zen Roshi Joan Halifax, insight meditation pioneers Jack Kornfield and Sharon Salzberg, and even the 17th Gyalwang Karmapa (the head of the Tibetan Buddhist Karma Kagyu lineage) have been discussants at contemplative conferences. Wisdom 2.0, the elite annual spiritual tech conference in San Francisco, has hosted other spiritual celebrities, such as Eckhart Tolle and Ram Dass.

In the last decade, some leaders of the contemplative movement have gained the status of charismatic leaders as well. Kabat-Zinn and his successor, Saki Santorelli, are held in more esteem now for their expertise in mindfulness than in molecular biology or education, which they studied in graduate school. Within the movement, other early leaders have attained near-celebrity status and serve as quasi-charismatic leaders of the movement, even though they do not publicly represent a religious tradition. Neuroscientist Richard Davidson, for one, has quite a gentle, affable presence and commands a great deal of respect within and outside of the movement.

Religious charismatic leaders stood to gain from membership in the mindful elite as well. Like others, the religious leaders could benefit from access to elite patrons, publicity, and media coverage of their partnerships and events. Through partnerships with top scientists, tech leaders, philanthropists, and program leaders, religious leaders also demonstrated their relevance and import in a rapidly changing, modern world.

Professional Elites and Funders

When I first started scouring the internet for contemplative organizations in 2009, professional elites like Chade-Meng Tan (Google engineer and Search Inside Yourself founder), Janice Marturano (former vice president and deputy general counsel at General Mills and founder of the Mindful Leadership Institute), and venture capitalists like Thomas Butler were nowhere to be found. Although professional elites and movement funders were involved in the contemplative movement by sitting on some organizations' boards and financially supporting the organizations, they had less of a public presence during the first several decades of the contemplative movement.[7]

Over the past decade, wealthy patrons and professional elites in business and other sectors, such as the media and politics, have become both more central leaders and public faces of the contemplative movement. This is in no small part due to the establishment of the Wisdom 2.0 conference in Silicon Valley in 2010. To bring mindfulness into the tech and business sector, Wisdom 2.0 conferences biannually convene tech royalty, such as founders and top management of eBay, PayPal, Zynga, and Google, and celebrities like Jewel and Alanis Morissette, with contemplative leaders and adept meditators. By bringing business leaders and social elites into the mix, conferences like Wisdom 2.0 contribute institutional legitimacy in business and others sectors, and public legitimacy to the mindfulness movement. Elite public support for contemplative practice has elevated the social status of the movement and its practices in America and abroad, attracted more resources for the movement , and amplified the message of mindfulness.

With the inaugural Wisdom 2.0 conference, the frenzy to make money from the meditation industry ramped up precipitously. This did not occur by accident. Wisdom 2.0 founder Soren Gordhamer had a larger vision of how he wanted to impact the world. In a conversation on his front porch in early April 2012, he shared with me some of his vision. After helping Richard Gere run a conference with the Dalai Lama and teaching mindfulness, Gordhamer wanted to foster an interest in mindful business among business elites. To do so, he emphasized how mindfulness could foster innovation and creativity, rather than focusing on how it could help employees cope with stress or hone attention the way that other contemplative pioneers did. "Innovation directly influences growth and potential," he told me, which is what funders and other business elites valued most. By the time I visited Silicon Valley in 2012, aligning mindfulness with profit-seeking was fairly commonplace among the tech elites in Northern California—and a distinct departure from the contemplative subcultures I encountered at MLI and CfM conferences.

At conferences like Wisdom 2.0, philanthropists and venture capitalists could scout out up-and-coming ideas, projects, and organizations in the burgeoning mindfulness space to invest in. This drew leaders of nonprofits and startups, who sought the attention, resources, and legitimacy of the professional elites and philanthropists. With elite patrons' endorsement and financial support, a nonprofit, or an adept meditator, could break out of the ranks and gain a near-celebrity status in the contemplative field. I saw this occur several times over the years. For example, Congressman Tim Ryan and his *A Mindful Nation* co-author, Mindful.org editor Barry Boyce, hit it off with Holistic Life Foundation (HLF) founders Ali and Atman Smith. The Smith brothers had a small mindfulness and yoga program in Baltimore. After connecting with Ryan and Boyce, Ryan helped HLF raise money by attending its fundraising events. Boyce showcased their work on his website and in the first edition of *Mindful* magazine. The Smith brothers were introduced to Kabat-Zinn and Davidson and were thereafter mentored and became integrated into the mindful elite contemplative circuit.

Contemplative leaders also had much to gain from connections with professional elites. Another Buddhist leader I met connected with one of Silicon Valley's most well-known entrepreneurs and venture capitalists (although not at a contemplative conference). This venture capitalist became a patron and supported his move to San Francisco. The contemplative teacher went on to teach mindfulness among top tech circles and even facilitated the first mindfulness teaching to business leaders at the World Economic Forum in Davos, Switzerland. This important connection provided the contemplative teacher not only with financial resources but also with social status, credibility, and legitimacy in the business and tech sector. This teacher's work with tech elites was featured in top tech publications.

Of course, it is important to recognize that these are exceptional stories. Most attendees at contemplative conferences did not have these incredible opportunities open up to them because of the connections they made at conferences. However, the promise and possibility of having such fortuitous events occur at contemplative conferences drew in many people. In addition, with the rise of social media, coaches, entrepreneurs, and others could take photos with professional celebrities or tweet words of wisdom from their talks to show how connected they were with change-maker elites; this amplified the contemplative message, sending it out to greater circles. By virtue of their associations with esteemed professionals and moneyed elites, coaches and entrepreneurs gained more professional and social legitimacy and credibility in their own right.

Why were professional elites, celebrities, and other wealthy patrons drawn to the mindfulness movement? Some professed a personal interest in humanist self-actualization, while others committed their lives to more meaningful activities after undergoing difficult life events. Maslow's (1943) hierarchy of needs, which many contemplatives were familiar with, suggests that after procuring basic needs, like safety, and psychological needs, such as social prestige and a sense of accomplishment, people will seek self-actualization and self-transcendence to attain their full potential. Spiritual practices like meditation, which seek to develop the self, can lead to transcendent sacred states and a greater sense of meaningfulness in one's life (Kucinskas, Wright, and Ray 2017; Kucinskas, Wright, and Riepl 2018). Philanthropy also contributes to a positive sense of self and of authenticity to one's values of aiding good causes that one believes in. Lastly, business and social elites interested in meditation were quite eager to be a part of a network that could provide access to the Dalai Lama and other charismatic Buddhist leaders. They appreciated learning about the neuroscience and the psychology of meditation from distinguished scientists as well.

Local Program Leaders

Although leaders and educators of mindfulness programs in K-12 schools, the military, social services, and other sectors had comparably lower social status than Ph.D. scientists, venture capitalists who founded and led Fortune 500 companies, and charismatic religious and spiritual figures such as the Dalai Lama and Eckhart Tolle, they were very important to the contemplative movement. In fact, the movement would not exist without them. They were on the frontlines actually doing the work to bring meditation to new audiences in need of help, such as underprivileged kids and war veterans. They provided pragmatic legitimacy and legitimacy in their respective institutions to the movement.

For example, while visiting K-12 educators Ali and Atman Smith in Baltimore, Atman showed me a video clip on his phone of one of his tougher students. The HLF, the Smith brothers' organization, taught mindfulness and yoga to underprivileged students in the neighborhood they had grown up in. Atman prefaced the video by saying that when they started working with this boy, he would hit everyone. In the video, this skinny black boy jumped around in front of the phone in the school gymnasium. He wanted to go play outside. Atman told him they were staying in the gym. The boy ran over to try to open the door and it was locked. He ran back to Atman, saying he wanted to go outside. At one point, as the boy's frustration escalated, a smiling girl crossed between him and the camera. Atman said that before meditating, the boy would have hit her. Now, with his mindfulness practice, the boy instead dropped to the ground and lay down, focusing on his breath.

Because of stories like this, elite funders, scientists, and others were eager to speak with leaders of successful mindfulness programs. Success stories showed that contemplative interventions were doing important work that had a positive social impact. This gave the movement pragmatic legitimacy and made funders and scientists feel good about the work they were doing.

Contemplative leaders, funders, and scientists additionally sought promising new programs to support and study. If they had evidence that contemplative programs did indeed help kids learn, increase active-duty military service members' resilience to chronic stress, heal veterans' posttraumatic stress disorder, and augment business professionals' health, creativity, and productivity, then it would be easier to expand the movement. With "scientific proof" that each kind of meditation intervention works, they would also be more likely to get federal funding and develop further studies and mindfulness interventions for people in more institutions.

The end result of all these interacting motivations and sources of legitimation for movement participation was that movement events were useful and important to all involved. Each participant group gained numerous legitimators and benefits from engaging in the movement.

The Many Purposes of Conferences and Stops on the Elite Circuit

Conferences served several main purposes for the contemplative movement. They attracted both long-time members and new people interested in the science of meditation or mindful interventions. The events invited new people and the media into the fold, where they showcased a parade of impressive people who meditated and had sophisticated reasons supporting why they did so. Scientific experts, wise adept contemplatives, professional and economic elites, and heroic mindfulness educators attested to the importance of mindfulness meditation; they legitimized the practice in many ways among successful, affluent people.

In addition, conferences and other informal visits on the mindful elite circuit helped convene contemplative leaders and pass along information on the movement's trajectory, challenges, and strategies. Leaders shared the latest scientific findings and met with esteemed religious and spiritual figures to seek guidance, with philanthropists to seek funding, and with program leaders to keep tabs on the latest and most effective contemplative pedagogies. Through it all, these movement leaders updated each other, raised questions about movement strategy, and sought feedback from other leaders on the current state of the contemplative field.

Based on the varied expertise of its leaders, the contemplative movement seemed to have what sociologist Marshall Ganz (2009) describes as *strategic capacity* in its conferences and in its organizational leadership. Organizations and fields with strategic capacity are run by teams of different people who have access to relevant skills and knowledge and the ability to draw on team members' diverse experiences. Collectively, teams with strategic capacity consider the many possible strategies at hand and settle upon innovative solutions. Having a diverse membership can provide organizations and movements with access to broad social networks, resources, and tactical repertoires of how to get things done in different settings. Due to the breadth of expertise and institutional membership of its leaders, the contemplative movement benefited from access to all of these resources.

Organizations with strategic capacity also tend to have leaders who are intrinsically motivated to do their work. Passionate personal commitments to meditation and progressive social change, as well as allegiance to top Buddhist leaders like the Dalai Lama, drove the contemplative leaders. As philanthropist Thomas Butler described during his talk at a contemplative conference in 2015, this movement was built on "passionate partnerships" that are "like a jazz band. It's like creating sounds with individuals who have different instruments to play, bringing them together and creating a sound that's beyond anything any one of them could do by themselves. And for me," he concluded, "that is spiritual."

A Downside to Elite-Driven Mobilization: Myopia

Despite the many advantages to convening elite contemplative leaders with their base at conferences, their format also had unintentional consequences. Especially in the beginning of the movement, leaders tended to recruit their friends, respected colleagues, and others who tended to be from similar sociodemographic backgrounds. Contemplative leaders tended to be affluent, white, well-educated, successful professionals. Thus, their culture tended to feel exclusive and highbrow—and it was. The cost of attending conferences was quite high. In addition to registration fees, most attendees had to travel to get to the meetings. And contemplative conferences were not always easy to get to: they were typically held in remote retreat centers or in expensive urban areas at reputable venues.

It is important to consider, beyond the sparkle and shine of the contemplative circuit, who was *not* present and what issues did *not* get raised. This became very apparent to Wisdom 2.0 organizers and attendees during the 2014 conference. Several protesters from Eviction Free San Francisco burst onto the stage during Google's talk on corporate mindfulness to bring attention to the housing crisis lower- and middle-class San Francisco residents faced due to the rapid growth of the tech industry in the area. Shouting on a bullhorn, one protester chanted, "Wisdom means stop displacement! Wisdom means stop surveillance! San Francisco's not for sale!" (Loncke 2014). Protester Amanda Ream explained in an article in the Buddhist magazine *Tricycle:*

> The tech industry's great economic boom is driving a housing crisis, with no-fault evictions increasing 175% since last year. The city doesn't keep track of how many people live in these apartments, but the Anti-Eviction Mapping Project estimates up to 3580 residents were no-fault evicted in 2013.
>
> I came to San Francisco like generations of people before me because I wanted to find the freedom to live out my ideals. And to practice the dharma—no other city has so many teachers and centers. It's a great place to find the teachings of the Buddha. The tech industry, Google and Facebook and their peers, have adopted the culture of this place.
>
> Just like the gentrification of a neighborhood where new, wealthy people displace people who have lived there longer, the dharma is undergoing a process of gentrification in San Francisco today. Lost is the bigger picture of the teachings that asks us to consider our interdependence and to move beyond self-help and addressing only our own suffering. The dharma directs us to feel the suffering of others . . .
>
> When I zipped up that banner in a bag to sneak it into the conference, I thought about the ways this action could contribute to a larger conversation among people of conscience about how to stop this crisis of economic inequality. But like our Mission District neighbors, the activists and the message of Eviction Free San Francisco were disappeared without a word, censored from the livestream of the event. As we were marched out of the hall by angry conference staff, the Google presentation carried on, asking the audience to

"check in with their body" about the conflict. No one addressed the issues we were raising, not then or later on in the conference. It was a case study in spiritual bypassing.

It's almost too easy to point this out at Wisdom 2.0. Most of the workshops offer lifestyle and consumer choices that are meant to help people heal from the harm, emptiness, and unsustainability associated with living under capitalism, but it does so without offering an analysis of where this disconnection comes from. The conference presents an evolution in consciousness of the wealthiest among us as the antidote to suffering rather than the redistribution of wealth and power.

Ream brought attention to the underbelly of spreading meditation by means of elites: structural inequalities and other social problems obvious to outsiders fail to be addressed within elite circles. This is not surprising given that people struggling to pay for rent or other basic needs will not be able to attend meditation retreats or other elite gatherings.

Ream additionally raised the question of whether instead of collectively addressing these complex, structural problems, elite contemplatives perpetuated a "gentrification of the dharma," which was increasingly detached from early contemplatives' Buddhist goals of increasing awareness of interdependence and feeling the suffering of others. Instead, she depicted contemplative elites as lost in the navel-gazing world of self-help. Instead of mobilizing to redistribute resources or political power to those in need, elites focused on improving their own well-being and interpersonal relationships. Ream suggested that the contemplative movement was teaching them to seek consumer-based lifestyle solutions to underlying feelings of anxiety, isolation, and a lack of meaning in their lives rather than attempting to build a broader, more inclusive community and initiate deeper social reform.

Ultimately, despite Ream's dramatic outburst at Wisdom 2.0, it seemed that her protest failed to have an impact on the affluent contemplative attendees. In the face of the contentious spike in inequality and subsequent housing crisis in the area that she raised awareness of—which tech workers were implicated in—conference attendees were instructed to merely check in with their body and soothe themselves rather than deeply consider and address the social problems Ream had raised. Such a response was a collective shrug in the face of others' suffering, and a return to self-centeredness, rather than a true reflection of interdependence. Affluent attendees seemed complicit in causing others harm. This response revealed hypocrisy at the core of the contemplative tech community.

Rich in Legitimacy and Resources, Yet Lacking in a Broader Perspective

At the helm of the contemplative movement were coteries of elites from various areas of expertise, including science, business, spirituality (Buddhist-inspired and other contemplative traditions), and mindfulness intervention programs. When working together, based on their various kinds of expertise, forms of established legitimacy, and access to resources (including cultural, social capital, and economic capital), the contemplative movement seemed to be a formidable, impressive force for social good. They had strategic capacity based on having an array of professional skillsets at their disposal. They seemed intellectually curious and argued that because of their devotion to contemplative practices, they were particularly adept at listening, learning, and growing from interactions with each other. At conferences, the movement came off as a group of incredibly competent, smart, successful, and kind people, who were sincerely devoted to helping others live more meaningful, impactful lives that could contribute to broader social growth and improvement. There is no doubt that the contemplatives' mobilization through elites, which enabled them to have so much social polish and to represent so many forms of legitimacy—scientific, professional, public, moral, and pragmatic—aided their rise in popularity among professionals and the broader American public over the past four decades. Through elites, contemplatives gained access to some of the most powerful institutions in the country and to considerable resources.

However, there were notable shortcomings due to contemplatives' choice to ground their initiatives in networks and organizations mainly comprising intellectual, economic, and spiritual elites. With their base in such groups, it was difficult for the movement to maintain awareness of the many privileges their members had that others who did not make it to their meetings lacked. Their movement risked becoming a solution for others like them rather than a source of broader social change that could address deep-seated social ills such as materialism and inequality.

PART III | Assessing the Contemplatives'
Success, 2013–2016

CHAPTER 8 | Collective Authenticity

THE MINDFULNESS MOVEMENT HAS surpassed its founders' initial expectations in many ways. Mindfulness and other contemplative practices have become wildly popular. They are not only embraced by professionals from institutions ranging from healthcare to sports, but are increasingly seen as legitimate aids to a litany of personal problems, such as stress, pain, burnout, and mental illness among the American public. In addition to countless mindfulness programs across healthcare, education, business, and other sectors, there is also a burgeoning market of mindful products available: you can scan your brain to assess your mental state; you can read about mindfulness; you can meditate through your phone; and you can even retreat from the world in total isolation in a hi-tech pod.[1]

Yesterday at a bookstore, I was shocked to see the number of mindfulness books offering advice on seemingly any life experience, ranging from pregnancy to nutrition. It was a noticeably different experience than when I started this project nearly a decade ago. Back then many scholars and friends had wondered why I wanted to investigate the source of practices they knew little about and considered unimportant. Now this is no longer the case: mindfulness has made it into the mainstream.

As a case in point, one of the first things I noticed upon entering the bookstore was a *Time* magazine special issue devoted solely to mindfulness. Flipping through its pages, I was surprised by the breadth of content included under the purview of mindfulness and the fact that I did not recognize the names of the articles' authors nor many of their quoted experts. One article caught my eye in particular. It encouraged people to stop and take more mindful breaks during the workday; the author suggested doing "mindful" activities throughout the day as wide-ranging as daydreaming and petting an animal.

As shown in Chapter 1 (with the media reporting on the American Enterprise Institute [AEI] event) and by the content at the bookstore, portrayals of mindfulness are increasingly shaped not only by contemplative leaders and by the growing field of mindful products, but also by portrayals of what mindfulness is from the media and from new advocates of mindfulness, many of whom may have little connection to the movement. Mindfulness has diffused beyond the bounds and influence of the mindful elite movement. Many reporters on the popularity of mindfulness depict it in far more secular and diffuse ways than contemplative program leaders (Van Dam et al. 2017). For example, a *Forbes* article on the Search Inside Yourself program at Google, which actually directly draws upon Buddhist tenets and practices, described it as

> a rock-solid business-friendly mindfulness course in three acts: train your attention, develop self-knowledge and self-mastery, and create useful mental habits . . . All Mindfulness is Good Mindfulness. It doesn't matter where or how you develop mindfulness. Doesn't matter why. Doesn't even matter what you do: meditation, yoga, prayer, therapy, gratitude, science-help practices, hiking, painting, exercise, etc. It's all *good*. (Essig 2012)

Such media attention may benefit contemplative programs by distancing the programs from their religious Buddhist roots, which may still be seen as problematic in secular spaces by some people. However, the attenuation of Buddhist influences is also evident as the contemplatives' work moves further into secular areas and into mainstream culture. As the Buddhist influences are taken out or transformed, new cultural products emerge. Even if many contemplatives can trace their work to Buddhist roots, by the time it reaches the public, it may seem completely secular—and by most measures (whether of descriptions, practices, or motives)—it may have become a new form of secular culture altogether. Contemplative culture is multivalent; it now has so many forms, and is sufficiently vague and amorphous, that it can appeal to nearly any audience.

I thought about how divergent the latest wave of mindful products was from the people I had met over the past decade. I reflected back on what I knew about the movement. The contemplative leaders' perspectives struck me as distinct from many of the pop-culture mindfulness books filling the bookstore's shelves. Most of the contemplatives I spoke with were committed to spreading Buddhist-inspired contemplative practice, which for many of them was inspired by transformative decade-long meditation practices, an optimistic progressive idealism, discontent with the capitalistic American status quo, and the belief that their experiences could be explained in part by scientific investigation. Knowing that contemplative practice had improved their lives in numerous ways, they hoped that spreading the practices throughout society would similarly transform others and make people more self-aware, thoughtful, caring, and compassionate to others. They believed contemplative practice would transform not only individuals but those around them in their everyday lives and communities. They truly believed that by spreading contemplative practice they would transform the world into a kinder, more socially engaged place. This is quite different from taking a break from work to daydream or to sit in isolation in a hi-tech pod.

At the center of the contemplative movement's work was a tension between their enduring commitments (1) to adapt contemplative culture to contemporary people's needs and subcultures in order to reach them and (2) to maintain authenticity to their Buddhist-inspired practices and their implicit ideologies. Critics viewed mindfulness proponents' commitment to adaptation as the biggest liability of contemplative culture and as compromising their authenticity to Buddhist values and practices. In the face of the considerable and often inaccurate media accounts of contemplative science, critics also questioned the veracity of scientific support for meditation. Given the competing tradeoffs and critiques about where to draw the line, how did the contemplative movement respond?

In light of these developments, many committed meditators—within the movement and outside of it—have raised questions about the authenticity of mindfulness to its Buddhist roots and to the progressive social values early contemplative founders were committed to. They have also brought into question scientific evidence supporting meditation. In this chapter I examine how contemplative leaders responded to the explosion in the popularity of mindfulness, which has dramatically increased their expert status domestically and internationally, while also growing beyond the reach of their influence. In the face of these changes and criticism about the expansion of mindfulness, contemplative leaders professed claims of authenticity, in which they renewed commitments to Buddhist-inspired contemplative practice, ethics, and social reform.

Individual and Collective Authenticity

Social psychologists suggest that, by virtue of having a self, humans are intrinsically motivated by a desire for authenticity. People want to view themselves favorably and to have authentic, meaningful, coherent lives in accordance with their most valued principles. Sociologists define *authenticity* as involving a person's assessments of what resonates or is false with regard to who they think they are. Typically, people are unaware of how authentic they are most of the time, but when value conflicts arise and one's character is called into question, one becomes aware of one's authenticity or inauthenticity (Erickson 1995). The authenticity of a person's character can be appraised by comparing their behavior to their identity standard of who they want to be and what they consider moral. After making this comparison, people feel good if they live up to their standard and bad if they fail to do so (Stets 2010). Consequently, based on the "authenticity motive," people strive for congruence between their values and their behavior, because incongruence leads to feelings of inauthenticity, and subsequent shame or guilt (Gecas 2000).

The most important basis of commitment to a group or movement may be authenticity, as authenticity can connect individuals' values with a group's moral and ideological systems. When a group's ideological and moral framework provides members with meaning, purpose, and significance, and thereby contributes to a sense of authenticity, members' commitment to a group will increase. Yet, little research exists on authenticity in social psychology and movements (Gecas 2000). The contemplative case fills this gap: authenticity claims and processes are at the core of this alterative movement. Most contemplatives strove to align their lives with Buddhist-inspired values such as compassion, kindness, and striving to relieve people's suffering. In kindling these commitments on and off the cushion, meditators also reaffirmed their commitments to contemplative practice and its proliferation.

When I spoke with Saki Santorelli, executive director of the Center for Mindfulness in Medicine, Health Care, and Society (CfM), in his office in Shrewsbury, Massachusetts, in 2015, he explained that "at the heart and soul of what happens" at CfM is the question of "How do you meet people in a way that translates to what seems to be called 'Eastern' into something that's available, accessible, understandable, commonsensical? And—and this is the big '*and*'—and not watered down?" Santorelli was fully aware of critiques that in translating religious spiritual practice to appeal to new audiences, important elements would be lost. "Most people, when you say to them that you want to take something and make it available to larger populations, the first thing they'll do is dilute it," he told me. Ultimately, however, he was not worried that would happen to the mindfulness movement.

"Why?" I asked.

Santorelli thought the contemplatives were different because they have "innate faith in the human genius, in the human capacity," which he thought was developed through mindfulness.

"So what are the most important facets you think that keep it [Eastern traditions] rich and keep them alive?" I asked.

"Well there's probably a lot of them," he responded. "The most essential one is my practice. I mean that," he said. He continued:

> It's my practice. And it's *your* practice. And it's every one of the teachers in this center's practice. And it's the staff members' practice. Because that's the way we are cultivating this capacity to be available. And awake. And to catch our habits, patterns, impulses. To be able to see them, to receive feedback about them even when it's uncomfortable. To look at the hard places. To argue and to still love each other. To hurt each other inadvertently and to still care about one another. So the practice is like the central axis around everything else. And you can say in a very real way, that if that's an axis, then it's really about awareness. That's the central axis.

Like most other contemplatives, Santorelli was not concerned about diluting and thereby losing the authentic contemplative practices they drew from Buddhism and other spiritual traditions. At their core, preeminent contemplative leaders I spoke with *had faith in the transformative power of devoted contemplative practice*. As new adopters developed committed practices under the guidance of good teachers, mindful proponents thought they would become more self-aware and better able to deal with challenges in collaboration with others. As a result, contemplative leaders assumed that with sufficient practice and mentorship, new generations of practitioners would, over time, become capable of responsibly passing on the torch of mindful practice.

However, since about 2013, a backlash from some reporters, Buddhist meditators, and academics has called into question the authenticity of the movement.[2] Such voices question the ways in which contemplatives have adapted Buddhism to appeal to secular professionals. Headlines such as "To Make a Killing on Wall Street, Start Meditating" (Burton and Effinger 2014) and press on the AEI event draw attention to examples in which Buddhist practices are being used to advance capitalistic pursuits. Critics wonder if contemplative programs have remained true to their Buddhist ethical roots or if contemplative leaders and educators have compromised Buddhist values to appeal to resource-rich professionals at the center of the capitalist system.

This sort of critique has a longstanding history in sociological theory on protest within organizations. Outsiders trying to work within dominant institutions can become coopted by powerholders (Selznick 1949).

Activist-minded institutional entrepreneurs are more susceptible to becoming "beholden" to the "institutions they intend to influence" than more autonomous movements (Katzenstein 1998: 9). This raises the question of whether meditators are succeeding in their goals of making society more compassionate and self-aware through their work bringing meditation into powerful secular institutions. Or, in the process of adapting meditation to make it attractive to professionals, perhaps meditation has been coopted as a tool to serve elites' self-interest, consolidate their power, and promote greater productivity, social control, and consumption.

A 2013 *Huffington Post* article by management scholar Ron Purser and Zen teacher David Loy illustrates the concern about the "McMindfulness" trend that has popularized meditation. First, they question the development of mindfulness into a "lucrative cottage industry" that draws new participants based on unfounded promises, such as the following:

> Business-savvy consultants pushing mindfulness training promise that it will improve work efficiency, reduce absenteeism, and enhance the "soft skills" that are crucial to career success. Some even assert that mindfulness training can act as a "disruptive technology," reforming even the most dysfunctional companies into kinder, more compassionate and sustainable organizations. So far, however, no empirical studies have been published that support these claims.

Second, Purser and Loy question the use of "Buddhist-inspired," arguing that it's a way of speaking out of both sides of one's mouth and makes no sense. Through pitching mindfulness as inspired by Buddhism, contemplatives set it in a tradition of "time-tested meditation methods"—while simultaneously declaring mindfulness as so thoroughly secularized as to relinquish "all ties and affiliations to its Buddhist origins."

Third, Purser and Loy note that, in decoupling Buddhist meditation from religious contexts to bring it to new audiences, contemplatives have changed the fundamental purpose of the practices. They have altered its intended ethical, transformative purpose to release practitioners from undesired, "unwholesome" mindsets in Buddhism, such as greed, attachment, and delusion to attain enlightenment, to instrumental aims such as improving health and aiding productivity at work.

Fourth, they bring attention to the importance of motivations in Buddhism. Rather than being an ethically neutral attention practice that reduces stress, Purser and Loy argue that in Buddhism there are good, "Right" applications of mindfulness (e.g., to help others) and bad "Wrong" uses of mindfulness (e.g., using focused attention to kill someone). Purser and Loy argue that mindfulness is a *distinct quality of attention* that is dependent upon and influenced by many other factors: the nature of our thoughts, speech and actions; our way of making a living; and our efforts to avoid unwholesome and unskillful behaviors, while developing those that are conducive to wise action, social harmony, and compassion . . . Right Mindfulness is guided by intentions and motivations based on self-restraint, wholesome mental states, and ethical behaviors—goals that include but supersede stress reduction and improvements in concentration.

Fifth, Purser and Loy argue that attention needs to be paid to serving the collective good rather than just relieving individual suffering. It is insufficient to teach people that institutional change will naturally follow from individual personal transformations. They argue that "today the three unwholesome motivations that Buddhism highlights—greed, ill will, and delusion—are no longer confined to individual minds, but have become institutionalized into forces beyond personal control," such as corporations, governments, and so forth, so the only way to pursue true change is to hold institutions accountable for the structural problems they perpetuate, such as overwork. They suggest that a mindful approach to business

> conveniently shifts the burden onto the individual employee: stress is framed as a personal problem, and mindfulness is offered as just the right medicine to help employees work more efficiently and calmly within toxic environments. Cloaked in an aura of care and humanity, mindfulness is refashioned into a safety valve, as a way to let off steam—a technique for coping with and adapting to the stresses and strains of corporate life.

According to this description, mindfulness operates as a Marxist "opiate," which comforts the suffering workers just enough so that they do not collectively organize to confront the structural sources of discomfort affecting them. This individualized "accommodationist" approach to change can lead to cooptation, Purser and Loy argue (c.f. Carrette and King 2004).

Authenticity as a Collective Performative Process

Critiques such as Purser and Loy's *Huffington Post* piece and the fallout from the AEI/Mind and Life Institute (MLI) event in 2014 provoked collective reflection within the contemplative movement. On multiple occasions over the past several years, contemplative leaders have convened to assess the movement's ideological commitments, mission, and mobilization strategy.[3] In these meetings, contemplatives maintained their sense of authenticity in multiple ways. In doing so, they demonstrated that authenticity could go beyond an individual motivation or reflective process in which a person assesses what rings true or false as it is commonly assumed to be; *collective authenticity could also occur as a group process through which movements assess whether their values, purpose, actions, and trajectory are in accordance with who they want to be as a group.* For the contemplatives, it seemed that the act of collectively meeting to assess group values, actions, purpose, and strategies served in itself as a rejoinder to critics' claims of inauthenticity. Such collective assessments not only could build strategic capacity to make a movement more efficacious in rapidly changing circumstances (as discussed in Chapter 7), but enable groups to *identify and enact cherished practices and values, thereby demonstrating their authenticity to members.* This served to further encourage loyalty and commitment among a movement's base. As canonical social theorists Emile Durkheim (1995 [1912]) and Randall Collins (2005) argue, convening around a group's key commitments and enacting esteemed group rituals create a sense of collective effervescence that fortifies collective identity and commitment to group membership. Collective affirmations of authenticity, I argue, are central to shaping and maintaining collective identity. However, to be truly effective in mobilization efforts, acts of collective authenticity must be used as an engine driving further collective action.

The contemplative movement enacted collective authenticity in various ways at the CfM's annual conference, titled "Meeting the World: Exploring Ethics, Values, and Responsibility of Bringing Mindfulness into Society," held at the University of Massachusetts in Shrewsbury, Massachusetts from April 10 to 12, 2015. First, in response to critiques of the movement, leaders grounded the meeting in contemplative ethics and a sense of social responsibility. Second, representing one of the largest contemplative organizations in the field and the movement as a whole, contemplative leaders embodied and modeled contemplative practice and values to their base of members. Third, contemplative leaders structured the meeting so that attendees could actively participate to enact democratic values and mindful collective inquiry. The group reflected on contemplative ethics and social responsibility, brainstormed collective strategy, and provided feedback to CfM. These strategies all created a sense of collective authenticity within the movement.

Collective Intention Setting

In response to the growing public critiques of mindfulness, CfM's 2015 annual conference initiated a process of reflecting upon, revitalizing, and deepening the movement's roots in Buddhist-inspired ethics. At the outset of the conference, contemplative leaders set the intention and agenda for the meeting to assess the values and social responsibilities of members' contemplative work. Santorelli opened the conference with the following speech:

> What brings us here is our values. What brings us here is our morality. What brings us here is a sense of responsibility. And I can tell you that for me, that always carries with it a deep undergirding sense of devotion. I'm not going to say to what. But that shouldn't be left out of our conversation, no matter what we call it. Because to be part of a lineage that has sustained itself across thousands of years—well more than 2,600 years—means we all carry something within us. We each actually are the lineage. It isn't as if it is some disembodied thing from some time ago. And yet, in another very real way, at least for me, there is a chain of beings. And this meeting is just an occasion to honor that and how we express that today in 2015 and beyond. So thank you for being in this living room.

Throughout his welcoming remarks, Santorelli sought to instill a sense of a moral, Buddhist-inspired community. He invited the people in the audience to participate in the organization's soul-searching, making them feel like important contributing members. He told the audience that the goal of the conference was to collectively "identify key ethical principles, values, and responsibilities for bringing mindfulness into society" through discussion and dialogue. As he spoke, he used inclusive language such as "we," "our," and "us." Such language fortified a sense of membership, reviving feelings of collective identity. Santorelli seemed to assume that as part of that identity, like him, other conference participants were not only committed to—but devoted to—promoting contemplative practices grounded in a Buddhist tradition dating back millennia.

Enacting Authenticity

During their conference presentations, contemplative leaders demonstrated authenticity in the following ways:

- They *addressed claims of inauthenticity by hearkening directly back to Buddhist and scientific primary texts and leaders.*
- In the face of critiques that their interventions did not enact social reform, they affirmed their commitment to use mindful practices to

advance social reform by *providing their own evidence of their past, present, and future commitments to social reform.*

- They *embodied their teachings and practices* in their meeting, modeling their values and practices.
- They *used the conference space as a trial classroom, where they experimented and brainstormed new ways of collectively addressing social problems,* thereby demonstrating the movement's commitment to collaborative inquiry, learning, and social reform and its willingness to innovate and improve its teaching techniques.

Below, excerpts from three contemplative leaders' conference presentations show the different ways they responded to critiques about mindfulness by cultivating collective authenticity. Although the examples are from a single conference, at all the other conferences I attended I witnessed similar performances in which contemplatives enacted authenticity by identifying, assessing, and thereby fortifying their movement's most cherished values, practices, and collective identity.[4]

Citing Buddhist Religious and Scientific Authorities

Following Santorelli's welcoming statement, neuroscientist Dr. Judson Brewer, the director of research at CfM, spoke about the ethical foundations of mindfulness and the need to further embed mindfulness in Buddhist ethics.[5] Brewer demonstrated the authenticity of the contemplative movement by hearkening back to Theravada texts, renowned Buddhist modernist and mindful teachers, and Buddhist philosophy on ethics. In doing so, he fortified ties between mindfulness and its foundational Buddhist elements among the contemporary base of the mindfulness community. In addition, he reaffirmed the movement's commitment to science, grounding his talk equally in Buddhist sources and scientific research.

In a culture dominated by rapid-fire online posting on social media and anonymous bullying, Brewer first emphasized the need for cultural change. Brewer explained that such phenomena resulted from people's addiction to short-term positive feelings of personal empowerment at the expense of others. Bullying, he explained, is a negative habit, but it continues because it briefly makes perpetrators feel more powerful. "Modern-day psychologists describe this process in terms of positive and negative reinforcement," he said. As his Buddhist teacher Joseph Goldstein had also taught him, he said, "We see the world through a certain view and if we keep seeing the world that way, we're gonna perpetuate habits that way." Brewer continued, "There's a saying that summarizes this from the [Pali Buddhist text] *Majihima Nikaya* 19: 'Whatever a person frequently thinks and ponders upon, that will become the inclination of the mind.' We reinforce habits this way."

In his talk, Brewer simplified and interwove perspectives from Buddhist texts and psychology to make his ultimate point that people develop both good and bad habits that have positive and negative outcomes, respectively, for the actors and those around them. Given the human proclivity for habit formation and the prevalence of bad habits, Brewer argued, "*there's got to be some kind of ethical quality here*" (italics added for emphasis).

In the face of such harmful habits, Brewer said that mindfulness, intertwined with Buddhist ethics, was needed. As "one of the nineteen universal beautiful factors" in the canonical Theravada Buddhist *Abhidharma* texts, he said, mindfulness was always interrelated with, and co-arose with, other ethical elements in Buddhism. Mindfulness derived from the Buddhist concept of *sati*, he said, which meant "to remember" and signified "attentiveness to the present." Mindfulness had the "characteristic of not wobbling. Not floating away from an object . . . Staying with the object. Its function . . . [is] the absence of confusion." Mindfulness from a Buddhist perspective, Brewer suggested, was "wholesome" and "skillful" because it enabled practitioners to see lucidly, free from the states that Buddhists avoid such as "craving, aversion, and delusion." Without those states, which make one's mind wobble and forget, mindful practitioners could "see clearly what we are doing so that we can begin to make wiser choices. So if we bring one of the meanings of mindfulness or roots to remember, to call to mind, we can call to the mind what increases or decreases suffering. We can remember what we did last time to see if it was harmful or helpful." Brewer concluded by arguing that the contemplative community needed to revise its definition to more explicitly incorporate Buddhist ethics, as his teacher Goldstein had advised:

> So let's bring this back to this definition of mindfulness. How does the definition that Jon [Kabat-Zinn] outlined fit with what Joseph was talking about and what I'm talking about this morning? Paying attention, so that's the observing. That fits pretty well. In the present moment nonjudgmentally—so free from reactivity: this is the mindfulness that's free from craving, aversion, and delusion.
>
> But I would add a third component here that it doesn't happen in a vacuum . . . We're constantly building who we are, and so if we remember previous actions we can iteratively learn. And I would argue that's what mindfulness can help us do. When we can see clearly with the intention of reducing suffering in the world, then suddenly there's a framework where we can iteratively learn. . . . So I'm going to put this out there for discussion, that there

actually is an ethical quality suffused in there, as Joseph argues in his talk. And it fits very nicely in the way in which ancient and modern psychology understand how the mind works and how we iteratively learn.

In his talk, Brewer performed authenticity in several ways. As the research director of CfM, he represented one of the central organizations in the movement. As such, he honored and fortified the Buddhist and scientific foundation of mindfulness by grounding his talk in Buddhist texts and teachers' perspectives as well as scientific convictions. Based on these perspectives, he concluded that to practice mindfulness properly, the Buddhist aspiration of reducing suffering in the world had to be invoked. Thus, he reaffirmed his Buddhist *vipassana* teacher, Joseph Goldstein's perspective. He also responded to critics who suggested that mindfulness needed to better incorporate Buddhist values into its teachings. He agreed, and he used such critiques to strengthen Buddhist values and authenticity in the heart of the mindfulness community.

Using Contemplative Culture in Social Engagement

Diana Chapman Walsh, former Harvard professor, president of Wellesley College and current MLI board member, began her talk by referencing Shakespeare's play *The Tempest*. For the contemplative movement, "The winds are blowing, the seas are rising. It's a little stormy," she said. "We are becoming so popular that we don't quite know what to do about our popularity, worrying that it will create all kinds of distortions." A particular distortion made about the contemplative movement, she said, was that it was out of touch and too disconnected from social problems.

Chapman Walsh addressed this claim by making the case that contemplatives have always been and remain committed to social reform. She argued that, based on her time with the Dalai Lama and "carefully" reading volumes on MLI's dialogues with "His Holiness," from the very beginning of MLI, the contemplative movement had always been committed to social reform. The Dalai Lama had "always" had a "larger vision" about the needs of the world, she said, citing a passage that he wrote in the introduction to a 2008 MLI publication: "The more we pursue material improvement, ignoring the contentment that comes of inner growth, the faster ethical values will disappear . . . Then we will all experience unhappiness in the long run, for when there is no place for justice and honesty in people's hearts, the weak are the first to suffer. And the resentments resulting from such inequity ultimately affect everyone" (Goleman 2008: xiv). This statement, Chapman Walsh argued, brought attention to the need for the contemplative movement to be more socially engaged, to think about long-term consequences, and to address the "overheated materialism [that] is crowding out the ethical values and the compassion more and more in our world." Thus, she returned to the initial values of key contemplative founders, such as CfM's Jon Kabat-Zinn and MLI's Adam Engle (as discussed in Chapter 3). She reiterated the importance of using contemplative culture to counteract materialism by reaffirming the importance of inner development, ethics, and compassion.

Chapman Walsh then cited the relationship of the Dalai Lama and MLI as an exemplar of contemplative values. She showed the audience a photo of MLI president Arthur Zajonc and the Dalai Lama greeting each other by bowing and touching foreheads. "I love this picture," Chapman Walsh declared. "In some ways it says it all, I think [on] Mind and Life and social engagement." It shows, she said,

> The affection. The shared concern about suffering, relieving suffering, promoting flourishing between these two individuals towards the ends of their careers with their great passion for their work and so much they have contributed. The power of that transmission. Transmission in this case from forehead to forehead, from mind to mind . . .
>
> I had the chance to experience it at a meeting in Mundgod, in South India, where in the middle of a program, I was moderating . . . all of a sudden he [the Dalai Lama] took ten minutes and spoke deeply from his heart about his concern about the suffering in the world and how comfortable we all were and the work that needed to be done. And so it stays with you.
>
> And this question about the erosion of ethical sensibilities . . . His Holiness contacted Arthur Zajonc and asked him to meet him in his hotel room for breakfast for a briefing to bring to him the results of work that had been done. And Arthur mentioned it briefly when he was here on the stage—to develop a curriculum and a program and a strategy for moving a compassion education together with emotional and social learning out into the world and schools in the U.S. and around the world. This is something the Dalai Lama had very much wanted.

Chapman Walsh tried to substantiate the authenticity of MLI in several ways. First, in showing the close relationship between MLI and the Dalai Lama and implicitly grounding MLI's work in the Dalai Lama's encouragement and support, she provided evidence that the movement remained true to its Buddhist roots. Second, she sought to show the authenticity of the Dalai Lama and Zajonc, as leaders of MLI, by providing personal examples of times when she had seen them reflect on their commitments to advancing Buddhist values such as relieving suffering, as well as the contemplative mission to initiate social reform through educational contemplative interventions.

Of course, critics may view the photo she referenced differently. After all, here are elites from higher education, including a former president of one of the best private liberal arts colleges in the world, who are collaborating with one of the most esteemed charismatic leaders in the world, to advance their own social agenda. Although the photo certainly shows the affection between the two, we could ask what they have accomplished on the ground to help "normal" people. This is the question Chapman Walsh next addressed.

She turned to the topic of the contemplative interventions MLI had promoted during Zajonc's leadership. In the face of MLI's support for applied contemplative interventions (and arguably in the wake of the AEI incident), MLI experienced an internal backlash from its "core constituency" of scholars, she said. These long-time members reminded MLI leadership that during the organization's twenty-seven-year history, the organization had been committed to upholding "scientific rigor." MLI scientists raised "concerns about whether we were getting out in front of the science, whether we should think twice before moving into applications, think carefully about how we did it," Chapman Walsh said. In response to the scientists' critiques, MLI board chair (and translator for the Dalai Lama) Thupten Jinpa and Chapman Walsh called thirty core members of MLI, wrote a report on their feedback, and used the report to reassess MLI's mission with the board. The board responded by revising MLI's mission to the "primary mission to promote critical inquiry, research and understanding. That's the raison d'être; that's where this organization has come from and how it has grown," Chapman Walsh acknowledged. But in moving forward, the board also approved the development of contemplative interventions, "emphasizing the iterative development of applications, selectively chosen, and avoiding always getting drawn into advocacy." Chapman Walsh assured the audience they took heed not to become "vendors . . . trapped in a sales mode where you've developed something and you really believe in it and you lose your objectivity. That's critically important." This is a very blurry boundary for her, and her organization, to be operating in.

In this messy boundary area, she said, in which it was unclear at times what the right thing to do was, she referred back to a contemplative "leadership lesson" from when she was a "rookie president" at Wellesley. "One of the things that a consultant told me early on," she explained, was "when you're lost in the forest, . . . you stand still. You stand still, you take a deep breath and then you remember to breathe out. And then you ask yourself, 'What is my role and what is my task?' It's an amazingly clarifying question to ask," she said. "It operates on many levels . . . It's also a vocational question if you move it to another level. What is my work? What is right work? . . . And on an ethical and spiritual [level], what is my life, my one wild and precious life? So it's a helpful compass, I believe."

Thus, in the face of an ethical quandary for MLI, Chapman Walsh exhibited her authenticity to the practice and to the movement: when in doubt, she resorted to her practice. Not only did she focus on her breath and take time to "be still," but she also raised deeper contemplative questions about what "right work," is, and what an "ethical and spiritual" life is, in order to choose next steps when facing challenges.

Chapman Walsh concluded her talk by discussing MLI's next big project: the Academy for Contemplative and Ethical Leadership. The Academy was led by highly regarded organizational and management scholars such as leadership professor Bill George from Harvard Business School, Chapman Walsh, Dan Goleman (Harvard Ph.D. psychologist and emotional intelligence expert), and MIT systems scholars Peter Senge and Otto Scharmer. The goal of MLI's leadership training program, Chapman Walsh said, was to help participants shift from an "ego system awareness to an ecosystem awareness." More specifically, they sought to open "hearts" and "minds" by deepening a focus on "the inner aspect of leadership and also to emphasize the collective systemic factors in leadership," Chapman Walsh explained. More specifically, they would facilitate inquiry into "situated ethics," as embedded in social systems and relationships, with "a focus clearly on contemplation and compassion."

On the one hand, this program exemplified how contemplative leaders developed interventions that incorporated Buddhist values and contemplative practices to inculcate a sense of social responsibility and serve as professional development. In addition, the program addressed shortcomings of the movement, such as critiques that the contemplative movement was not sufficiently aware of systemic and institutional social contexts. Thus, from the perspectives of program developers, and even of the contemplative audience at CfM's conference, such work aligned with the values and mission of the contemplative movement; it seemed an authentic response to critics.

However, when considering MLI's new focus on leadership development from a perspective of inclusion and socioeconomic inequality, the program could be viewed as discordant from the movement's lofty aspirations to promote democracy and equality. With a heightened focus on developing leadership, MLI continued to apply mobilization strategies the movement had used for decades. What was particularly evident with their new leadership training initiative was that MLI continued to use elite-led and elite-focused interventions to advance social reform, rather than developing direct applications for underprivileged groups. This provided further evidence of MLI's, and arguably many parts of the movement's, strategy of initiating social change by transforming the hearts and minds of society's most privileged, rather than grounding change initiatives in under-resourced communities. This raised further questions of who, in fact, contemplative programs were designed to serve.

An Innovative Application: Using Mindful Collective Inquiry to Raise Awareness of 'the Other'

In many ways, the contemplative community is a social bubble. As discussed in Chapter 7, the core membership of the movement was far more likely to be affluent, educated, and white than the typical American. At CfM's conference, there were only a handful of nonwhite folks, including two renowned contemplative leaders: Rhonda Magee, a law professor at the University of San Francisco, and George Mumford, the mindfulness teacher of Phil Jackson's basketball teams (including the likes of Michael Jordan and Kobe Bryant). Mumford discussed with me over lunch, as well as in his public talk at the conference, the discomfort he continued to experience in the contemplative community due to his race. He said that fewer people tended to approach him at conferences than other speakers. Another black contemplative leader I had met at a prior conference recounted similar experiences of feeling marginal and devalued compared to white leaders at some contemplative meetings. (For example, at a Kabat-Zinn and Santorelli retreat, the black educator had been asked if he was a member of the staff.)

During her talk, Magee did something I had not seen at any prior contemplative gathering: she talked explicitly about the dehumanizing and even lethal effects of racial prejudice and discrimination in America to a predominantly white group of meditators. To show the contemplatives present how dire racial inequality is in the United States, she showed video footage of Eric Garner's 2014 death at the hands of New York Police Department officers.

Before showing the video, she invited audience members to settle "into the depth of your practice right now as a support for turning toward . . . the suffering around this issue." She then explained that, based on her insight meditation practice over the past twenty years, she believed mindfulness practice inherently supports ethical means of addressing social problems:

> For me the insights of the practices are really what assist me in the sense of the right and wrongness of the actions that I need to take in the world. Some

of those insights include the interconnectedness of every single entity of all of us, my brothers and sisters in this room, recognizing that in this space we are creating a community together and in every space in which we exist with any other human being, there's something deep and interconnecting already existent between us that we have the potential to tap into. All of that can help be a guide for right action around these challenging issues around race. They really can if we can be present to them. And mindfulness as a way of helping deepen again the capacity of working with the challenges, learning from, growing together through them. Not . . . denial around these issues, or minimizing these issues, but really turning into them. How it is that both we have the capacity to do this that's strengthened by our practice and the commitments that come from them, but also we have a way of sensing into the joy, if you will. And I don't mean that as a light word: I mean joy as in the joy that undergirded Martin Luther King in his work, Gandhi in his work, a joy that comes from a deep abiding sense of love that is coming from that sense of interconnectedness, of the light and the treasure that is in every single human being. So those are the kind of touchstones that I want to turn us toward but with some spaciousness. Yes. And with some capacity to sort of breathe in and turn toward, bearing witness to what's going on in our world.

Magee radiated authenticity by practicing mindfulness during her talk to prepare the audience to witness a tragic, unjust event. In accordance with Buddhist ideology, she explained that contemplative practices transform one's perspective by raising awareness of the interconnectivity among people, fostering care and love, and enabling practitioners to develop the ability to turn toward, rather than away from, suffering. Furthermore, like other CfM conference speakers, Magee articulated mindfulness as a practice that honed both ethical inquiry and "right action," from Buddhist and social justice perspectives.

Magee then facilitated an experimental lesson on racial injustice for the contemplative audience by showing them a video of the last moments of Garner's life. As a professor, Magee said, she had used the lesson to teach her law students, but she had never taught a contemplative audience about race and police brutality before. With this lesson, she sought to pose "a radical question" to the mindfulness community. She suggested that her lesson modeled how "we might infuse some of our teachings of MBSR [Mindfulness-Based Stress Reduction] with at least some of these kinds of practices" to bear witness, turn "toward suffering," and raise awareness of suffering not only in "our daily communities" but among "people who are suffering at the bottom of a system of kind of ongoing and historically generated oppression." This, she said, "is some of the hardest" suffering.

As she started the video, she reminded everyone to pause and bring to bear their practice in witnessing challenges, "right here, right now, together with the support of this community." Initiating mindful practice among the audience, she asked them to notice "what arises for you as we turn toward this right now."

The clip started rolling. It showed a prolonged conversation between Garner and two NYPD officers on a sidewalk. The police officers surrounded Garner on two sides. Garner said he was not doing anything. The police accused him of selling cigarettes. Another male voice supported him, saying he was just sitting there. Garner got frustrated with the police. He said, "Every time you see me, you want to mess with me. I'm tired of it . . . I'm minding my business, officer. Why don't you just leave me alone?" The four officers surrounded him and forcibly took him down onto the ground. One officer put him into a headlock. The officers handcuffed him. As they held him down, he began to say, "I can't breathe."

Watching this video, my heart raced and the hair on my arms stood on end. It was horrifying. I looked around and everyone was raptly watching the video.

Garner continued repeating, "I can't breathe," as officers held down all parts of his body, smashing his face into the sidewalk. More police appeared in the video and no one intervened. Garner continued to say, "I can't breathe."

Magee turned off the video. She was visibly upset. Hesitating, she turned toward the video and then back toward the audience. She took a deep breath. "I can't even . . .," she started to say and then trailed off. Then, more matter-of-factly, she stated, "Fourteen times they say, he said, 'I can't breathe,'" she said. "Fourteen times he was ignored there." We need to "turn toward this as an example of what is actually happening in our communities and what people who come to our classes in MBSR, who we meet on the street have witnessed, might be carrying with them, might have actually maybe experienced some version of," she said. "You'd be surprised how many people have experienced some version of painful interaction with the police."

She next made a proposal. Rather than bringing mindfulness to where it was strategically convenient, Magee raised the question of how mindfulness interventions could be used to bring people's attention to issues that were morally and socially important, such as "the injustice that we've just witnessed . . . [of] a man losing his life in an altercation with police" over a claimed "misdemeanor of selling loose cigarettes on the street. How can mindfulness help us address this kind of injustice that is happening with alarming frequency," such as "guns being pulled on people after being stopped and people being let go, no apology? So again, this is touching into a large set of issues that we often don't take mindfulness to, but this conference is about bringing mindfulness into the world, looking where the suffering is and asking how can our practices, how can these beautiful teachings that have been translated for delivery, if you will, into a world that is starving for much. How can we bring these practices to bear?"

To answer that question, Magee brought up more examples of black men killed by U.S. police officers, suggesting that teaching mindfulness practice to deepen "focus, concentration, and understanding what's going on" and emotional regulation in the face of anxiety might not only help prevent more deaths of people of color, but also avoid the negative repercussions that officers face from such actions, like jail time. When triggered, Magee explained, people experience what Buddhists described as an "internal knot." Bringing "benevolent awareness to those knots can really transform them. And again, that can be both in the officers and the people who are being accosted by the police."

She then provided an example in which staying calm throughout a life-threatening situation with police saved the life of Brian Stevenson, a famous African-American death penalty lawyer and graduate of Yale Law School. He was pulled over by a cop and a gun was put to his head, she said, but he survived in part "because he was able to say to the officer, 'This is gonna be okay. We're gonna get through this.'" Magee concluded:

> Increasing capacity for perspective taking and compassion, which in part was a bit of what was going on with Brian Stevenson: he was aware that that cop was already seeming triggered against him, calling him the N word. And still Brian was able to say, "We're gonna get through this." What does it take to be able to do that in the face of that kind of threat? Something profound. A kind of grace. A kind of inner strength that these practices, actually I can say in my own experience, have helped develop.

Magee once again demonstrated authenticity by drawing upon her personal experience with contemplative practice to support her claims that mindfulness could be used to address racial injustice. The expansion of mindfulness content to include issues of racial inequality, she suggested, would align with the goals of Buddhist-inspired contemplative practice, the movement's goals, and the purpose of the CfM conference by increasing awareness of injustice and reducing suffering in the world.

Magee reiterated that lessons like the one she facilitated were a way to create an "opening to asking how can MBSR make a particular contribution to how we as individuals, we in interaction together in our personal communities and our families, in our schools, our job sites, and in our MBSR classrooms, how can we work more effectively and be more better prepared to change the world around these issues?"

To answer these questions, Magee provided examples of how mindfulness could be used to ameliorate the effects of personal experiences with racism, subtle interpersonal racism, and systematic racism. At a personal level, for example, stereotype threat can occur. "Stereotype threat," she explained, "is a psychological concept that helps us understand what happens when you're afraid you're going to be stereotyped. All your energies start to go toward avoiding being stereotyped. They get in the way of performing well in school. They get in the way of performing well in all kinds of areas." She said that this contributed to persisting performance gaps between black and white American students.[6] "It's not just about kids and students not being well prepared and coming from bad families and all those kinds of dominant narratives," she said. "Stereotypes are being dropped on them and they are not thriving in these environments." Mindfulness, she thought, could help reduce subtle forms of racism pervading education and stereotype threat by helping people "recognize both when we might be stereotyping someone – and check that – and when we might be starting to feel the effects as a victim or target of stereotypes." There is "at least one really good study," she said, "that indicates that a bit of training in mindfulness can help inoculate against the effects of stereotype threat."

At an interpersonal level, Magee explained how racism occurs through subtle microaggressions and stereotypes, such as when teachers ask racial minority students to speak on behalf of their whole race, or when white people ask to touch black people's hair. Although many white Americans do not notice and define these experiences as "racist," these acts make salient and reinforce essentialized views of race, and contribute to enduring interpersonal, structural, and systemic inequalities between whites and racial/ethnic minorities. People such as police officers, teachers, and students could become more aware of their unconscious, unintentional racism through lessons such as Magee's, which could be taught in conjunction with mindfulness training.

Finally, in the tradition of engaged Buddhism, Magee advocated for a bold new vision of mindfulness training in which mindfulness practice would be combined with other social justice traditions to more directly address systemic injustice and inequality:

> I just wanted to put the systemic piece up there because that's a piece we typically don't talk about in MBSR or don't see as part of our work. I think there

are ways that we can practice together that do bear on systemic solutions. So practices: a curated set of mindfulness-based practices that assist people in working with these experiences. Processing them more effectively with compassion for ourselves and for each other as we go through this that can actually help us in this sort of a tradition we might call *engaged mindfulness*. Picking up off Thich Nhat Hanh and other teachers who use the notion of engaged Buddhism, but engaging mindfulness to actually help change the world. So we're talking about familiar practices—sitting with awareness, compassion, self-compassion as examples.

But we're also talking about some new practices, storytelling practices, interweaving our stories together so we see that we are a beautiful mosaic, we are both individual and part of systems whose experience co-arise. There isn't a black woman's experience without a white man's experience. What's that about? There isn't a subordinated, segregated, ineffective school experience without some privileged effective school experience somewhere else. How are our lives intertwined and what can we do better to resolve the inequities around that? We can talk about it in stories, we can do sending and receiving practice borrowed from Tibetan Buddhism—the *tonglen* practice. We could do restorative justice circles, which come from more indigenous traditions [and out of South Africa] in terms of their contemplative practice. So these are not all Buddhist-based; it's a broader set of contemplative approaches, but things that are working.

Similar to Chapman Walsh, Magee ended her talk by responding to perceived shortcomings of the contemplative movement. She suggested new ways the movement could address systemic problems. She focused on enhancing mindfulness programs by adding content and practices that would raise awareness of people's different experiences due to their social positions, while also emphasizing their connections despite those differences.

Like Brewer and other contemplative leaders, Magee walked a fine line between maintaining authenticity to the movement's Buddhist roots and addressing contemporary social problems. She justified updating mindfulness interventions based on Buddhist modernist precedents, noting Zen master Thich Nhat Hanh's support for socially engaged Buddhism. However, to appeal to more diverse audiences, she also recommended bringing in practices and insights from other wisdom traditions, such as indigenous and South African trust and reconciliation practices. Importantly, Magee's talk was distinct from Brewer's and Chapman Walsh's appeals to collective authenticity because she laid out a multifaceted path forward that explained how contemplatives could engage more directly with systemic structural problems, such as racism and police violence, on the ground in local communities.

Magee's talk was followed by a question-and-answer session with the audience and an afternoon breakout discussion on racial injustice and the mindfulness community. CfM leaders had designed the conference so it would be more amenable to community building and brainstorming using the "collective intelligence of members," as Santorelli said on the first day. The format included more time for audience discussion and feedback than prior annual conferences. Santorelli explained that CfM hoped to elicit key points of interest from its members, so at the end of each session, a facilitator took notes on the collective lessons learned during the session. Time was also allotted for breakout sessions where attendees could further discuss topics of interest in small groups following the morning sessions. On the last day of the conference, a final cumulative session was held to reflect on the sessions and synthesize the main points covered for CfM leaders.

These structural innovations to the conference format were, in themselves, a means of authenticating CfM leaders' democratic values and aspirations to be inclusive and transparent, to listen to their members, and together to commit to shared values and responsibilities with regard to promoting mindfulness. The changes signaled an effort to shift more responsibility onto the members, who helped establish the parameters and standards of the movement's authenticity and brainstorm how to advance their work together.

As an audience member, the open dialogue portions with all conference attendees in the CfM auditorium and during breakout sessions seemed chaotic. Anyone could participate, and people brought very different ideas and concerns to the forum. For example, in the discussions that followed Magee's talk on racial injustice in the United States, conference attendees juggled a lot of challenges simultaneously, such as how to address racial homophily and ignorance, racial and socioeconomic privileges in the mindfulness community, pervasive forms of racial and economic inequality in the country, and how to confront such problems with mindfulness in an authentic way.

In a two-hour afternoon breakout group on race and mindfulness, several dozen people crammed into a corner of CfM's large dining room. We were arranged in a sort of oval, with people sitting wherever they could fit on chairs and tables. Participants struggled with what to focus on during their limited time together. Some attendees shared what they had learned emotionally and cognitively from Magee's lesson on police brutality. One woman said she realized she had a "thirst" to know more, and that the talk brought to light a symbolic internal Buddhist "knot" she had been unconsciously carrying. A few folks reflected on the privileges they have that others do not due to the color of their skin, such as feeling safe around police. Another man recommended that others read scholar Peggy McIntosh's 1988 article on "the invisible knapsack" of privileges that white people carry.

Others struggled with the tension of whether to practice mindfulness in the face of the challenge of American racism, or whether to act in order to initiate social reform. As one older man with white hair sitting to my right said at the beginning of the meeting, "it's frustrating to want to hear from" as well as "be with and have this feeling with" everyone and to have "this wonderful opportunity to . . . give suggestions back to the center." While several women mentioned the "urgency" of creating a plan as soon as possible, suggesting that CfM work to increase the number of practitioners of color in the mindfulness community, as well as to incorporate more content on social diversity and inequality in courses, others disagreed. After the women made suggestions for new organizational strategies, for example, the older man with white hair interjected that the group should stop and reflect before jumping into action. He recommended that the group "sit [in meditation] for a few minutes."

Witnessing this discussion, I wondered if this democratic conversation, which represented various perspectives yet seemed to be meandering aimlessly across a lot of topics, would yield any practical results. At that point, midway through the conversation, Kabat-Zinn stepped in, tying the wandering discussion back to the core of contemplative philosophy and practice. "Even in this room, every single one of us is in a different room," he said. Yet:

> part of the beauty of being human and social creatures is that we're co-constructing a community and a nest and a space that holds us in this room at this moment. But every single one of us has a different sunlight coming in differently—the angles, the colors, where we are positioned in the room. We're all in different rooms and we're all the same. And I think it's really important to recognize the unity in the duality and the duality in the unity.And then note: [a] wisdom orientation would be to deny none of it . . .
>
> But this is where the rubber meets the road in terms of liberative mindfulness, embodied practice. And *none of us* has the inside angle on it. We need each other to co-create something that I *do* believe unifies this element. Unifies CNN and Fox News. Unifies the Republicans and Democrats. Recognizes a kind of core humanity where fear is fear: doesn't matter whether you're black or white—fear is fear. We all experience it . . . We all have that

experience of disregard, so we need to in some sense generate an entirely new *ethic* . . . around how we are to conduct ourselves moment by moment. And how we are to be in relationship to narrative, so it is both nurturing, and not ultimately, or romantically, or unromantically, traumatically, or racefully, a prison. And in order to do that I think you need a *collaborative* inquiry. And that is exactly what we're adding here at this conference and at this circle. And I just want to give to the conversation. Every single person who gets up and speaks, offers something; it is *profoundly valuable*. And where it's going? We don't really know. But just as I emphasize with MBSR, the point is not to jump to magical solutions—it is to actually to remain inside the holding of, the naming of, the externality of things as they really are. And by doing that, we have already transformed things as they are. These are just the thoughts off of the top of my head—because you know, I find this so *emotional*. (Italics indicate speaker's emphasis)

Here Kabat-Zinn grounded the conversation in contemplative values and ideology by applying the contemplative philosophy of nonduality. Like other contemplatives, Kabat-Zinn believed that to be human was to be involved in a process of life in which people simultaneously had their own seemingly separate experiences, yet also shared universal experiences, emotions, and interactions with others; this created a simultaneous experience of independence and interconnectivity, as he alluded to above. Learning to see and accept that these seemingly paradoxical truths about human existence was at the heart of contemplative belief and practice.

Race, Kabat-Zinn suggested, was one of many examples that could be used to delve into contemplative insights. He suggested that through collaborative inquiry, like that occurring in the breakout group, people could bridge differences, realize they shared some common experiences, and enact a sense of a whole community rather than only seeing its disparate parts. Such conversations, he argued, bridged people's stories and could tear down siloed experiences.

Kabat-Zinn ended his soliloquy by attesting to the authenticity of the work. As he told the group, in being part of the conversation, they were engaged in a mindful process of collective inquiry that took into account multiple, different, important perspectives on race and mindfulness. This process was mindful in that the group was collectively examining the situation they were in to figure out together where to go next. Participants were simultaneously collectively practicing their democratic values, their listening skills, and mindfulness to where they were, as both individuals and members of the contemplative community, in the present moment with regard to racial injustice and the role of the mindfulness community in working to ameliorate it. In doing so, he suggested, they had already transformed the status quo. This discussion was therefore in and of itself a performance of collective authenticity and action to initiate social change. Personally, as he stated, he found this process of dialogue, of engaging with each other in the moment, resonant and deeply emotional.

Of course, some critics may disagree with Kabat-Zinn's interpretation of the event, wondering in fact what tangible steps had been taken to address the problem of racial inequality in American society. After the conference, CfM did launch several fundraising initiatives in an attempt to broaden their base. In December 2015, CfM ran an annual fund drive, seeking money in part for their new projects that included a mission to work toward "diversity, inclusion, and equity through mindfulness."[7] To implement this mission, CfM raised money for a tuition-assistance fund to help support more diverse MBSR program participants and an MBSR teacher education scholarship fund to provide "greater access to MBSR for underserved and underrepresented people and . . . to attract, nurture, and sustain a diverse and inclusive cadre of MBSR teachers."[8] In the summer and fall of 2016, CfM continued raising money through its "Hearts Open Wide," campaign, in which they sought to (1) educate a new, more inclusive cadre of MBSR teachers from underrepresented cultures and communities, (2) collaborate with urban colleagues to make mindfulness and MBSR accessible to underserved and diverse communities, (3) create jobs and new economic opportunities for people, and (4) diversify the healthcare field.[9]

MLI is also diversifying contemplative science. The theme of its 2018 Summer Research Institute gathering is "Engaging Cultural Difference and Human Diversity." Such efforts to diversify the mindfulness community represent a step toward addressing the racial homophily and privilege within the group. To members of the movement, this might demonstrate further collective authenticity. However, the CfM did not take up Magee's suggestions to fundamentally transform the content of interventions and movement tactics to try to address deep-seated social problems more directly; instead, CfM's proposed solutions seemed to follow their previous model of social change, which hoped that transforming select individuals would lead to later social change.

Strengths and Weaknesses of Contemplatives' Response to Critics

In response to critiques, leaders of the contemplative movement's main organizations convened their base and enacted individual and collective authenticity in various ways. They hearkened back to Buddhist texts and teachers' articulations of Buddhist ethics. They engaged in collective inquiry, assessing their movement's hallowed sources of knowledge in both contemplative traditions and in science, and together reaffirmed their commitments to contemplative ethics, shared social responsibility, and social reform.

Contemplatives noted their successes and the ways they and their leaders had embodied and acted upon contemplative ethics. They demonstrated collective authenticity by incorporating mindful practices, such as breathing and reflection exercises, into their meetings. They listened to others' perspectives, which were at times contemplative, at times critical, and at times strategic. Through these processes, they learned from each other and engaged in personal and collective processes of growth and transformation. Furthermore, following the CfM conference, the center altered its course of development. It took into account the feedback from its leadership and base, which recommended diversifying its membership, and created scholarships for teachers and MBSR program attendees from underrepresented groups. Such meetings thereby served to enact and affirm the authenticity of the movement to itself.

However, social scientists, religious studies scholars, and other critics, such as Purser and Loy, may continue to find fault with certain elements of the movement. They may wonder to what extent values and aims are explicitly incorporated into the actual content of mindful intervention programs embedded across the different institutional contexts discussed in this book. They may also continue to criticize the choices of many mindfulness programs, such as MLI's leadership program, which focused on developing the contemplative and social skills of elites rather than on under-resourced communities most in need of aid. Lastly, they may continue to identify shortcomings of the movement's primary focus on transforming the hearts and minds of select groups rather than directly seeking institutional and policy change to address the deep-seated problems of materialism and inequality that our contemporary society continues to face.

CHAPTER 9 | In Conclusion

THE MORE ONE DELVES into the contemplative movement, the more its internal tensions, which may not be visible at first, become visible. On the one hand, Buddhist-inspired mindfulness has gone mainstream, embraced not only by professionals of all stripes, but increasingly by a public audience. Mindful breathing and other contemplative practices are everywhere, including in magazines at the grocery store, in healthcare solutions, in workplace training programs, and in children's television programing. Yet the very factors that led to its proliferation—its simple, digestible, modular tips and practices for individual well-being and success—simultaneously carry seeds of the contemplative movement's failures.

Buddhism comes from Asia, where monastics devoted to contemplative practice make a total commitment to engrossing themselves—in body, behavior, and mind—to the pursuit of personal liberation and the end of suffering through habitual practice throughout their daily lives. A profound commitment to the Buddhist path requires sacrifices; most monastics seriously committed to the path give up the pursuit of financial gain, excess material comforts, a family of their own, a sense of self-control, and other personal ambitions. Moreover, they are not alone in such pursuits and sacrifices; they are embedded in religious communities designed to support the Buddhist path.

To those familiar with Asian Buddhist monastic communities, the success of mindfulness—the watered-down, Westernized forms of Buddhism contemplation in rational, ambitious capitalist societies – may come at best as a surprise, and at worst as an affront. What is lost when religious cultures embedded in other societies' values, practices, and norms are systematically adapted to appeal to new audiences in quite different contexts, which contain elements antithetical to the originating cultures? What happens when elites—even elites earnestly devoted to maintaining the authenticity of the practices—guide this transmission process? What does success—and failure—look like in expanding alterative cultural and social movements?

These are the questions I raise in this book.

Many factors contributed to the elite-led contemplative movement's successful expansion over the past forty years. Although its success is in part due to having access to many of "the usual suspects" that aid most social movements (e.g., the media, resources, support from elites and academics, subcultures to build upon, and centralized organizations to train and support members), the contemplatives sought a different path to cultural change than typical protest-oriented social movements. Led by meditators who came of age in the midst of the 1960s and 1970s American counterculture, this group was disillusioned with the prospect of pursuing social reform through conventional politics or social movements. Some key contemplative leaders had participated in the protests of that era and were aware of the shortcomings of typical social movement mobilization. They also were wary of Buddhist meditation becoming merely a cultural fad, which would then quickly blow over, as some contemplative leaders reported occurring with Transcendental Meditation in the 1970s. Instead, contemplative leaders used their access to and power within powerful institutions, like science, healthcare, education, and business, to try to legitimize Buddhist-inspired contemplative practices and institutionalize them in people's daily lives across social sectors.

Like other spiritual and religiously motivated movements, contemplatives sought to spread their sacred practices and beliefs to convert and transform more individuals. With this strategy, their goals were more akin to the spiritual movements often included in the canon of New Social Movements and/or religious movements (e.g., Smith 1998) than to social movements or conventional politics that target structural legal or policy changes. However, unlike most Western religious movements or New Social Movements, contemplatives deliberately recruited and trained people in their meditation practices in groups within or contiguous to esteemed professional institutions.

To popularize and spread meditation, contemplatives strategically avoided contention with other institutional powerholders to the utmost extent possible. Instead, they used consensus-based mobilization, convening and collaborating with professional insiders to create meditation interventions that aligned with localized professional cultures. Contemplatives adapted Buddhist-inspired meditation in countless ways to align with host institutions' structures, professional norms, and motivations. Mindfulness leaders and educators deliberately disguised and altered any potentially controversial, off-putting elements of their culture. With these new forms of specialized contemplative culture, they could more easily attract professionals.

Thus, from the beginning, mindfulness and other adapted forms of meditation for professional sectors have been an amalgam of Buddhist ideas, values, and practices and Western motivations, values, and justifications. Contemplative forms of meditation have been shaped to fit into niches in capitalist-oriented organizations and deliberately adapted to appeal to pragmatic, individualistic, secular Western audiences. Mindfulness and other contemplative practices were formed in order to fit into capitalism and to appeal to consumers within that system. Jon Kabat-Zinn created his Mindfulness-Based Stress Reduction program as a therapeutic alternative to Western medicine for patients with chronic illness. Because capitalism pervades the field of Western medicine, contemplatives like Kabat-Zinn had to consider how to make their programs marketable and financially solvent in such contexts from the beginning. It is not surprising that some segments of the contemplative community and their offshoots then further adapted contemplative practice to appeal to and support corporate profit-seeking interests. Yoga emerged in the United States through a similar process (Jain 2015).

To contemplative leaders, the changes made to Buddhist modernist culture were not only acceptable but necessary to spread meditation more broadly. But they thought adaptations could be made while maintaining the authentic core of contemplative culture: personal commitment to one's meditation practice. Contemplatives believed that if their members maintained devout, disciplined, regular meditation practices, they would make ethical decisions about how best to promote Buddhist-inspired contemplative practices. Furthermore, incremental alterations to contemplative practices, and even to the motivations for the practices, were viewed as necessary and only superficial changes to spread the contemplative culture through Buddhist "skillful means," to meet new people "where they are." In accordance with Buddhist ideology, changes to the practices were seen as altering the surface-level elements of the culture, but not the transformative core experience that contemplative practice evoked in its members. Due to the spiritual ideology they ascribed to, contemplative leaders never mandated a formal regulated training system through which they could control how, why, and where mindfulness and other forms of contemplative culture could and should be developed.[1]

Although contemplatives changed many facets of Buddhist modernist culture, one cultural boundary they did not alter or challenge was that of social respectability and stature; this is particularly ironic for a group seeking to honor and diffuse a Buddhist culture that is critical of attachment to social status and material assets. To legitimize meditation, contemplative meditators deliberately kept their ranks socially credible and legitimate—which meant revering those with social and symbolic power while distancing themselves from those who might tarnish the movement's image of respectability.[2] Their unapologetic desire for social respectability and legitimacy, as well as their reliance on elite donors, the support of celebrities, and endorsements by scientists at top academic institutions, created a lack of awareness about the many forms of privilege that influenced their work. It is likely that this unintentionally distanced them from some of the communities they purportedly wanted to serve.

Through these tactics, the contemplative movement has impacted millions of people's lives in ways great and small.[3] Many people previously uninterested in Buddhism have tried their hand at meditation. Some have seriously adopted a regular meditation practice as a spiritual foundation of their lives, using contemplative practices regularly to reflect; to invoke Buddhist-inspired values such as kindness, compassion, and equanimity; and to refocus attention on taken-for-granted aspects of their lives. As some meditators became more committed to their practice, their professional and lifelong goals changed; some even went so far as to quit their jobs and begin doing contemplative work.

Of course, not everyone who came into contact with meditation has become a committed meditator, as teachers readily admit. But over the past several decades, enough people have adopted contemplative practice to move it into many powerful mainstream organizations. The movement has been extraordinarily successful at moving into spaces of institutional power through sympathetic insiders. It has spread broadly across the fields of healthcare, education, science, and business, not only in the United States but also in Canada, the United Kingdom, and increasingly, other locations around the world. Contemplatives are now even exporting mindfulness back to schools and groups in Asian Buddhist countries. The contemplative movement's spread of mindfulness into so many institutions and countries has provided a foundation for further cultural diffusion of meditation, in even more varying forms.

With this success, however, have come challenges and growing awareness of the weaknesses of consensus-led mobilization within powerful institutions. Critics raise important questions about the shortcomings of working so closely with elites within institutions in need of reform. As discussed in Chapter 8, questions remain about whether contemplatives continue to neglect Buddhist values that oppose materialism, self-centeredness, greed, and attachment. Critics wonder if mindful interventions are indeed initiating any true reform in institutions or if they are aiding corporate interests in producing ever-more-productive workers.

In response to such criticism, contemplatives have performed various kinds of authenticity. Although, as an alterative movement, demonstrating authenticity through individual contemplative practice and modeling contemplative culture has been central to the movement from the beginning, showing collective authenticity became especially important after the rising sea of criticism since 2013. Contemplative leaders have responded by demonstrating individual and collective authenticity to members of the movement in multiple ways, such as by modeling contemplative practice, listening and learning from others in the movement, referring back to Buddhist and contemplative canonical texts and leaders' perspectives, and highlighting their commitments to social reform.

So where does this process leave us? Were the contemplatives ultimately successful in their endeavors to change the world through the spread of mindfulness to new audiences, or did they fail? Or is the underlying story a more complex admixture of both—depending on which motives you focus on, and the way the movement is defined? At heart, is the movement merely a cultural self-help movement, or is it something more? Does it retain deeper social and political importance, offering a critique of the individualistic, capitalist status quo, as intended by some early contemplative leaders?

Thus far, portrayals of the mindfulness movement have seemed Janus-faced, with each side looking at the same cultural movement and obtaining very different results with limited data. On the one hand, many contemplative leaders I spoke with were effusively optimistic about the potential of their work to transform the world. On the other hand, critics accuse movement leaders of falsely promoting the benefits of contemplative practice and ultimately serving the gods of neoliberalism who hunger for greater productivity and profit (Whippman 2016). In this book, I have attempted to show the story of the movement from multiple angles in an effort to eschew overly simplistic portrayals assuming that one side is "right" and another is "wrong."

In doing so, I hope to advance understandings of both contemplative practice and non-contentious cultural movements by exploring the consequential tradeoffs that leaders of cultural and institutional change initiatives must make at the intersection of clashing cultures and objectives. Better questions can be asked, such as: How much oppositional content is actually being taught in targeted sectors? Have participating organizations committed enough to mindfulness practices so that a sufficient number of employees have been trained and can actually have an impact on the broader company culture? Without explicit company buy-in to change as a whole organization, are the activists' aims to reform institutions unrealistic? Without full buy-in, will oppositional practices, which are adapted and "snuck in," be weakened to the point in which they represent only an anemic solution to deep-seated structural problems? Will mindfulness end up more like yoga practice—which for many people is merely a way to relax and maintain physical and mental fitness rather than a transformative spiritual practice? Or does mindfulness have the potential to initiate deeper cultural change in how people conceive of themselves, their level of self-awareness, how they prioritize Buddhist-inspired values such as compassion, and how they treat others in the workplace?

There remains much to learn about the outcomes of the contemplative movement's consensus-based mobilization tactics, and of how other elite-driven movements may mobilize in similar ways. The contemplatives were effective in moving their cultures into some of the most esteemed secular institutions in American society. They were greatly aided by elites' resources, support, and social influence. They are also buoyed by countless success stories about how the practices have transformed their leaders' and educators' lives, and the lives of their clients, in manifold positive ways. People from seemingly all walks of life—ranging from corporate leaders, to underprivileged kids, to star athletes, to the chronically ill—report improved mental health, better emotion regulation, and a greater capacity to reflect on and inhabit their lives. In addition to contemplatives' anecdotal evidence, many scientific studies buttress various claims on the benefits of mindfulness and other contemplative practices on well-being, memory, attention, meta-awareness, cognitive flexibility, and emotion regulation (Britton et al. 2013; Chiesa, Calati, and Serretti 2011; Farb et al. 2007, 2010; Lao, Kissane, and Meadows 2016; Taylor et al. 2011).

However, in working with the deeply ingrained institutional cultures that activists seek to alter, the movement risks becoming susceptible to cultural cooptation. Activists inevitably learn from and grow more sympathetic to the motivations, interests, and perceived constraints of those they want to recruit. They also may become reliant on their access to resources and social power granted from institutional collaborators. As such, activists and institutional entrepreneurs can become more "beholden" to their institutional collaborators, who have more vested in maintaining the status quo than more independent movements (Katzenstein 1998: 9). Boundaries between "us" and "them," and "our mission" and "their mission," can become murky and dynamic, as seen in the contemplative movement. Furthermore, without regulation about which adaptations and compromises can be made, it is likely that elements of an elite-led, consensus-driven movement will veer in different, and possibly contradictory, directions over time, again as seen in the contemplative movement. Although some parts of a large movement may remain committed to longstanding cultural values and practices (such as long-time founding members), others (such as contemplative coaches in the profit-driven world of business) might be more likely to stray farther from a nascent movement's core values over time in order to resonate in their institutional world.

Perhaps one of the greatest risks for elite-driven alterative movements like the contemplatives is the myopia that can occur as members focus their inherently limited attention on the world around them, forgetting the problems of the people who never make it into the room with them because they lack the economic, cultural, or social capital. For a movement inspired and motivated by democratic aspirations, progressive politics such as reducing consumption and material inequality, and spiritual liberation for all, it is striking how the contemplative base was composed of such a privileged, seemingly homogenous, group of people. This intellectual and class homophily was hard to see from the inside at times because members were deliberately chosen based on their ability to bring in new intellectual and practical insights. However, new members mainly came from a pool of already successful people who were rich enough in intellectual and cultural capital to be able to confidently articulate their perspectives in convincing, charming, and humorous ways to other accomplished intellectuals and professional elites. As one contemplative leader told me wryly, all you need to get a seat at the decision-making table (rather than in the balcony at conferences watching the action) is to be famous, with a best-selling book. Alternatively, you could get a seat at the table by having wealth, or a powerful position in a highly esteemed institution such as the U.S. government, a top university, or a well-known company like Google or General Mills. Without such achievements, resources, or status, you could always pay your way into the network. However, the conferences are costly. I spent thousands of dollars in conference fees and retreat fees just to get access to this group of people. It also is nearly a prerequisite to be well educated, and it helps a great deal to have a Ph.D or M.D. degree. The movement also continues to be predominantly white.

Although the contemplatives have been successful in recruiting members who continue to expand the breadth of mindfulness and contemplative practice, and reach ever more niche audiences in the West and internationally, the question remains about the depth of the movement's impact on the institutions they inhabit. Although mindfulness interventions seem to affect a considerable amount of people who commit to and complete their programs, it remains unclear if they produce any greater structural changes in the institutions they work in.

I suspect that, like yoga programs in many workplaces, mindfulness interventions have yet to make much of an imprint on the larger organizations they inhabit. It is important to consider the limited proportion of people in targeted institutions impacted by contemplative programs, even in some of the movement's most heralded programs such as at Google and the Center for Mindfulness in Medicine, Health Care, and Society. Even at the University of Massachusetts and at Google worldwide, it is likely that only a small percentage of all employees have taken a mindfulness course.[4] Furthermore, the inhabited organizations have yet to consider implementing new missions aligned with mindfulness, or making structural changes to safeguard the health and well-being of all their members, such as by reducing work hours. There is also no evidence that contemplative practice within companies and other organizations leads members to be more socially considerate of those in their surrounding communities, in the way that contemplatives would hope with their aspirations of inculcating greater awareness of interconnectivity.

Ultimately, the movement's focus on individual transformation superseded deeper institutional changes. Contemplative leaders appear to hope for rather than push for deep social reform to institutional structures. While some contemplative leaders have made changes to how their specific groups operate, without addressing the institutional root causes of social problems, they risk proving their critics correct by implementing programs that are palliative rather than truly transformative.

A Shift to Consensus-Based Mobilization?

Importantly, examining the rise, the successes, and the shortfalls of the contemplative movement shows how elites can shape mainstream culture by building collaborative networks across powerful institutions and by bringing in and adapting previously marginal cultures so they are suitable for new contexts. These consensus-based tactics are a form of "activism lite," which may be particularly suited for the overworked people in contemporary Western society. "Activism lite" enables employees, and professionals in particular who have a great deal of power in their workplaces, to bring their personal causes and values into work in a way that efficiently enables them to seemingly "do it all." They thereby leverage their institutional power to contribute to creating positive social change while also advancing their professional goals and making a living. Such work can provide professional activists with a sense of authenticity because they are acting on their values on a regular basis at work. However, as some critics may note, engaging in "activism lite" at work may deflect the attention of potential activists from more committed, but less convenient, alternative forms of civic and political engagement.

Contemplatives are not alone in mobilizing through non-contentious tactics to change local cultural practices in various institutional fields.

Proponents of many movements from the 1960s and 1970s such as feminists, environmentalists, LGBTQ activists, and civil rights proponents have entered powerful mainstream organizations in their careers.[5] To what extent do they change these organizations from the inside by mobilizing their networks with similar others in powerful institutional positions across fields, like the contemplatives? How do they do so? Like the mindful elite, to what extent are other "activists lite" at risk of becoming so socialized into the institutions that they are a part of that they fail to sufficiently and directly address deep-seated systemic problems?

While much remains to be known about unobtrusive mobilization within and across institutions, we can look to other movements' mobilization processes to get a sense of how the contemplatives' mobilization was not unique—and may even be an increasingly common engine of cultural and political change. In particular, environmental activists have used similar tactics to establish credibility and legitimacy, influence institutions, and gain public support through a variety of paths. Climate change initiatives have been supported and facilitated by elites who organize through social movement organizations as well as through their professional organizations. Climate scientists have published peer-reviewed research, organized through conferences and institutional coalitions, and tried to reach the public through celebrities and popular media.

Al Gore is perhaps the most famous climate change advocate. As vice president, he brought climate change initiatives to the forefront within the federal government, and outside of office, he has raised awareness of climate change and helped the issue gain public legitimacy by traveling around the world giving talks and promoting his documentaries. Gore's advocacy work is connected to other movement organizations raising awareness of climate change such as the Business for Innovative Climate and Energy Policy coalition, a group of businesses committed to raising awareness of climate change and changing the way their companies operate to reduce emissions and increase energy efficiency, and the American College & University Presidents' Climate Commitment, an advocacy coalition that is building academic institutions' commitments to prevent climate change.[6] The group describes itself on its website as

a high-visibility effort to address global climate disruption undertaken by a network of colleges and universities that have made institutional commitments to eliminate net greenhouse gas emissions from specified campus operations, and to promote the research and educational efforts of higher education to equip society to re-stabilize the earth's climate. Its mission is to accelerate progress towards climate neutrality and sustainability by empowering the higher education sector to educate students, create solutions, and provide leadership-by-example for the rest of society.

These organizations used the same tactics as contemplatives. Their business and academic leaders mobilized to address climate change using their professional positions to initiate changes in the organizations they worked for. Like contemplatives, leaders of these institutional climate change initiatives aimed to lead by example and make their workplaces benchmarks for the rest of society, which they hoped others would mimic. Their work has some more easily measurable successful outcomes, such as reducing their organizations' greenhouse gas emissions and increasing organizational energy efficiency, in addition to promoting research on climate change. However, researchers could also assess if collaborating organizations' members have experienced more subjective changes, such as in their values, attitudes, and personal behaviors with respect to climate change. Comparisons of cases that enact consensus-based tactics in similar—yet different—ways, like advocacy for climate change and meditation, are needed to further disentangle the strengths and weaknesses of elite-driven consensus-based mobilization.

I hope that, in evaluating the contemplatives and other movements attempting to initiate change from within and across powerful social institutions, we are all left with more questions than answers. In the murky area between cultural and social movements, how do we define and assess success? Ultimately, are consensus-based, elite-driven movements handicapped by their commitment to working with elites and existent power structures, or are the inherent compromises made by consensus-based change advocates worth the opportunities they afford? Can such collaborations lead to the creation of innovative new organizational vehicles for change, which can lead to deeper structural social reform, or do they merely serve as palliative Band-Aids to entrenched social problems? Can lifestyle movements, which aid in developing certain personal values and innovative cultural practices in daily life in powerful social domains, be as efficacious as contentious social movements? To what extent can they complement or work alongside more contentious collective movements? Perhaps we should be more sensitive to the multiple measures of movement success, posing such assessments with a battery of outcomes, ranging from individual to organizational to broader social change, and inclusive of both cultural and structural reforms made. Only then can we more fully compare and understand the efficacy of collective strategies of making the world a better place.

APPENDIX | Data Collection and Analysis

I STARTED THIS PROJECT using a grounded theory perspective (Corbin and Strauss 2008). I attended meditation retreats and teachings from various Buddhist traditions to learn more about Buddhist philosophy and meditation, to gain a Buddhist metacommunicative cultural and linguistic competence (Briggs 1986), and to better understand the embodied, subjective kinds of knowledge meditators experience (see Pagis 2010).

I collected ethnographic data at a nonsectarian, interfaith Tibetan temple in the Midwest from November 2009 to November 2011. I attended two book discussion groups, Sunday dharma teachings, and Thursday meditation instructions. I also attended three Tibetan Gelugpa and Kagyu Buddhist retreats. This preliminary research provided me with a baseline understanding of how Buddhism is practiced in the United States in Asian temples that teach lay American audiences. Through the intensive embodied Buddhist training I underwent, I physically, emotionally, and cognitively became a more sensitive listener to my respondents. Feedback from the contemplatives during my interviews affirmed to me that my knowledge on meditation was not only important but critical to gaining trust and asking the right questions so that I could understand their work, their motivations, and their aspirations beyond a superficial, front-stage comprehension.

I also realized that if I wanted to understand how Buddhism was changing, I had to understand what it had been and the context through which it had come to the West. To learn about the history of Buddhism in the West, I attended a course offered through the Department of Central Eurasian Studies at Indiana University taught by renowned Tibetologist Professor Elliot Sperling.

I first became interested in the contemplative movement when I heard lay Buddhist practitioners at the Buddhist center I attended speak about how neuroscientific research had "proven" that Buddhist meditation was beneficial. As a sociologist who was very aware of how few scientific studies reach the public and quite skeptical about religious practitioners using "science" to legitimize their practices, I became curious about who was conducting research on Buddhist meditation and how their research was being received within their disciplines. At about this time, several

Buddhist monks came to the Midwest dharma center to lead retreats who had been to Mind and Life Institute (MLI) events and incorporated neuroscientific research on meditation into their teachings. I interviewed them, officially starting this project. The first person I interviewed knew an MLI founder, whom she had met while meditating in Nepal in the 1970s. She emailed him directly in 2011, shooting me into the center of the contemplative movement.

To investigate how the contemplative movement has spread meditation, I used mixed qualitative methods, including interviews, multisite ethnography, and content analysis, as described in more detail below. I drew upon different data sources, research methodologies, and multiple informants from organizations when possible to check the validity of sources and address recall bias (Kumar, Stern, and Anderson 1993; Rizzo, Corsaro, and Bates 1992).

Interviews

This book draws upon 108 interviews I conducted with contemplatives from 2011 to 2016. When I began this project, I sought meditators who were connected with the primary, publicly known organizations bringing Buddhist-inspired meditation into secular professional fields (e.g., MLI, Center for Mindfulness in Medicine, Health Care, and Society [CfM], Center for Contemplative Mind in Society [CCMS], and their affiliated research laboratories and centers at universities) in an attempt to get to the core of the network.

When I started, I did not know what to call the members of these organizations; in fact, there was not an obvious consensus on what they called themselves or if they were in fact a "movement" at all. I was not convinced at the time they were actually a movement, so I approached the network of contemplative organizations with an open mind as to whether it represented a movement, a social network, or separate initiatives. I first selected the largest, most established, and most heavily resourced organizations in order to reach contemplatives committed to bringing meditation into new institutional spaces, and then used snowball sampling to work my way out through their members and networks. For the contemplative movement in science I began interviews in Boulder, Colorado, with MLI founders and leaders, and at the laboratory of another MLI leader. I also spoke with a long-time program manager at the Fetzer Institute in Kalamazoo, Michigan, which funded some of the first peer-reviewed research on meditation and first brought national media attention to meditation in the 1990s.

After these initial interviews, I moved on to different research institutions, university departments, and collaborators in the movement in other areas. In 2011 and 2012, I conducted 101 in-depth, semistructured interviews with the leaders of 61 contemplative programs and organizations, their protégées, and new adopters of the movement. During interviews, I asked respondents about how their programs were founded, their program content, their social networks, their strategies for expansion, and the challenges their initiatives faced. I also inquired about their religious affiliations and identities, when they began meditating, and the forms of religious, spiritual, or secular meditation they practiced. The interview schedule I used was flexible and allowed for adaptations for each respondent. Before every interview, I Googled the informant, gathering all the information I could. I then went over my standard interview schedule, slightly adapting it for each respondent based on the information I had gathered and marking specific topics I wanted to probe for more information on. I used Gordon's (1980) probing techniques and tried ask questions that did not contain implicit bias or lead informants to give particular responses.

I interviewed most contemplatives in their homes or offices, in coffee shops, at meditation retreats, and at academic conferences in Boulder and Denver, Colorado; Ann Arbor, Michigan; Kalamazoo, Michigan; Bloomington, Indiana; Madison, Wisconsin; Santa Fe, New Mexico; Los Angeles, San Diego, San Francisco, Oakland, and Berkeley, California; New York City, New York; Lancaster, Pennsylvania; Washington, D.C.; New Haven, Connecticut; Garrison, New York; Providence, Rhode Island; and Northampton, Massachusetts. Interviewing participants in their work and home environments helped me to build rapport and provided some insight into their workplaces. Interviews lasted from twenty minutes (at conferences) to six hours. After interviews, many respondents invited me to dinner with their families, business meetings, or dharma teachings. The additional informal interviews and ethnographic data allowed me to see into the informal, backstage workings of movement leaders' lives and their work, and how they often seamlessly intersected.

Through my interviews, I learned about the best-known mindfulness education programs, programs for members of the military, and the burgeoning interest in mindfulness in business. The people I spoke with connected me with their contacts and told me of planned events in all of these areas. For educational programs for children and youth and for law enforcement and military servicemen, I interviewed principal members of various prominent organizations in the field, including leaders of the Garrison Institute (Garrison, New York), the Impact Foundation (Boulder), Inner Kids (Los Angeles), Mindful Schools (Oakland), The Still Quiet Place (Menlo Park), UCLA's Mindfulness Awareness Research Center, and various other organizations (some of which preferred anonymity).

In business, I entered the field by attending the Wisdom 2.0 conference in Silicon Valley, California. Building on contacts made there, I met and interviewed business leaders who then connected me with the names of philanthropists, venture capitalists, midlevel managers, and life coaches bringing meditation and mindfulness into corporate settings. Networks from the Wisdom 2.0 conference connected me with additional neuroscientists, Buddhist contemplative teachers, and members of the media involved in the movement as well.

Over time, I learned how interconnected leaders, funders, and members of the different contemplative organizations were. Some of their relationships dated back decades (as discussed in Chapter 3). Conferences often convened leaders of contemplative organizations bringing meditation into various fields (see Chapter 7). In addition, many contemplative leaders told me about the many informal ways they communicated with leaders of other initiatives, seeking information and feedback. Often, they developed friendships over the years, which I witnessed in both formal conference events and social events. The dense social networks I unearthed and the primary contemplative leaders' commitments to social reform (explained in

Chapter 3) over time led me to conclude that the contemplatives did in fact make up a movement, as defined by social movement scholars (see p. 12).

Readers may wonder how my sample fits into the larger landscape of Buddhism in America. Respondents were connected to the primary organizations that at the time were bringing Buddhist-inspired meditation into secular institutions (namely MLI, CfM, CCMS, Wisdom 2.0, and the other organizations referred to above); they were either members of such organizations or attendees at their events. Contemplatives drew from a lot of different Buddhist and non-Buddhist contemplative traditions, including Tibetan Buddhism, Zen, Burmese and Thai Theravada Buddhism, insight meditation, Advaita Vedanta, mindfulness-based stress reduction (MBSR), and yoga. However, as discussed in the book, they were mainly affluent, educated, white, and willing to adapt Buddhist meditation to make it appeal to a broader audience. They by no means represent ethnic Asian Buddhists in America and are a small, particular subset of converted American Buddhists. Yet, they have disproportionate influence on how Buddhism and mindfulness are perceived in America.

I am often asked how much the contemplatives I spoke with were inspired by socially engaged Buddhism, a movement to apply Buddhism to address social problems such as war, human rights violations, disease and natural disasters, and environmental destruction. Perhaps due to the diffuse nature of socially engaged Buddhism in America (Sigalow 2014), surprisingly only a few people I spoke with directly referred to being involved in it, or even familiar with it.

I am also asked by many scholars if I think my sample represents the whole movement. During the height of my data collection, in 2011 and 2012, I think my respondents did represent the core parts of the contemplative movement. However, such assessments are difficult to conclusively assess, especially because the contemplative/mindfulness movement grew so rapidly after I did the bulk of my interviews. Mindfulness and other contemplative practices have become so diffuse in America and internationally at this point that such an assessment would be impossible to make. In fact, I believe my study was possible only because I happened to conduct it at the historical juncture I did: I caught the movement just as it was exploding in size and influence. Had I started my study a few years earlier, I could not have imagined how rapidly mindfulness would become popular in business and among the public; had I started it later, I doubt I would have been able to gain access to the people I did.

Because I collected data as various parts of the contemplative movement were coalescing, increasingly overlapping, and rapidly growing, as I gathered information, members of the movement were increasingly interested in my findings. Their interest in the study and in better understanding the expanse and cutting edge of this growing movement undoubtedly helped me gain access to other important members of the movement. After interviews, if informants asked about what I was finding, I told them about the patterns I saw. As I attended more events, I began repeatedly seeing certain leaders of the movement. This also helped me build relationships with them and gain access to others in the movement. I began keeping touch with some of these members of the movement, whom I encountered in various locations, via social media such as Facebook and Twitter, through email, and, for some, by phone. Several of the contemplatives have become key informants whom I have spoken with on various occasions over the years. These key informants have been helpful in providing updates on the movement's progress as well as in verifying and elaborating upon my perspectives and accounts.

I conducted a second round of interviews with an additional seven contemplative leaders in 2015 and 2016 to get an update on where the field was at after the media backlash against their work. In addition to questions from the prior interview guide, I added more questions about critiques of their work, their authenticity, and their commitments to institutional reform.

All interview data were transcribed, verified, and de-identified for respondents requesting confidentiality. Some informants, who are public figures and regularly speak about their contemplative work, gave me permission use their names. I also supplemented my interview data with eleven additional publicly available interviews with influential movement leaders that contained information on the questions I asked.

After completing all interviews, I reviewed my total sample (114 interviews) and decided to include only the 108 people who were trying to bring meditation into secular institutions and/or had attended contemplative events in the final sample used in this book. I removed six interviews with Buddhist meditators who, I learned upon interviewing, were not part of the broader contemplative movement. Removed interviewees included Buddhist meditators or translators who have been involved in neuroscientists' research but were not involved in the larger contemplative movement, dedicated meditators who aspired to bring their practice into their workplaces but had yet to do so, and Buddhist scholar-practitioners who were not involved with the movement.

Participant Observation

I was a participant observer at various contemplative events. At two contemplative scientific retreats, Zen and the Brain at the Upaya Zen Center in Santa Fe and the MLI Summer Research Institute in Garrison, I attended meditation sessions and scientific talks and ate with other attendees. I spent down time with attendees, getting to know them more informally before, after, and in between sessions. I also attended four conferences: Wisdom 2.0 in Silicon Valley; the first International Symposium for Contemplative Studies, hosted by MLI in Denver; the 2015 UC Davis Center for Mind and Brain Research Summit; and the 2015 CfM annual conference.

Additionally, I participated in three Gelugpa Tibetan Buddhist meditation retreats with Buddhist monastics who have been involved in the movement (in Bloomington, Indiana, and Fairplay, Colorado, as discussed above), two one-day events, five contemplative organizations' meetings, and eight insight and mindfulness meditation sessions led by leaders in the contemplative movement (in San Francisco, Berkeley, and Los Angeles; Providence, Rhode Island; and New Haven, Connecticut).

In 2014 and 2015, I attended additional events (e.g., a multiday conference, one-day events, mindfulness trainings, speaker events, and informal social events such as group lunches and a movie night) at CfM. During January 2015, I spent two weeks as a participant observer at the center. I took detailed field notes during my time at the organization as well as conducted formal and informal interviews with its members.

Over the past decade, I have spent hundreds of hours with contemplatives. During my time with them, I deliberately chose to be as authentic and myself as much as possible. Although some ethnographers and interviewers try to be more detached observers, I did not do this for several reasons. First, the group of people I studied were incredibly intelligent intellectuals and elites. Had I been not authentic and candid, they would have picked up on this immediately and would not have trusted me or helped connect me with their contacts, some of whom they were protective of due to their high social status. Second, given Buddhist culture and the importance of being present in the moment, if I was not open-hearted and authentic, I would not have fit into the culture I was investigating; I would not have been able to do my project. I had a turning point during the Wisdom 2.0 conference when I realized that if I ran up to every high-status meditator at the conference and asked for an interview, I would get no interviews. I did this to several people, and although they said they would do an interview, those I had approached too directly later reneged on their promises for interviews. Those who I instead spoke with more casually and connected with on personal values, intellectual interests, or other common interests not only met me later for interviews but also openly shared candid perspectives with me and connected me with other elites in the movement.

Throughout my participant observation, I was comfortable taking detailed field notes, as many other practitioners took notes on dharma teachings and scientific talks. Afterward, I wrote up and filled in my field notes with all the details I could remember about the events I'd attended (in keeping with Emerson et al. 2011). During my second round of data collection in 2015, I began audio-recording events as well as taking handwritten notes. The recordings were transcribed. During and outside of these retreats, teachings, and events, I conducted numerous informal interviews with both leaders and participants in the movement.

Content Analysis

I tracked and analyzed hundreds of media articles, websites, and publicly available interviews on contemplative leaders and their organizations from 2008 to 2016. Many leaders also gave me their publications and other documents from their organizations, which I analyzed as well. In addition, I followed movement activity via members' posts on social media outlets such as Facebook and Twitter. Content from these sources is included throughout my analysis.

Multiple Analytical Strategies

I used different kinds of data analysis for the research in this book. While conducting research, I wrote memos identifying common themes or patterns in the data. During the second half of my data collection and analysis process, I relied mainly upon abductive analysis (Timmermans and Tavory 2012). As I collected data, I identified surprising results and iterated between reading different literatures in sociology and organizational studies so I could identify why the results were surprising and how they could contribute to a better understanding of the social change processes in these literatures. An interest in certain perplexing results also led me to collect additional data on these areas of interest in subsequent interviews.

To make sense of the thousands of pages of data I collected, I coded interview data, documents, and field notes partially with ATLAS.Ti and partially by hand. I went through ATLAS.Ti coding first for the strategies contemplatives used in diffusing meditation; their personal religious, spiritual, or secular relationship with Buddhist meditation and other religious or spiritual traditions; the content of their programs; and their basic sociodemographic information. When writing the specific chapters in this book, I returned back to my data and conducted another coding for these larger themes and for the specific mechanisms and tactics I discuss in each chapter. In later coding iterations, I checked the data for cases that affirmed the patterns I saw while I collected data and about which I wrote in my memos. I looked for negative or alternative cases to the patterns I perceived to check my results, as well as to add complexity to findings I may have initially oversimplified.

I also juxtaposed timelines of the movement organizations', leaders', and members' histories at numerous points in my data collection and analysis process to gain a sense of how the overall contemplative sub-movements, and later the overarching movement, evolved. I assessed movement members' individual timelines, paying attention to when and where they began meditating, what motivated their initial experiences with meditation, how they were introduced to it, and how they began bringing it into their work and connecting with the larger movement. I mapped out the networks of the movement as well, analyzing how different leaders and their organizations were connected through personal and professional connections.

NOTES

Chapter 1

1. Transcripts and video footage from this event accessed at: http://www.aei.org/events/happiness-free-enterprise-and-human-flourishing-a-special-online-event-featuring-his-holiness-the-dalai-lama, August 30, 2014.

2. At the time, MLI did not have a communications specialist to respond. The organization has since hired a director of communication.

3. When I began this research, I was perplexed about what contemplatives all had in common, because the common praxis they shared did not register on the long list of ways scholars typically identify religious people. Although all meditators in this book had some form of training in Buddhist-derived meditation (and, in some cases, Buddhist philosophy) and they participated in contemplative events or meetings, they did not share a particular history, Buddhist lineage, set of beliefs, or holy book, like many American Christians do. Most did not identify publicly solely as Buddhists, but many would admit that by certain definitions, they were Buddhist. Like self-acknowledged Buddhists, the contemplatives do not even share an exact canon of practices. Contemplatives additionally did not share an explicit religious or spiritual identity or attend a common religious organization to practice. They spoke of doing a wide range of Buddhist practices and engaging in multiple other sacred traditions. It was not uncommon for a respondent to say he was raised in a Judeo-Christian tradition, had a committed Buddhist meditation and yoga practice, and read widely on Eastern wisdom traditions. Others said they were anti-religion, but read Buddhist texts, or identified as Buddhist if they had to pick a tradition, but largely didn't choose to self-identify in any religious or spiritual categories.

The contemplatives I spoke with were careful in the way they described their motivations, beliefs, and personal meditation practices, aware that using certain words associated too much with religion or certain variants of spirituality would jeopardize the legitimacy and credibility of their work. Many of the contemplatives would qualify as spiritual according to definitions from prior research, which describe spirituality as privileging primary first-order personal experiences as central elements of their religious experience, rather than second-order religious traditions, authorities, and institutions (Bender 2009; Cadge 2012). Spirituality has also been defined as the presence of the human spirit, and as characterized by individual quests for meaning and experiences of wholeness (Roof 2003; Wuthnow 1998); the contemplatives I spoke with would agree. However, contemplatives are a particular subset of spiritual people who believe in personal quests for spiritual and secular meaning and understanding through meditation and science. They are quick to distinguish themselves from other spiritual and religious groups, such as those associated with the New Age, and Transcendental Meditation.

4. Practitioners can also focus on other neutral (not positive or negative) points of focus, such as their steps during walking meditation, their food while eating mindfully, or other objects.

5. Web of Science, accessed June 3, 2014.

6. For more on my research design and methods, see Appendix.

7. Prior to the official beginning of this project, I spent a year learning how to meditate at a local Tibetan Buddhist center by attending several weekly sitting meditation sessions, attending a few book discussion groups, and attending short two- to four-day meditation retreats.

8. For exceptions see Collins (2000); Duffy et al. (2010); Lindsay (2008, 2010).

9. See also Armstrong and Bernstein (2008: 84).

10. In the book, in accordance with Ganz (2000), in referring to contemplative leaders, I indicate people "authorized to make strategic decisions" (1014) in the movement.

In referring to contemplatives, I speak of the people in the movement and of those learning contemplative practices from members of the movement (whom I do not necessarily consider members of the movement). As Bert Klandermans and Dirk Oegema (1987) discuss, there is a process through which people become committed to a movement. New movement participants have to agree with movement goals, be exposed to movement activity, choose to attend movement events, and then actually attend. Taking this all into consideration, the best way to explain the contemplatives is that the center of their field operates like a movement, but like all movements, on the fringes of the networks of the movement, there is a conceptual gray area between movements and collective action. In this area, there are people who learn about contemplative culture but do not become involved in the movement. There are also people who learn about contemplative culture secondhand rather than directly by attending movement activities. They may read about contemplative culture through the internet or books, or be exposed to similar resonant ideas through other cultural influences, and integrate parts of contemplative culture into their lives to varying degrees. These people are likely to become new participants in the movement, but must take action and actively connect with the movement to become a part of it (Klandermans and Oegema 1987).

11. This movement built upon some justifications for meditation that had existed in earlier manifestations of mindfulness, as described in Chapter 2.

12. For more on unobtrusive tactics, see Katzenstein (1999) and Kucinskas (2014).

13. For more on the history of movement scholarship, see Kucinskas (2018).

14. Everyone I spoke with sat in meditation at least intermittently. Many contemplatives also practiced walking meditation, and other Buddhist forms of meditation to cultivate a sense of calmness or caring for others.

15. Socially skilled institutional entrepreneurs use a variety of well-known tactics such as theorization of ideas and practices (Maguire et al. 2004; Strang and Meyer 1993) and effective framing of narratives to inspire cooperation in others by appealing to their identity, ideology, and interests while also providing a contrasting perspective to their opponents' outlook (Benford and Snow 2000; Goffman 1974; Snow et al. 1986). Socially skilled actors can play an important role in new field development (Fligstein and McAdam 2012). For a review on institutional entrepreneurship, see Batilliana et al. (2009).

16. While neoinstitutionalist theory offers a powerful analytic lens on "how conformity occurs in already existing fields" (Fligstein and McAdam 2012: 28) that has yielded a considerable body of research, it has several shortcomings. It fails to sufficiently account for the agentic capacity of actors (DiMaggio 1988) or how fields emerge (Fligstein and McAdam 2012), which scholarship on institutional entrepreneurship and my book seek to address. Neoinstitutionalism also fails to account for the incremental social change that occurs as actors pursue their interests using resources at hand through interactions with others in their organization and field and how actors can use deviant local cultures to struggle against coercive, normative, or mimetic isomorphism (Binder 2007; Hallett 2010; Hallett and Ventresca 2006). Because Bourdieu's field theory (Bourdieu 1984; Bourdieu and Wacquant 1992) and neoinstitutionalist theories say little on field emergence, field interdependence, and agentic collective action, other scholars studying field development, such as Fligstein and McAdam (2002: 24–26) and I rely more heavily upon social movement scholarship to explain field emergence and change processes.

17. The study also builds upon scholarship on how movements and fields form, such as Blee and Currier (2005) and Fligstein and McAdam (2012).

18. I published some of the ideas and quotes from this book in a 2014 article in *Sociology of Religion.*

19. See Reich (2007).

Chapter 2

1. For example, in an informal conversation with me in 2014, Mindfulness-Based Stress Reduction founder Jon Kabat-Zinn espoused a similar perspective. He argued that his conceptualization of mindfulness took the "spiritual essence" of Buddhism and left behind less important rituals and other cultural trappings of Asian Buddhist traditions.

2. For more on the history of Buddhism in America, see Jeff Wilson's *Mindful America* (2014), Richard Seager's *Buddhism in America* (2012), and Rick Field's *How the Swans Came to the Lake* (1992).

3. Contemplative leaders Mirabai Bush, Daniel Goleman, Joseph Goldstein, Sharon Salzberg, and Ram Dass met at Goenka's first retreat for Westerners in India in 1970. For more information, see Sigalow (2014).

4. Interestingly, eastern Massachusetts was also the home of Transcendentalists Ralph Waldo Emerson and Henry David Thoreau as well as Jack Kerouac.

5. However, this case suggests that Rochon's theoretical distinction between critical communities and movements as distinct entities overemphasizes the distinctiveness of the two. The core social foundation of the contemplative movement was based firmly in the critical community of scholar-practitioners discussed above.

6. Several contemplative scientists I interviewed told me about the backlash against TM research and their experiences during this period. See also Tøllefsen (2014) on stigma of TM meditation during the late 1970s.

Chapter 3

1. Scholars might expect contemplatives to be inspired by Socially Engaged Buddhism, a movement to apply Buddhism to address social problems such as war, human rights violations, disease and natural disasters, and environmental destruction. However, perhaps due to the diffuse nature of socially engaged Buddhism in America (Sigalow 2014), surprisingly only a few people I spoke with directly referred to being involved in it, or even familiar with it.

2. In her research on engaged Buddhists, Yukich (2017) suggests that they have a similar perspective on how Buddhism leads to social change: they think that Buddhism promotes positive social change through transforming individuals, who then integrate Buddhist principles into their daily lives.

3. Contemplative organizations can be considered social movement organizations (SMOs), as defined by McCarthy and Zald's (1973; 1977) resource mobilization theory. SMOs, they argued, operated like purposive business firms that made rational decisions to pursue resources and their goals to generate social change. SMOs depended most on affluent outsiders for skilled labor, leadership, and material resources (McCarthy and Zald 1973; 1977; Morris and Herring 1984).

4. Accessed from *Toward a Mindful Society*, May 5, 2014: http://www.mindful.org/the-mindful-society/vision/toward-a-mindful-society.

5. It is also important to acknowledge that different Buddhist traditions emphasize different paths to the cessation of suffering (Dalai Lama in Ribush 2005; Field Notes November 6, 2010).

6. Pseudonym used.

7. In accordance with the way Buddhism is traditionally taught, others chose not to disclose their experiences meditating. They said they discuss such experiences only with their teachers.

8. See also Stiles (2011).

9. Scholarship on movement development and institutional entrepreneurship discusses the importance of theorization and cultural development early in a program or movement's development (Maguire et al. 2004; Rochon 2000; Strang and Meyer 1993).

10. Weber (1978) defines instrumental rational action as expectations of the behavior of other people and objects in one's environment that guide an actor's pursuit of a rational end.

11. Pseudonym used upon request.

Chapter 4

1. Although studied by movement scholars in the late 1980s and early 1990s (Klandermans 1988; McCarthy and Wolfson 1992; Michaelson 1994), consensus-based mobilization has received little attention in recent research (Pellow 1999). This movement also operates similar to other religious and spiritual movements (see Davis and Robinson 2012; Kucinskas 2014; Yukich 2013) that try to create cultural and institutional change in multiple institutional fields simultaneously.

2. The fields of K-12 education and some business initiatives developed in a more grassroots way, in which people with sustained meditation practices (with origins in many traditions, including Tibetan Buddhist, *vipassana*, MBSR, and Advaita Vedanta) began bringing contemplative practice to new audiences in their workplaces, such as to kids or to colleagues. In the early to mid-2000s, leaders of some of the first mindfulness programs for kids began to attend contemplative organizations' events and in effect joined the movement. Other mindful education programs I visited developed in a manner similar to the process depicted in Figure 4.1. Although the contemplative movement, and its field of members and organizations, formed through both the establishment of central organizations (e.g., MLI, CfM, and CCMS) *and* grassroots initiatives in business and education, I begin by emphasizing how the former mobilized because without the organizational groundwork and social networks they developed, the movement would not have been able to legitimize and spread contemplative practice to the extent they have.

3. In its early years, CCMS met at Fetzer or Roshi Joan Halifax's Upaya Zen Center, for instance. The Center for Mind and Life met at private residences, such as the Dalai Lama's residence in Dharamsala, India, during its first few years. MLI and mindful educators have also met at the Garrison retreat center in Garrison, New York.

4. Because Bush was the only contemplative leader who told me about this report, I think this working paper was not followed directly like a playbook by other contemplative leaders. Instead, I think the strategies laid out in the report shaped Kabat-Zinn's and other early founders' organizations more implicitly.

5. For the sake of simplicity here I am painting the history in broad strokes. Although Bush and the CCMS began bringing meditation into select businesses such as Monsanto and *Marie Claire* of Hearst Publications in the early 2000s, this field did not take off until Soren Gordhamer convened a critical mass of people in business and tech in the Wisdom 2.0 conference in 2010. K-12 mindfulness programs first developed in a more grassroots rather than centralized process, which is similar to how mindfulness developed in the United Kingdom (see the Mindfulness All-Party Parliamentary Group Report 2015). Mindfulness in the United Kingdom was developed in dialogue with mindfulness in America.

6. Cited from CCMS website: http://www.contemplativemind.org/archives/business; downloaded October 7, 2017.

7. Excerpt from Twerkov (2001) interview for *Tricycle*.

8. Twerkov (2001).

9. For more on cooptation, see Selznick (1949).

10. In the Monsanto case, it is not possible to answer this question; after Shapiro left, the program was eliminated.

11. Cited from CCMS website: http://www.contemplativemind.org/archives/business; downloaded October 7, 2017.

12. Google's mission is "to organize the world's information and make it universally accessible and useful." Accessed from: https://www.google.com/about/company; accessed August 29, 2016.

13. This case builds upon and informs scholarship on how new fields form (Fligstein and McAdam 2012) and how institutional fields change through

isomorphism. The contemplative movement shows how mimetic isomorphism can be initiated by movements external to institutional fields in which changes occur. For more information on how new practices and institutional logics can travel within institutional fields, see DiMaggio and Powell (1983) and Meyer and Rowan (1977).

14. They likely have increased references to scientific research on mindfulness meditation since 2014.

15. See Isaac (2008) for more on how movement culture moves.

16. Although Klandermans (1988) pointed out that this was a promising area of research, this book is the first empirical study I know of that supports this mechanism as contributing to movement mobilization and field development.

17. Disinhibition theory (which dates back to Freud) posits that contagion processes can occur based on "imitation mediated by restraint release due to observing another perform an action that the individual is in conflict about performing himself" (Freedman 1982 c.f. Marsden 1998). Thus, behaviors or ideas that are already part of an actor's repertoire but are restrained due to social stigmas or a lack of perceived legitimacy may be released when the actor sees similar others engaging in such behaviors or ideas.

Chapter 5

1. Pseudonym.

2. From their website: https://www.umassmed.edu/cfm/mindfulness-based-programs/mbsr-courses/about-mbsr/history-of-mbsr/, downloaded November 4, 2017.

3. From the University of Virginia School of Medicine's website: https://med.virginia.edu/mindfulness-center/programs/mindfulness-based-stress-reduction-mbsr, downloaded November 4, 2017.

4. My analysis in this chapter builds upon the framing literature in social movements. For more on framing, see Benford and Snow (2000), Snow and Benford (1988, 1992), and Snow et al. (1986).

5. Meyer and Rowan's neoinstitutional theory (1977) argues that loose coupling and decoupling between formal cultural structures and everyday work processes occurs so that technical efficiency can be maintained on the ground. These authors speak to how decoupling processes, in which gaps are formed between organizations' macro-cultural myths and practical activity on the ground, and the "maintenance of face" are both mechanisms that occur based on the assumption that actors generally act "in good faith" for the best interests of their organization (Meyer and Rowan 1977: 358). However, this perspective fails to account for the multiple fields actors are simultaneously embedded in (Fligstein and McAdam 2012), and how actors' allegiances to their work organizations vary and can become attenuated.

More recent theory on "inhabited institutionalism" (such as Binder 2007, Hallett 2010, and Hallett and Ventresca 2006) shows how actors can attach and decouple localized organizational cultures to/from their larger organizations in a number of ways. My work adds to inhabited institutionalist perspectives on how coupling occurs in various ways. First, I address a lack of scholarly attention to how decoupling processes occur due to the multi-institutional contexts actors are embedded in. Second, I investigate how a movement can use coupling and decoupling simultaneously in its institutional work initiatives to bring in an alternative cultural system without opposition. Third, examining the contemplative movement's spread of Buddhist-inspired meditation into secular organizations shows how targeting change in local interactional culture, which may already deviate from formal organizational rules and logics, is a way through which movements can initiate cultural change. Local inhabited institutional culture is a vulnerable entry point in an organization, and contemplatives use it strategically as a platform from which to change an organization from within. Fourth, this case shows that some actors may be most loyal to other organizations or identities rather than their occupational identity. For example, some people's allegiances to their family or religion may be more salient than their loyalty to their work. Lastly, this case suggests that contemplative change agents are neither the "cultural dopes" (Garfinkel 1967: 68–75) neoinstitutionalists are accused of portraying, nor heroic, overly rational, decontextualized change agents depicted in some research on institutional entrepreneurs (Batilliana et al. 2009). Instead, contemplative meditators navigate a complex multilevel organizational environment embedded in multiple fields simultaneously. These meditators strategically initiate organizational changes gradually and cautiously while also affirming certain institutional norms, rules, and logics.

6. There were a handful of incidents in which contemplative initiatives were not received favorably. Taylor, for example, failed at his first attempt to get Buddhist-inspired mind training into a military base. Several professors reported a backlash from colleagues. One educator mentioned a program in which the superintendent ordered that a school have a mindfulness education program without getting sufficient teacher buy-in first; the program did not go well. However, overall, the vast majority of stories I heard from respondents were success stories, even though I specifically asked for challenges and failures. Admittedly, respondents likely had a positivity bias. I do think the contemplatives' success was also due to the combination of the familiarity of other similar Buddhist-inspired, spiritual and countercultural ideologies, their aid from insiders, and the efficacy of their efforts to adapt Buddhism so that it resonated with specific targeted audiences.

7. Goldie Hawn's MindUP program alone has influenced this many people. From the MindUP website: https://mindup.org/thehawnfoundation, downloaded November 29, 2017. See also numbers of children influenced by Mindful Schools at: https://www.mindfulschools.org/about-mindfulness/our-organization, downloaded May 24, 2018.

8. Mirabai Bush described how a similar process occurred in bringing meditation into higher education: "In the beginning, people would have a regular course and maybe five minutes of silence in the beginning of class . . . But over the years scholars have begun to 'penetrate the core' of the curriculum."

9. From Buddhist Geeks Interview 211: http://www.buddhistgeeks.com/2011/03/bg-211-optimizing-awareness-in-organizations, accessed April 30, 2013.

10. Choices made in how to navigate the boundary between contemplative culture and science did not seem to be based on academics' field of expertise.

11. *Abhidharma* is the portion of Buddhist literature on "abstruse philosophy or psychological matters" (Prebish and Keown 2010: 286).

12. Pseudonym used.

13. Pseudonym used.

14. From *Humans of New York, The Series*. Uploaded on Facebook November 26, 20 17 at 6:41 p.m.: https://www.facebook.com/humansofnewyork, downloaded November 29, 2017.

Chapter 6

1. In these contemplative intervention programs, meditation facilitators' pedagogical strategies are similar to other religious movements' conversion tactics, which involve graduated exposure to religious ideology and practice-based, embodied training (Davis and Robinson 2012; Pagis 2010).

2. Mindfulness for Children: Q & A with Susan Kaiser Greenland; http://www.tricycle.com/blog/mindfulness-children-q-susan-kaiser-greenland. Posted by Philip Ryan on October 4, 2011, downloaded May 12, 2014.

3. There remains a lack of scientific consensus on the effects of mindfulness interventions on attention and cognitive functioning. For example, see Chiesa, Calati, and Serretti (2011) and Lao, Kissane, and Meadows (2016).

4. Pseudonym used upon request of interviewee.

5. This finding aligns with Hafenbrack and Vohs' (2018) conclusion that mindfulness practice can impair task motivation at work.

6. See Kucinskas (2014) for more examples of how religious movements can build upon and around powerful nonreligious systems to gain power and influence.

7. However, based on my research, I suspect that most mindfulness programs have not led to deep structural changes in the institutions they are a part of.

8. For example, Bush said the following about the impact of Search Inside Yourself at Google: "I hear it's had a big influence, impact on the culture at Google . . . I know anecdotally it made a huge difference." "How did it make a difference?" I asked. She responded:

> They were better able to communicate with each other. It's not only that they're young engineers, it's also . . . culturally there are a lot of differences as well as the fact that engineers . . . take very little in the liberal arts and there's no emphasis on communication in their education. Because, at least at Google, it was always like about a third Indian, a third Chinese, and a third everybody else—so those are big cultural differences in terms of communicating. And so that would get into the mix as well. So the potential for miscommunication was huge. So people reported that it felt that they could hear others better and therefore communicate with them better. The mindful listening practice is powerful . . .
>
> But I remember one young engineer saying, "When I was sitting I realized that, since I've come to Google, I'm so focused on my Google life that when my parents or my old friends call me up, I'm just like waiting for the call to be over so I can get back to my Google life." And he said, "But I realized when I was sitting that I really love my parents and I really love my old friends and so I've decided . . . I was gonna set a goal of noticing one thing every day here that would be interesting to my parents." . . . So inasmuch as their lives can be better integrated, they can be better at everything.

She concluded that at Google, those who have completed the Search Inside Yourself program are

> really better at communication and more in touch with their own values. And part of the work is to get in touch with your own deepest values and then look at the ways in which they are aligned or not with the corporate values, and then there's a set of concerns around that. But can you move them closer together? Or is it impossible and should you be doing something else? But that's something that came up a lot.

Chapter 7

1. For a survey of inequality research, see Grusky (2018).

2. Pseudonym used to protect respondent.

3. Annette Lareau's (2011) book *Unequal Childhoods* shows how this sense of deservingness and ability to communicate with people in positions of power is developed among the middle and upper classes as early as elementary school.

4. Lauren Rivera's (2015) book *Pedigree* shows how much race-, class-, and gender-based homophily shapes comfort in interactions in interviews at top professional firms.

5. MLI neuroscientists Richard Davidson and Cliff Saron told me on different occasions that the current contemplative movement could not have attained the scientific legitimacy it has without numerous advances in the scientific technology at their disposal. Brain imaging and other scientific tools have become more sophisticated and allowed them to study meditation with greater precision than was possible in the late 1970s. These advances surely contribute to the burgeoning field of contemplative science.

6. From the Dalai Lama Trust website: http://www.dalailamatrust.org/grants, downloaded August 24, 2016.

7. I interviewed four main funders of the movement. Most had prior interests in meditation and sought out the contemplative organizations to fund them or learned about them through their social networks.

8. Because I used a convenience sample, these numbers cannot be generalized to the movement as a whole. They merely indicate the elite stature of the majority of the contemplative leaders I spoke with (who formed the foundation of the movement during the time I collected data).

Chapter 8

1. For more information on some of these products see Muse (http://www.choosemuse.com) or the Somadome (http://somadome.com) (accessed January 16, 2017).

2. Critiques of contemplative mobilization have come from both within and outside the movement.

3. I attended two such conferences. The first was a meeting of scientists at the University of California, Davis at the Center for Mind and Brain on May 21, 2015. The second was the annual conference of the CfM at the University of Massachusetts held April 10 through 12, 2015, in Shrewsbury, Massachusetts. I saw similar social

processes of authenticity unfold at both, but for the sake of brevity, I share my experience at only one conference.

4. I describe contemplative "performances" of collective authenticity in the tradition of Goffman's dramaturgical (1959) theory of people's actions in public settings with others; my choice of the word "performances" is not used to undermine contemplatives' authenticity practices.

5. Brewer's talk was a summary of a talk Goldstein gave at CfM in the fall of 2014, as a part of its Public Speaker Series. The talk, Brewer said, had come out of a conversation among a small group of New England mindfulness researchers (who are also affiliated with MLI) who meet about three times per year. In the spring of 2014, with Kabat-Zinn, the group of researchers discussed the definition of mindfulness in response to the growing critiques of mindfulness in the media. Their discussion led to a continued online discussion in CfM's Home platform on whether ethics are inherent in the definition of mindfulness. Out of these discussions, CfM invited Goldstein to give his talk on mindfulness from a Buddhist teacher's perspective (which has since been posted on CfM's Home website).

6. For more information on stereotype threat, see scholarship by Claude Steele and Joshua Aronson (1995).

7. From a December 7, 2015, CfM mass email to members.

8. Ibid.

9. Cited from CfM mass emails to members sent on June 21,2016 and October 6, 2016.

Chapter 9

1. Contemplative leaders could collectively support or fail to include certain people who they thought lacked the personality, intellect, or appropriate understanding of contemplative culture. I encountered several examples in which MLI leaders collectively rejected the involvement of certain individuals by failing to award grants, leadership positions, and so forth.

2. I am grateful to Tim Hallett for helping see this point more clearly.

3. It is extremely difficult to pinpoint how many people have been influenced by the movement. According to a CfM email from December 28, 2016, it served nearly 3.5 million people in 2016 alone. However, the figure is likely overestimated because it relies on website hits and video content views without taking into account users who may have repeatedly visited their website. To date CfM has taught over 22,000 people their eight-week MBSR program. (Downloaded from CfM webpage History of MBSR, December 28, 2016: http://www.umassmed.edu/cfm/stress-reduction/history-of-mbsr). Goldie Hawn's MindUP program has taught nearly a million children (MindUP website: https://mindup.org/thehawnfoundation, accessed January 3, 2017). Mindful Schools has also impacted over a million and a half children (Mindful Schools website: https://www.mindfulschools.org/about-mindfulness/our-organization, accessed May 25, 2018).

4. This assertion is based on information shared with me by people working with these programs and others in the movement. Although I asked for the official statistics on program clientele served, neither organization has shared their data with me.

5. See research on other movements that gained legitimacy via support from established, esteemed institutions (e.g., Lounsbury et al. [2003] on how recycling gained legitimacy through the support of industry and the government; Raeburn [2004] on convening elites in conferences and developing LGBT rights in businesses, which could be used as benchmarks to initiate further change).

6. Downloaded from http://www.takepart.com/an-inconvenient-truth/action, October 18, 2013.

REFERENCES

Armstrong, Elizabeth A., and Mary Bernstein. 2008. "Culture, Power, and Institutions: A Multi-Institutional Politics Approach to Social Movements." *Sociological Theory* 26(1): 74–99.

Aronson, Harvey. 2004. "Ego, Ego on the Wall: What Is Ego After All?" In H. Aronson, ed., *Buddhist Practice on Western Ground*. Boston: Shambhala, 64–90.

Batillana, Julie, Bernard Leca and Eva Boxenbaum. 2009. "How Actors Change Institutions: Towards a Theory of Institutional Entrepreneurship." *Academy of Management Annals* 3(1): 65–107.

Baum, Will. 2010. "Mindfulness-Based Stress Reduction: What it Is, How it Helps." Posted March 8, 2010: https://www.psychologytoday.com/blog/crisis-knocks/201003/mindfulness-based- stress-reduction-what-it-is-how-it-helps, downloaded November 4, 2017.

Bender, Courtney. 2009. *The New Metaphysicals: Spirituality and the American Religious Imagination*. Chicago: University of Chicago Press.

Benford, Robert D., and David A. Snow. 2000. "Framing Processes and Social Movements: An Overview and Assessment." *Annual Review of Sociology* 26: 611–639.

Binder, Amy. 2002. *Contentious Curricula*. Princeton, NJ: Princeton University Press.

Binder, Amy. 2007. "For Love and Money: Organizations' Creative Responses to Multiple Environmental Logics." *Theory and Society* 36(6): 547–571.

Blee, Kathleen M., and Ashley Currier. 2005. "Character Building: The Dynamics of Emerging Social Movement Groups." *Mobilization: An International Quarterly* 10(1): 129–144.

Bodhi, B. 2011. "What Does Mindfulness Really Mean? A Canonical Perspective." *Contemporary Buddhism* 12(01), 19–39.

Bourdieu, P. 1984. *Distinction: A Social Critique of the Judgment of Taste*. Cambridge, MA: Harvard University Press.

Bourdieu, Pierre, and Loïc J. D. Wacquant. 1992. *An Invitation to Reflexive Sociology*. Chicago: University of Chicago Press.

Boyce, Barry. 2011. *The Mindfulness Revolution: Leading Psychologists, Scientists, Artists, and Meditation Teachers on the Power of Mindfulness in Daily Life*. Boston: Shambhala Publications, 57.

Brewer, Judson A., Patrick D. Worhunsky, Jeremy R. Gray, Yi-Yuan Tang, Jochen Weber, and Hedy Kober. 2011. "Meditation Experience Is Associated with Differences in Default Mode Network Activity and Connectivity." *Proceedings of the National Academy of Sciences* 108(50): 20254–20259.

Briggs, Charles L. 1986. *Learning How to Ask: A Sociolinguistic Appraisal of the Role of the Interview in Social Science Research.* Cambridge, UK: Cambridge University Press.

Britton, Willoughby B., Anne-Catharine Brown, Christopher T. Kaplan, Roberta E. Goldman, Marie DeLuca, Rahil Rojiani, Harry Reis, Mandy Xi, Jonathan C. Chou, and Faye McKenna. 2013. "Contemplative Science: An Insider Prospectus." *New Directions for Teaching and Learning* 134: 13–29.

Brooks, Arthur. "His Holiness the Dalai Lama at AEI." *AEIdeas*, February 20, 2014: http://www.aei.org/publication/his-holiness-the-dalai-lama-at-aei, retrieved May 11, 2018.

Burton, Katherine, and Anthony Effinger. 2014. "To Make a Killing in the Markets, Start Meditating." *Financial Post*, May 29: http://business.financialpost.com/investing/to-make-a-killing-in-the-markets-start-meditating, retrieved December 29, 2016.

Cadge, Wendy. 2008. *Heartwood: The First Generation of Theravada Buddhism in America.* Chicago: University of Chicago Press.

Cadge, Wendy. 2012. *Paging God.* Chicago: University of Chicago Press.

Carrette, Jeremy, and Richard King. 2004. *Selling Spirituality: The Silent Takeover of Religion.* New York: Routledge.

Chiesa, A., R. Calati, and A. Serretti. 2011. "Does Mindfulness Training Improve Cognitive Abilities? A Systematic Review of Neuropsychological Findings." *Clinical Psychology Review* 31(3): 449–464.

Collins, Randall. 2005. *Interaction Ritual Chains.* Princeton, NJ: Princeton University Press.

Corbin, Juliet, and Anselm Strauss. 2008. *Basics of Qualitative Research: Techniques and Procedures for Developing Grounded Theory.* 3rd ed. Los Angeles: Sage.

Davidson, Richard J., and Daniel J. Goleman. 1977. "The Role of Attention in Meditation and Hypnosis: A Psychobiological Perspective on Transformations of Consciousness." *International Journal of Clinical and Experimental Hypnosis* 25(4): 291–308.

Davidson, Richard J., Daniel J. Goleman, and Gary E. Schwartz. 1976. "Attentional and Affective Concomitants of Meditation: A Cross-Sectional Study." *Journal of Abnormal Psychology* 85(2): 235.

Davis, Nancy J. and Robinson, Robert V., 2012. *Claiming Society for God: Religious Movements and Social Welfare in Egypt, Israel, Italy, and the United States.* Bloomington: Indiana University Press.

DiMaggio, Paul J. 1988. "Interest and Agency in Institutional Theory." In Lynne Zucker, ed., *Institutional Patterns and Organizations.* Cambridge, MA: Ballinger.

DiMaggio, Paul J., and Walter W. Powell. 1983. "The Iron Cage Revisited: Institutional Isomorphism and Collective Rationality in Organizational Fields." *American Sociological Review* 48(2): 147–160.

Duerr, Maia. 2011. "Assessing the State of Contemplative Practices in the United States." In Mirabai Bush, ed., *Contemplative Nation: How Ancient Practices Are Changing the Way We Live.* Kalamazoo, MI: Fetzer Institute, 9–34.

Duffy, Meghan M., Amy J. Binder, and John D. Skrentny. 2010. "Elite Status and Social Change: Using Field Analysis to Explain Policy Formation and Implementation." *Social Problems* 57(1): 49–73.

Durkheim, Emile. 1995 [1912]. "The Elementary Forms of the Religious Life." Karen Fields (trans.). New York: Free Press.

Emerson, Robert M., Rachel I. Fretz, and Linda L. Shaw. 2011. *Writing Ethnographic Fieldnotes.* 2nd ed. Chicago: University of Chicago Press.

Erickson, Rebecca, J., 1995. "The importance of authenticity for self and society." *Symbolic Interaction,* 18(2), 121–144.

Farb, Norman A. S., Adam K. Anderson, Helen Mayberg, Jim Bean, Deborah McKeon, and Zindel V. Segal. 2010. "Minding One's Emotions: Mindfulness Training Alters the Neural Expression of Sadness." *Emotion* 10(1): 25–33.

Farb, Norman A. S., Zindel V. Segal, Helen Mayberg, Jim Bean, Deborah McKeon, Zainab Fatima, and Adam K. Anderson. 2007. "Attending to the Present: Mindfulness Meditation Reveals Distinct Neural Modes of Self-Reference." *Social Cognitive and Affective Neuroscience* 2(4): 313–322.

Fields, Rick. 1992. *How the Swans Came to the Lake: A Narrative History of Buddhism in America.* Boulder, CO: Shambhala Publications, 223.

Fligstein, Neil. 2001. "Social Skill and the Theory of Fields." *Sociological Theory* 19(2): 105–125.

Fligstein, Neil, and Doug McAdam. 2012. *A Theory of Fields.* Oxford: Oxford University Press.

Fronsdal, Gil. 1998. "Insight Meditation in the United States: Life, Liberty, and the Pursuit of Happiness." In Charles S. Prebish and Kenneth K. Tanaka, eds., *The Faces of Buddhism in America.* Berkeley, CA: University of California Press, 163–180.

Gamson, William A. 1975. *The Strategy of Social Protest.* Homewood, IL: Dorsey Press.

Ganz, Marshall. 2000. "Resources and Resourcefulness: Strategic Capacity in the Unionization of California Agriculture, 1959–1966." *American Journal of Sociology* 105(4):–1003–1062.

Ganz, Marshall. 2009. *Why David Sometimes Wins: Leadership, Organization, and Strategy in the California Farm Worker Movement.* Oxford: Oxford University Press.

Garfinkel, Harold. 1967. *Studies in Ethnomethodology.* Englewood Cliffs, NJ: Prentice-Hall.

Gecas, Viktor. 2000. "Value Identities, Self-Motives, and Social Movements." In S. Stryker, T. J. Owens, and R. W. White, eds., *Self, Identity, and Social Movements (Social Movements, Protest, and Contention, Vol. 13).* Minneapolis: University of Minnesota Press, 92–109.

Gieryn, Tom. 1999. *Cultural Boundaries of Science: Credibility on the Line.* Chicago: University of Chicago Press.

Giugni, M.G. 1998. "Was It Worth the Effort? The Outcomes and Consequences of Social Movements." *Annual Review of Sociology* 24: 371–393.

Goffman, Erving. 1959. *The Presentation of Self in Everyday Life.* New York: Anchor Books.

Goffman, Erving. 1974. *Frame Analysis: An Essay on the Organization of Experience.* Cambridge, MA: Harvard University Press.

Goleman, Daniel. 1976. "Meditation and Consciousness: An Asian Approach to Menal Health." *American Journal of Psychotherapy* 30(1): 46.

Goleman, Daniel. 2008. *Destructive Emotions: A Scientific Dialogue with the Dalai Lama*. New York: Bantam.

Gorden, Raymond L. 1980. *Interviewing: Strategy, Techniques, and Tactics*. Homewood, IL: Dorsey Press.

Greenland, Susan K. 2011. "Mindfulness for Children: Q & A with Susan Kaiser Greenland." *Tricycle*, October 4: http://www.tricycle.com/blog/mindfulness-children-q-susan-kaiser-greenland, downloaded May 12, 2014.

Grusky, David. 2018. *Social Stratification: Class, Race, and Gender in Sociological Perspective*. New York: Routledge.

Gyatso, Tenzin. 2005. *The Universe in a Single Atom*. New York: Broadway Books.

Gyatso, Tenzin, and Nicholas Vreeland, ed. 2011. *A Profound Mind: Cultivating Wisdom in Everyday Life*. New York: Harmony Books.

Hafenbrack, A.C. and K.D. Vohs, 2018. "Mindfulness Meditation Impairs Task Motivation but Not Performance." *Organizational Behavior and Human Decision Processes* 147:pp.1–15.

Hallett, Tim. 2003. "Symbolic Power and Organizational Culture." *Sociological Theory* 21(2): 128–149.

Hallett, Tim. 2010. "The Myth Incarnate: Recoupling Processes, Turmoil, and Inhabited Institutions in an Urban Elementary School." *American Sociological Review* 75(1): 52–74.

Hallett, Tim, and Marc J. Ventresca. 2006. "Inhabited Institutions: Social Interactions and Organizational Forms in Gouldner's Patterns of Industrial Bureaucracy." *Theory and Society* 35(2): 213–236.

Hawn, Goldie. 2006. *A Lotus Grows in the Mud*. New York: Berkeley Books.

Hori, Victor. 2000. "Koan and Kensho in the Rinzai Zen Curriculum." In Steven Heine and Dale S. Wright, eds., *The Koan Texts and Contexts in Zen Buddhism*. Oxford: Oxford University Press, 280–316.

Isaac, Larry. 2008. "Movement of Movements: Culture Moves in the Long Civil Rights Struggle." *Social Forces*, 87(1):33–63.

Isaac, Larry W., Daniel B. Cornfield, Dennis C. Dickerson, James M. Lawson, and Jonathan S. Coley. 2012. "Movement Schools and Dialogical Diffusion of Nonviolent Praxis: Nashville Workshops in the Southern Civil Rights Movement." *Research in Social Movements, Conflicts and Change* 34: 155–184.

Isaac, Larry W., Anna W. Jacobs, Jaime Kucinskas, and Allison McGrath. Forthcoming. "Social Movement Schools: Sites for Consciousness Transformation, Training, and Future Social Development."

Jain, Andrea. 2015. *Selling Yoga: From Counterculture to Pop Culture*. New York: Oxford University Press.

Jennings, P. A., and M. T. Greenberg. 2009. "The Prosocial Classroom: Teacher Social and Emotional Competence in Relation to Student and Classroom Outcomes." *Review of Educational Research* 79(1): 491–525.

Kabat-Zinn, Jon. 1994a. *Wherever You Go, There You Are: Mindfulness Meditation in Everyday Life*. New York: Hyperion Books.

Kabat-Zinn, Jon. 1994b. *Catalyzing Movement Towards a More Contemplative/ Sacred Appreciating/Non-Dualistic Society*. Pocantico, NY: Center for Contemplative Mind in Society.

Kabat-Zinn, Jon. 2011. "Some Reflections on the Origins of MBSR, Skillful Means, and the Trouble with Maps." *Contemporary Buddhism* 12(1): 281–306.

Katzenstein, Mary F. 1998. "Stepsisters: Feminist Movement Activism in Different Institutional Spaces." In D. S. Meyer and S. Tarrow, eds., *The Social Movement Society: Contentious Politics for a New Century.* Lanham, MD: Rowman & Littlefield Publishers, Inc., 195–216.

Katzenstein, Mary F. 1999. *Faithful and Fearless: Moving Feminist Protest Inside the Church and Military.* Princeton, NJ: Princeton University Press.

Kerouac, Jack. 1976 [1958]. *The Dharma Bums.* New York: Penguin Books.

Khan, Seamus. 2011. *Privilege: The Making of an Adolescent Elite at St. Paul's School.* Princeton, NJ: Princeton University Press.

Khorsandi, Yasaman. 2016. "The Movement of Meditation Replacing Detention in Schools." *Newsweek,* September 30: http://www.newsweek.com/education-meditation0-after-school-program-holistic-life-504747, downloaded November 29, 2016.

Klandermans, Bert. 1988. "The Formation and Mobilization of Consensus." *International Social Movement Research* 1: 173–196.

Klandermans, Bert, and Dirk Oegema. 1987. "Potentials, Networks, Motivations, and Barriers: Steps Towards Participation in Social Movements." *American Sociological Review* 52(4): 519–531.

Kohler, Robert E. 2002. "Labscapes: Naturalizing the Lab." *History of Science* 40(130): 473–501.

Kucinskas, Jaime. 2014. "The Unobtrusive Tactics of Religious Movements." *Sociology of Religion* 75(4): 537–550.

Kucinskas, Jaime. 2018 "Bridging Social Movements and Social Problems." In *Cambridge Handbook of Social Problems.* New York: Cambridge University Press, 99–117.

Kucinskas, Jaime, Bradley R. E. Wright, D. M. Ray, and J. Ortberg. 2017. "States of Spiritual Awareness by Time, Activity, and Social Interaction." *Journal for the Scientific Study of Religion* 56(2): 418–437.

Kucinskas, Jaime, Bradley R. E. Wright, and Stuart Riepl. 2018. "The Interplay Between Meaning and Sacred Awareness in Everyday Life: Evidence from a Daily Smartphone Study." *The International Journal for the Psychology of Religion* 28(2):71–88.

Kumar, Nirmalya, Louis W. Stern, and James C. Anderson. 1993. "Conducting Interorganizational Research Using Key Informants." *Academy of Management Journal* 36(6): 1633–1651.

Lao So-An, David Kissane, and Graham Meadows. 2016. "Cognitive Effects of MBSR/MBCT: A Systematic Review of Neuropsychological Outcomes." *Consciousness and Cognition* 45: 109–123.

Larana, Enrique, Hank Johnson, and Joseph Gusfield. 1994. *New Social Movements: From Ideology to Identity.* Philadelphia: Temple University Press.

Lindsay, D. Michael. 2008. "Evangelicals in the Power Elite: Elite Cohesion Advancing a Movement." *American Sociological Review* 73: 60–82.

Loncke, Katie. 2014. "Why Google Protesters Were Right To Disrupt Wisdom 2.0." Buddhist Peace Fellowship: http://www.buddhistpeacefellowship.org/

why-google-protesters-were-right-to-disrupt-wisdom-2-o, accessed October 2, 2016.

Lounsbury, Michael. 2001. "Institutional Sources of Practice Variation: Staffing College and University Recycling Programs." *Administrative Science Quarterly* 46(1): 29–56.

Lounsbury, Michael, and Ellen T. Crumley. 2007. "New Practice Creation: An Institutional Perspective on Innovation." *Organizational Studies* 28(7): 993–1012.

Lounsbury, Michael, Marc Ventresca, and Paul M. Hirsch. 2003. "Social Movements, Field Frames and Industry Emergence: A Cultural-Political Perspective on US Recycling." *Socio-Economic Review* 1(1): 71–104.

Maguire, S., C. Hardy, and T. B. Lawrence. 2004. "Institutional Entrepreneurship in Emerging Fields: HIV/AIDS Treatment Advocacy in Canada." *Academy of Management Journal* 47(5): 657–679.

Marsden, Paul. 1998. Memetics and social contagion: Two sides of the same coin. *Journal of Memetics-Evolutionary Models of Information Transmission*, 2(2):171–185.

Maslow, Abraham H. 1943. "A Theory of Human Motivation." *Psychological Review* 50(4), 370.

Mayer J.D. & Salovey P. 1997. "What is emotional intelligence?" In P. Salovey & D. Sluyter, eds., *Emotional Development and Emotional Intelligence: Implications for Educators*. New York, NY: Basic Books, pp. 3–31.

McAdam, Doug. 1999. *Political Process and the Development of Black Insurgency, 1930– 1970*. Chicago and New York: University of Chicago Press.

McAdam, Doug, and David A. Snow. 1997. *Social Movements: Readings on Their Emergence, Mobilization, and Dynamics*. Los Angeles: Roxbury Publishing Company.

McAdam, Doug, Sidney Tarrow, and Charles Tilly. 2001. *Dynamics of Contention*. Cambridge, UK: Cambridge University Press.

McCarthy, John D., and Mark Wolfson. 1992. "Consensus Movements, Conflict Movements, and the Cooptation of Civic and State Infrastructures." Aldon Morris and Carol Mueller, eds., *Frontiers in Social Movement Theory*. New Haven, CT: Yale University Press, 273–297.

McCarthy, John D., and Mayer N. Zald. 1973. *The Trend of Social Movements in America: Professionalization and Resource Mobilization*. Morristown, NJ: General Learning Press.

McCarthy, John D., and Mayer N. Zald. 1977. "Resource Mobilization and Social Movements: A Partial Theory." *American Journal of Sociology*. 82: 1212–1241.

McIntosh, Peggy. 1988. "White Privilege: Unpacking the Invisible Knapsack." Paula S. Rothenberg, ed., *Race, Class, and Gender in the United States: An Integrated Study* 4th ed. New York: Worth Publishers: 165–169.

McMahan, David L. 2008. *The Making of Buddhist Modernism*. Oxford: Oxford University Press.

Mead, George Herbert. 1934. *Mind, Self, and Society*. Chicago: Chicago University Press.

Meiklejohn, J., C., Phillips, M. L. Freedman, M. L. Griffin, G. Biegel, A, Roach, J. Frank, C. Burke, L. Pinger, G. Soloway, and R. Isberg. 2012. "Integrating Mindfulness Training into K-12 Education: Fostering the Resilience of Teachers and Students." *Mindfulness* 3(4): 291–307.

Meyer, J.W. and Rowan, B., 1977. "Institutionalized Organizations: Formal Structure as Myth and Ceremony." *American Journal of Sociology*, 83(2):340–363.

Michaelson, Marc. 1994. "Wangari Maathai and Kenya's Green Belt Movement: Exploring the Evolution and Potentialities of Consensus Movement Mobilization." *Social Problems* 41(4):540–561.

Mindfulness All-Party Parliamentary Group. 2015. "Mindful Nation UK": http://www.themindfulnessinitiative.org.uk/images/reports/Mindfulness-APPG-Report_Mindful-Nation-UK_Oct2015.pdf, accessed May 25, 2018.

Morris, Aldon D., and Cedric Herring. 1984. "Theory and Research in Social Movements: A Critical Review." In S. Long (Ed.), *Annual Review of Political Science*.

Pagis, Michal. 2010. "From Abstract Concepts to Experiential Knowledge: Embodying Enlightenment in a Meditation Center." *Qualitative Sociology* 33(4): 469–489.

Pagis, Michal. Forthcoming. *Inward: Vipassana Meditation and the Embodiment of the Self*. Chicago: University of Chicago Press.

Pellow, David N. 1999. "Framing Emerging Environmental Movement Tactics: Mobilizing Consensus, Demobilizing Conflict." I *Sociological Forum*.14(4): 659–683.

Platt, Gerald M, and Rhys H Williams. 2002. "Ideological language and social movement mobilization: A sociolinguistic analysis of segregationists' ideologies." *Sociological Theory* 20(3):328–359.

Prebish, Charles S., and Damien Keown. 2010. *Introducing Buddhism (World Religions)*. 2nd ed. New York: Routledge.

Purser, R., D. Forbes, and A. Burke, eds. 2016. *Handbook of Mindfulness: Culture, Context, and Social Engagement*. Switzerland: Springer.

Purser, Ron, and David Loy. 2013. "Beyond McMindfulness." *Huffington Post*, August 31: http://www.huffingtonpost.com/ron-purser/beyond-mcmindfulness_b_3519289.html, retrieved December 12, 2016.

Raeburn, Nicole. 2004. *Changing Corporate America from the Inside Out*. Minneapolis: University of Minnesota Press.

Reich, Robert B. 2007. *Supercapitalism: The Transformation of Business, Democracy, and Everyday Life*. New York: Vintage Books.

Reich, Robert. 2015. *Saving Capitalism: For the Many, Not the Few*. New York: Vintage Books.

Reuben, Julie A. 1996. *The Making of the Modern University*. Chicago: University of Chicago Press.

Rivera, Lauren A. 2016. *Pedigree: How Elite Students Get Elite Jobs*. Princeton, NJ: Princeton University Press.

Rizzo, Thomas A., William A. Corsaro, and John E. Bates. 1992. "Ethnographic Methods and Interpretive Analysis: Expanding the Methodological Options of Psychologists." *Developmental Review* 12(2): 101–123.

Rochon, Thomas R. 1998. *Culture Moves: Ideas, Activism, and Changing Values*. Princeton, NJ: Princeton University Press.

Roof, Wade Clark. 2003. "Religion and Spirituality: Toward an Integrated Analysis." In Michele Dillon, ed., *Handbook of the Sociology of Religion*. Cambridge, UK: Cambridge University Press, 146–148.

Rose, David. 2014. "Why Was the Dalai Lama Hanging Out with the Right-Wing American Enterprise Institute?" *Vanity Fair* magazine, February 26, 2014.http://www.vanityfair.com/culture/2014/02/dalai-lama-american-enterprise-institute, retrieved May 23, 2018.

Ryan, Tim. 2012. *A Mindful Nation*. Carlsbad, CA: Hay House.

Sampson, Robert, Doug McAdam, Simon Weffer, and Heather MacIndoe. 2005. "There Will Be Fighting in The Streets: The Distorting Lens of Social Movement Theory." *Mobilization: An International Quarterly* 10(1): 1–18.

Santorelli, Saki F. 2011. "'Enjoy Your Death': Leadership Lessons Forged in the Crucible of Organizational Death and Rebirth Infused with Mindfulness and Mastery." *Contemporary Buddhism* 12(1): 199–217.

Schmidt, Leigh Eric. 2012. *Restless Souls: The Making of American Spirituality*. Berkeley: University of California Press.

Schonert-Reichl, K. A., E. Oberle, M. S. Lawlor, D. Abbott, K. Thomson, T. F. Oberlander, and A. Diamond. 2015. "Enhancing Cognitive and Social–Emotional Development Through a Simple-to-Administer Mindfulness-Based School Program for Elementary School Children: A Randomized Controlled Trial." *Developmental Psychology* 51(1), 52–66.

Seager, Richard Hughes. 1999. *Buddhism in America*. New York: Columbia University Press.

Selznick, Philip. 1949. *TVA and the Grass Roots: A Study in the Sociology of Formal Organization*. Berkeley and Los Angeles: University of California Press.

Sigalow, Emily. 2014. "The JUBUs: The Encounter Between Judaism and Buddhism in America." Ph.D. Dissertation, Brandeis University.

Smith, Christian. 1998. *American Evangelicalism*. Chicago: University of Chicago Press.

Snow, D. A., and R. D. Benford. 1988. "Ideology, Frame Resonance, and Participant Mobilization." *International Social Movement Research* 1(1): 197–217.

Snow, D. A., and R. D. Benford. 1992. "Master Frames and Cycles of Protest." In Aldon Morris and Carol McClung Mueller, eds., *Frontiers in Social Movement Theory*. New Haven, CT: Yale University Press, 133–154.

Snow, David A., E. Burke Rochford, Jr., Steven K. Worden, and Robert D. Benford. 1986. "Frame Alignment Processes, Micromobilization, and Movement Participation." *American Sociological Review* 51(4): 464–481.

Snow, David A., Sarah A. Soule, and Hanspeter Kriesi. 2007. *The Blackwell Companion to Social Movements*. Malden, MA: Wiley-Blackwell.

Soule, Sarah A. 2009. *Contention and Corporate Social Responsibility*. New York: Cambridge University Press.

Stark, Rodney. 1987. "How New Religions Succeed: A Theoretical Model." In David Bromley and Phillip Hammond, eds., *The Future of New Religious Movements*. Macon, GA: Mercer University Press, 11–29.

Steele, Claude M. and Aronson, Joshua, 1995. "Stereotype threat and the intellectual test performance of African Americans." *Journal of Personality and Social Psychology*, 69(5), 797–811.

Stets, Jan E. 2010. "The Social Psychology of the Moral Identity." In S. Hitlin and S. Vaisey, eds., *Handbook of the Sociology of Morality*. New York: Springer, 385–409.

Stiles, Kaelyn. 2011. "New Universalism: The Rise of Mindfulness-Based Meditation in the U.S." In *Sociology*. University of Wisconsin, Madison.

Strang, D. and J. W. Meyer. 1993. "Institutional Conditions for Diffusion." *Theory and Society* 22(4): 487–511.

Strang, D., and S. A. Soule. 1998. "Diffusion in Organizations and Social Movements: From Hybrid Corn to Poison Pills." *Annual Review of Sociology* 24(1): 265–290.

Tan, Chade-Meng. 2012. *Search Inside Yourself: The Unexpected Path to Achieving Success, Happiness (And World Peace)*. New York: Harper Collins.

Taylor, Véronique A., Joshua Grant, Véronique Daneault, Geneviève Scavone, Estelle Breton, Sébastien Roffe-Vidal, Jérôme Courtemanche, Anaïs S. Lavarenne, and Mario Beauregard. 2011. "Impact of Mindfulness on the Neural Responses to Emotional Pictures in Experienced and Beginner Meditators." *Neuroimage* 57(4): 1524–1533.

Thoreau, Henry D. 1982 [1954]. *Walden*. In Carl Bode, ed., *The Portable Thoreau*. New York: Penguin Books, 197–467.

Tøllefsen, Inga B. 2014. "Transcendental Meditation, the Art of Living Foundation, and Public Relations." In James Lewis and Jesper Petersen, eds., *Controversial New Religions*. Oxford and New York: Oxford University Press, 159–175.

Timmermans, Stefan, and Iddo Tavory. 2012. "Theory Construction in Qualitative Research: From Grounded Theory to Abductive Analysis" *Sociological Theory* 30(3): 167–186.

Tucker, Robert C., ed. 1978. *The Marx-Engels Reader*. 2nd ed. New York: W. W. Norton & Co.

Tweed, Thomas A. 2000. *The American Encounter with Buddhism, 1844–1912: Victorian Culture and the Limits of Dissent*. Chapel Hill: University of North Carolina Press.

Tweed, Thomas A. 2013. "Night-stand Buddhists and other creatures: Sympathizers, adherents, and the study of religion." In Christopher Queen and Duncan Ryuken Williams, eds., *American Buddhism*, London: Routledge, 109–128.

Twerkov, Helen. 2001. *Tricycle* magazine.

Van Dam, N. T., M. K. van Vugt, D. R. Vago, L. Schmalzl, C. D. Saron, A. Olendzki, T. Meissner, S. W. Lazar, C. E. Kerr, J. Gorchov, and K. C. Fox. 2017. "Mind the Hype: A Critical Evaluation and Prescriptive Agenda for Research on Mindfulness and Meditation." *Perspectives on Psychological Science* 13(1):36–61.

Varela, Francisco J., Evan Thompson, and Eleanor Rosch. 1991. *The Embodied Mind: Cognitive Science and Human Experience*. Cambridge, MA: MIT Press.

Versluis, Arthur. 1993. *American Transcendentalism and Asian Religions*. Oxford: Oxford University Press.

Washington, Peter. 1995. *Madame Blavatsky's Baboon*. New York: Schocken Books.

Weber, Max. 1978. *Economy and Society: An Outline of Interpretive Sociology*. Berkeley: University of California Press.

Weber, Max. 2012 [1934]. *The Protestant Ethic and the Spirit of Capitalism*. New York: Routledge.

Weick, Karl E., and Ted Putnam. 2006. "Organizing for Mindfulness: Eastern Wisdom and Western Knowledge." *Journal of Management Inquiry* 1593: 275–287.

Whippman, Ruth. 2016. "Actually, Let's Not Be in the Moment." *New York Times*, November 26: (http://www.nytimes.com/2016/11/26/opinion/sunday/actually-lets-not-be-in-the-moment.html?_r=0), retrieved December 28, 2016.

Williams, Rhys H. 2006. "Collective Action, Everyday Protest, and Lived Religion." *Social Movement Studies* 5(1): 83–89.

Wilson, Jeff. 2014. *Mindful America: The Mutual Transformation of Buddhist Meditation and American Culture*. New York and Oxford: Oxford University Press.

Winter, Gibson. 1961. *The Suburban Captivity of the Churches: An Analysis of Protestant Responsibility in the Expanding Metropolis*. Vol. 124. Doubleday.

Wuthnow, Robert. 1998. *After Heaven: Spirituality in America Since the 1950s*. Berkeley: University of California Press.

Wuthnow, Robert, and Wendy Cadge. 2004. "Buddhists and Buddhism in the United States: The Scope of Influence." *Journal for the Scientific Study of Religion* 43(3): 363–380.

Yukich, Grace. 2013. *One Family under God: Immigration Politics and Progressive Religion in America*. New York: Oxford University Press.

Yukich, Grace. 2017. "Progressive Activism among Buddhists, Hindus, and Muslims in the U.S." In Ruth Braunstein, Todd Nicholas Fuist, and Rhys Williams, eds., *Religion and Progressive Activism*. New York: New York University Press.

Zietsma, C., and T. B. Lawrence. 2010. "Institutional Work in the Transformation of an Organizational Field: The Interplay of Boundary Work and Practice Work." *Administrative Science Quarterly* 55(2), 189–221.

INDEX

activism, 23, 33, 103, 194
Alpert, Richard. *See* Dass, Ram
alterative movement, 32, 42, 110, 164, 188, 190, 193
American College and University Presidents' Climate Commitment, 195
American Council of Learned Societies, 61
American Enterprise Institute, 3–8, 162
American Idol, 140
American Madha Bodhi Society, 24
Anti-Eviction Mapping Project, 155
Aronson, Harvey, 125
Association for Mindfulness in Education, 86
authenticity, 163–164, 167–187, 190–191, 194, 213–214n3

Baba, Neem Karoli, 47
Beat poets, 25, 29–30, 39
Being Human conference, 137
Belzer, Marvin, 108–109, 112
Blavatsky, Helena, 21
Boyce, Barry, 151
Brewer, Judson, 170–172, 181
Britton, Willoughby, 123
Brooks, Arthur, 3–6

Brown Contemplative Studies Initiative, 37
Buddhify, 96
Buddhism
    American Buddhist modernizers, 19, 24, 32, 92, 200
    ethnic Buddhism, 19, 22, 30, 32, 200
    Socially engaged Buddhism, 181, 200, 208n1
    See also Theravada Buddhism; Tibetan Buddhism; Zen Buddhism
Buddhist Geeks podcast, 118
Burdulis, Greg, 38, 42, 114, 122–123, 127
Bush, Mirabai, 27, 47–63, 69, 83, 93, 101–103, 129–136
Business for Innovative Climate and Energy Policy coalition, 195

Cambridge Zen Center, 52
capitalism, 4–7, 34, 48, 58, 102–103, 156, 189
Carus, Paul, 22, 30
CCMS. *See* Center for Contemplative Mind in Society
Center for Contemplative Mind in Society, 12, 34, 47–54, 66, 68–70, 138, 147, 198
    Education, 61–63, 86
    See also Bush, Mirabai

Greenland, Susan Kaiser, 114
Gunatillake, Rohan, 96, 118

Halifax, Joan, 27, 50, 82, 139, 149
Halpern, Charlie, 50, 55
Hanh, Thich Nhat, 25, 181
Hanuman, 47
Hearst Publications, 58
Hinduism, 21
HLF. *See* Holistic Life Foundation
Hoffmann-La Roche, Inc., 58
Holistic Life Foundation (HLF), 151–152
Horn, Vincent, 118
Huffington, Ariana, 64–65
Humans of New York, 104

ideology, contemplative, 10, 32–33,
    36–38, 40, 97–101, 111–113, 116–119,
    124, 177, 184, 189
Impact Foundation, 199
impermanence, 26, 111
individualism, 20, 23
Inner Kids, 114, 199
Insight Meditation Society, 27, 29,
    32, 47, 52
Institute for Mindful Leadership, 63
institutional entrepreneurs, 14, 166,
    192, 207n15
    insiders, 48–49, 53–60, 68–70, 188
institutional isomorphism, 14, 207n16,
    209–210n3, 210–211n6
interdependence, 36–38, 43, 89, 98,
    155–156
International Symposium for
    Contemplative Studies, 98,
    139, 201
intervention programs, 4, 8, 33–34, 43,
    52–54, 84–85, 112–137
    business, 55–56, 63–65, 84–85, 90–93,
    96, 101–105, 107, 114, 118–119, 123, 125,
    127–128, 131, 134–135, 162
    education, 61–62, 86–90, 97, 100–101,
    108–110, 113–114, 120–122, 128–129,
    133, 152–153
    healthcare, 52, 74–78, 84–85
    military, 65, 71–74, 84–85, 127, 129
    science, 66, 78–82, 84–85, 131–132

See also Mindfulness-Based Stress
    Reduction (MBSR); Search Inside
    Yourself
Isaac, Larry, 110

Jha, Amishi, 71
Jinpa, Thupten, 100, 174

Kabat-Zinn, Jon, 4, 27, 33–36, 83, 115,
    146, 149, 171–173, 189
    1994 Center for Contemplative Mind
    in Society report, 74
    Contemplative practice, 50–53,
    94–98, 183–184
    Program establishment, 75–78
    See also Center for Mindfulness in
    Medicine, Health Care, and Society;
    Mindfulness-Based Stress Reduction
Karmapa, 17th, 149
Kerouac, Jack, 25, 29
Kerr, Catherine, 82
Khan, Seamus, 143–144
Klandermans, Bert, 68
Kohler, Robert, 111–112
Kornfield, Jack, 26–27, 149

legitimacy, 100, 139, 148, 190, 195
    elite legitimacy, 151–152
    institutional legitimacy, 48–49,
    62–64, 69, 146, 150–152, 215n5
    interdependent forms of legitimacy,
    145–153
    moral legitimacy, 4, 7, 146
    normative legitimacy, 105
    organizational legitimacy, 16, 49,
    62–63
    pragmatic legitimacy, 76, 146, 152–153
    public legitimacy, 9, 64–66, 94, 146,
    150, 195
    scientific legitimacy, 9, 12, 40, 52,
    61–63, 66–69, 72, 78–79, 80–83,
    93, 108, 146–147, 213n5
Lehman, Rob, 50
Lindisfarne Association, 27–28
Lindsay, Michael, 48–49, 141
loose coupling, 75
Loy, David, 166–167